Teddy Wilson Talks Jazz

TEDDY WILSON

TALKS JAZZ

TEDDY WILSON

With ARIE LIGTHART
and HUMPHREY VAN LOO

Foreword by BENNY GOODMAN

CONTINUUM

NEW YORK ■ LONDON

2001

The Continuum International Publishing Group
370 Lexington Avenue, New York, NY 10017

The Continuum International Publishing Group
The Tower Building, 11 York Road, London SE1 7NX

First published in Great Britain in 1996 by Cassell
by arrangement with Bayou Press Ltd

Printed in the United States of America

Library of Congress Cataloging-in-Publication Data

Wilson, Teddy, 1912-
    Teddy Wilson talks jazz / by Teddy Wilson, with Arie Ligthart and Humphrey van Loo.
       p. cm. -- (Bayou jazz lives)
    Includes discography and indexes.
    ISBN 0-8264-5797-5 (pbk.)
       1. Wilson, Teddy, 1912- 2. Jazz musicians--United States--Biography. I. Ligthart,
Arie. II. Van Loo, Humphrey. III. Title. IV. Series.

ML417.W52 A3 2001
786.2'165'092--dc21
[B]
                                                                          2001047040

Contents

Publisher's Note

(from 1996 Cassell hardback edition)

This book was originally written between 1976 and 1978, and was to have been published during Teddy Wilson's lifetime. The original publisher then underwent a change of policy, and the book never appeared. For many years up to and following Teddy's death in 1986, Arie Ligthart sought a new publisher, and with the help of pianist Martin Litton, the book was originally announced by Bayou Press to appear in 1991. As so long had passed since the book was written, it was agreed to delay the book slightly, so that the fairly slender manuscript could be augmented by material from Charles Fox's BBC interviews with Teddy, which took place the week after one of the main interviewing sessions with Ligthart and van Loo, and which covered a number of subjects obviously fresh in Teddy's mind, from a slightly different perspective. Charles's death in May 1991 further delayed matters, and we are grateful to Howard Rye for integrating this material with the story, and for preparing the comprehensive recording chronology, based on an original compilation by Gerard Bielderman. A number of further delays held the book up in production and we are glad that it will now appear under our arrangement with Cassell. Despite the passage of time, we have preserved Teddy's words exactly as they were set down in the 1970s, and so there are some obvious anachronisms, notably in the comments on South Africa and the former Soviet Union, that reflect the views of the time.

Alyn Shipton
Bayou Press 1996

Foreword

By Benny Goodman

This is a foreword, but not an introduction, because Teddy Wilson does not need one. Through his records and personal appearances, he is well known to millions of jazz fans throughout the world. His superb music has already spoken for him, but musically eloquent though he is, it may well be asked: "Who is the man behind the music?"

Teddy Wilson is of a retiring disposition. Publicity stunts and cavorting before the footlights to gain the favors of the public are not for him. I can speak with authority, because of course I worked with him during an important era in jazz music from July 1935, after I met him at a party given by singer Mildred Bailey, until 1939, when he left me to form his own band. It was a memorable period, both for me personally, and for jazz. We made history not only with the big band but also with the Trio and Quartet, featuring myself, Teddy, Lionel Hampton and Gene Krupa. It was the first inter-racial music group and marked an important milestone in race relations in the United States. We were not bothered ourselves, however, and to us it was the music that mattered.

During that time I got to know Teddy intimately and I have retained a high respect for him both as a musician and as a person. I have gone on record as saying that my pleasure in playing with Teddy Wilson equalled the pleasure I got out of playing Mozart, and that's saying something. I've said it before and I'll say it again today.

Teddy is a walking history of some of the most vital periods in jazz, and fortunately he has a retentive memory. He has played as an equal with countless jazz greats and I am happy that the time has now come for a summing up, valuable now that jazz is experiencing a revival, and valuable to posterity as an authentic document. I wish him luck and I hope the book gets the readership it deserves.

Introductory Note

To say this is an autobiography would perhaps too pompous: it is rather a book of reminiscences and comments on an important era in the American music we call jazz , in which I had the luck and honour to participate with – I may say in all modesty – some distinction.

In making my acknowledgements for the birth of this book I should in the first place say thank you to my close collaborators, Mr Humphrey van Loo and Mr Arie Ligthart.

It was Arie Ligthart, as manager and guitar and banjo player of the Dutch Swing College Band, who first suggested to me the idea of recording some of my impressions for posterity. It was Mr Humphrey van Loo, for 30 years a writer and correspondent of Reuters News Agency, who was found willing to look after the presentation of the material I provided in book form. Thus was formed what I might call a new "Teddy Wilson Trio" and we spent many hours together with the tape recorder in The Hague, Netherlands. It goes without saying that we learned to value each other in those long hours, all of us having a deep-seated love of jazz music.

I would also like to express my sincere thanks to that great jazz musician, who has had such incalculable influence throughout the world, Benny Goodman, with whom I experienced some of the most crucial and successful years of my life. My profound thanks are also due to *Downbeat* for the generous way in which they have made photographic material available.

Finally, my thanks are, and of course always be, due to the millions of jazz enthusiasts and fans throughout the world whose loyalty and affection have made my art possible.

Teddy Wilson
The Hague, 1978

1

Early Beginnings

How encouraging to look back on more than forty active years in jazz music and realize that, far from being just a fad, one of the many rages of the public that have come and gone, it is durable and viable and just as alive and kicking in this day and age of the 1970s as it was when I first started playing professionally in 1929. How grateful I am too to be in the swim today as I was then and hope to remain so, even though I am now in my sixties. You may be getting older all the time, but the important thing is not to feel old, and I don't.

Not only is a long and richly varied life in the essential music of America something to be grateful for, so is the opportunity it afforded me to play with and get to know at close range many of the key figures in the important phases of the development of jazz; people whose names are now household words all over the world: Louis Armstrong, Benny Goodman, Fats Waller, Earl Hines, Art Tatum, Billie Holiday, Gene Krupa, Lionel Hampton, Benny Carter – the list is endless.

Let's begin at the beginning and see how I ever got caught up in the first place in this tremendous maelstrom of jazz which swept me along, sometimes into the most unexpected and fascinating situations, and was to determine the whole course of my life and make me, in turn, a "jazz influence".

I was born in Austin, Texas, on November 24, 1912, the son of James Augustus Wilson and Pearl Shaw. My father was born in Pennsylvania in 1877 and my mother in Tennessee in 1880, and both were teachers at the Sam Houston College in Austin, where my father was Dean and my mother taught elementary grades. I grew up with my brother Gus, who is a year and two months my senior and who also became a

musician, successfully playing trombone with jazz orchestras. His full name was James August Wilson Jr. and he was
born in Montgomery, Alabama. There were only the two boys
in the family, no sisters.

In due course my parents got better jobs at Tuskegee
College in Alabama, a boarding school for Negro students
from all over the USA, about forty miles east of Montgomery.
It stood very much on its own amidst woods and forests and
had its own farm for milk and vegetables.

My father was in charge of the English language and literature department of the college and my mother taught the
ordinary grades, reading and writing, chiefly to adults up to
twenty who were still on the elementary level because of conditions under which Negroes were living in the southern
states of the US in those days. Having to deal with adults
who had not had the advantage of elementary education as
children naturally required a great deal of tact and insight on
the part of the teacher, but my mother fortunately possessed
these qualities in ample measure. There was a great deal of
illiteracy in Alabama then and my mother had to teach her
pupils the alphabet and simple arithmetic, without humiliating them so that they shut their minds to education altogether. Many pupils used to scrape together their school fees
from the work they did, which included raising food on the
school farm. For those who had no money at all there was the
possibility of a scholarship.

This was a trade school where all students, besides an aca-
demic education, had to learn a trade. You had a selection of
twenty-two. I took printing, which involved setting the type
by hand. I learned that at the beginning, then proof-reading,
operating what they called the job-press (which you feed one
piece of paper at a time) and then graduated to the cylinder
press, on which you could make a newspaper. In my last two
years I learned to operate a Linotype machine, which does all
the printing of a newspaper with many columns of type. I
was pretty thorough with that, but the opportunity to play
jazz was much more compelling and more attractive than to
be a professional printer.

Gus and I started studying music at a very early age, when we were about seven or eight. Both my parents were fond of music. Neither of them were highly skilled musicians, although both could read music on the piano: they knew the bass clef and the treble clef on paper and on the keyboard. My father was sufficiently knowledgeable to rehearse small groups of students to do special programmes of really fine classical vocal music – Christmas and Easter music – for about eighteen voices, although he did not work with the big choir of between sixty and eighty voices, which was under a Mrs Lee. My mother's sister, Leora, was a skilled classical pianist and I heard her play a lot. So all in all there was plenty of music "in the air" in the family. I became attracted to music at such an early age because hearing an instrument played well is a very strong force in shaping a child's likes and dislikes and is very inspiring. Fortunately, I was in a position to hear some excellent violinists and some good piano playing.

Now it was much appreciated by the Tuskegee faculty if pupils learned music in addition to the ordinary curriculum. This was done through a private teacher and quite a lot of music teaching was done during the summer vacation when there was only a small resident staff.

The Tuskegee musical scene was therefore lively and, although my first instrument was the piano. I also studied the violin for a while, but I found it a difficult instrument and it was a considerable effort to keep in tune. I had a very good violin teacher although, as my life has proved, the piano was my first love.

It was very important of course, that I learned to read music. My first contact with music was with the "straight" or "classical" kind, and my life in jazz has in no way diminished my interest in classical music. I learned to read music with great facility at an early age and I have successfully put my memory to the test since with such things as the Grieg Piano Concerto, Chopin études, Chopin preludes, Bach and so on. I might mention that, round about 1936 or 1937, when I was about 24, I played a Concerto for two harpsichords and a small orchestra at the Town Hall in New York. (The "Town

Hall" was not what Americans call the City Hall, it was just the name of a public auditorium in New York used for concerts and other performance.)

So at the age of about eight I started my musical education with a very gifted woman pianist and singer named Mrs Sims and I owe her a great debt of gratitude for being the first person to have a big influence on my musical growth.

I got to know the piano fairly well and learned how to read the bass and treble clefs and give little piano recitals in company with Mrs Sims, my brother Gus, and the other students. Sometimes I would accompany Mrs Sims when she sang at recitals.

When I was about ten or eleven I became, through the High School department, the pupil of a very fine violinist named Maceo Williams, who also conducted the chapel orchestra. He played the most beautiful violin I had ever heard and I promptly fell in love with the instrument and got Maceo Williams to teach me. I played violin in the chapel orchestra under his direction.

At that time I also cast further afield and became interested in the High School band, which was conducted by Captain Frank Dry, who had been a bandmaster in the First World War. The Captain did a wonderful job licking High School boys into shape to get them to sound like a first class marching brass band. I played oboe and E flat clarinet in this band, and it was a very enjoyable experience. We used to play at football games and travel with the High School team, as well as giving a one-hour band concert every Sunday afternoon, outdoors on the college campus, weather permitting.

The credit for my proficiency on these instruments cannot go to Captain Dry, but to one of his talented assistants, a student named Leonard Bowden. He was very advanced with the whole reed family: clarinet and saxophones. He could play a little jazz, but he was best at classics. So he helped me along with the oboe and clarinet.

Meanwhile, I hadn't given up the piano. I was playing in the High School orchestra under the leadership of a very gifted trumpet player named Philmore Hall, whom everybody called "Shorty" Hall. Shorty was an exceptional trumpet player for a student High School orchestra and he was an assistant to both Maceo Williams and Leonard Bowden. He organized a little dance orchestra among the students and we played mainly for the teachers and doctors at the nearby government hospital and for dances at villages and towns among what was a fairly sparse population in the Alabama of those days, around Tuskegee.

So far I have been talking about the normal musical education of a young boy with aptitude, without any special reference to jazz. It is of course difficult to say exactly when jazz as a musical form dawned on my consciousness, but there is no doubt it was love at first sight and circumstances were such that I met people who encouraged and stimulated my interest in it.

In this respect my original keyboard instructor was John Lovett who, after graduating from school, was employed at the local drug store on the campus. Today he is a teacher at an Alabama school, but in those days he was working as a clerk at the school drugstore. John Lovett was himself an excellent jazz pianist and he would often have students down to his house to listen to 78 rpm records he had managed to pick up in other towns. This, for example, was my first acquaintance with Duke Ellington's early piano solos. John taught me a lot about the use of the tenth and about the technique of the bass in the left hand. As far as that goes, I got my first knowledge of it from him.

All this would have been about 1926 and 1927 and I was around John Lovett a great deal then, listening not only to the Duke Ellington solos I've already mentioned but also to recorded solos by Earl Hines and Fats Waller. Lovett had a fine collection of records. We didn't have record shops anywhere near the campus at Tuskegee, which was miles from anywhere, so John used to order a lot of his records by mail from the big cities.

It was a very large school, set in a rural area of the South, so it was a boarding school. The students all lived there, the faculty and the personnel who operated the school, plus their children and families, all lived there. A lot of the boarding students and teachers too used to bring in records from outside. They were all 78s of course and were played on an acoustic gramophone with adjustable speed, a piece of equipment which was to prove very useful to me when I was following in the footsteps of my masters, Fats Waller and Earl Hines. Looking at the great strides that have been made since then in electronic and stereo equipment, the way I studied jazz in those early college campus days seems a very far cry indeed from all that and I envy the modern jazz enthusiast for his technical and listening resources.

So the first real jazz I ever heard was on record: people like Bix Beiderbecke, Frankie Trumbauer, Eddie Lang and Joe Venuti, Louis Armstrong, and pianists Hines and Waller, and very exciting it all was. Of course, it was even more exciting to hear such people in person and in this I was very lucky. I had an aunt in Detroit, where I used to stay during the summer vacation, and McKinney's Cotton Pickers, fronted by Don Redman, were actually stationed in Detroit at the time. In addition, other important bands were passing through the city: bands like those of Fletcher Henderson and his brother Horace, who played at the Graystone Ballroom in Detroit, and tenor saxophonist Coleman Hawkins. I heard clarinettist Jimmie Noone there in an overnight stand, maybe once.

In 1926 my father died and in the following year my mother took Gus and me to Detroit for a summer vacation and that is how we got to hear so much live jazz of quality. The Graystone Ballroom was the main showcase for the big jazz orchestras in those days and in addition to the names I have already mentioned I can recollect hearing trumpeter Rex Stewart, that great musical all-rounder Benny Carter, who is a great personal friend of mine today, Buster Bailey on clarinet, Kaiser Marshall on drums; so many men who are now household names in the jazz world.

I have spoken of McKinney's Cotton Pickers and Don Redman. Redman had come out to Detroit from New York as musical director of the band and he stood out in front, conducting and playing saxophone. He shared the arranging chores with a very talented trumpet player named John Nesbitt and, between the two of them, they had a wonderful big band repertoire of arrangements and original music. Redman himself wrote several hits, one in particular called *Cherry*, which later became very successful on records in versions by trumpeter, Harry James, the Erskine Hawkins band and the Mills Brothers in New York.

I shall always remember hearing the Fletcher Henderson and McKinney's Cotton Pickers bands at the Graystone Ballroom as the highlight of one of my happy summer vacation jaunts in Detroit.

After the vacation I would go back to school at Tuskegee for the new term and the jazz thread would be taken up again at regular intervals through records and my contacts with pianist John Lovett.

With all this going on, I was inspired to copy jazz piano solos by giants like Fats Waller and Earl Hines whom I admired and wanted to emulate. I copied the solos from records note for note and memorized them. I did that, for instance, with Fats Waller's *Handful Of Keys*. That was the way all pianists learned in those days and there was a standard way of doing it. I have told you that the old gramophones had a speed regulator attached. This made it possible to slow down the record to the pitch you yourself were playing in. You could hear exactly what a player was doing in a particularly intricate passage and match it to your own piano pitch. I didn't always write the solos down; I often memorized them and imitated them at the keyboard.

Later, when I went in for piano teaching myself, I would teach my pupils both to memorize and write down accurately. This applies especially to the intricacies of jazz rhythm, the little shades which are not easy to write: the delaying of a note, or the difference between a dotted eighth and sixteenth rhythmic pattern, and a triplet with the middle notes, a rest. They are close together, but not exactly, and in jazz the phrasing was generally the triplet pattern and the middle note rest would be a little closer than the dotted eighth note, with the sixteenth just a shade closer. It might not be exactly what you heard on the record, but it would be as close as you could notate, and that would make your knowledge more secure: to be able to write it as well as to do it at the keyboard by ear. In this way you could analyse what the player had done.

While on the subject of my early jazz activities at Tuskegee I should also mention, in addition to John Lovett, a student named Melvin Smalls, who was a very good pianist and used to play for the movies in the chapel. That was before the advent of "talkies". Then again, there was one of the English literature teachers, a man named Neil Heriford from Kansas City, who played beautiful jazz piano at the movies for the pleasure of the students. Sometimes, after supper, he'd get hold of one of the pianos from the auditorium and give the students a treat , both classical and jazz.

In September, 1927, I went back to school for the new term. But, in the following summer vacation off I went again to Detroit just to hear those bands again. That did it. When I got back home I told my mother I wanted to become a professional jazz pianist.

2

Off To Detroit

Mother took it quite calmly. I told her that I had made friends with local musicians in Detroit and found that, if I joined the Musicians' Union, I could get work at 50 dollars a week, which was more than my father, with his job, had made in Tuskegee as head of the English Department! Of course, there were a lot of fringe benefits, like the house we lived in, since my parents were members of the faculty. But still, 50 dollars cash a week was more than he earned and, to me, who wasn't earning any money at all, it looked like a wonderful way to live! At that point, it seemed to me a waste of time to go on studying and becoming a teacher or a doctor.

So when I told my mother I wanted to become a professional jazz pianist, she said "Well, go to college first for one year and, if you still want to be a jazz musician, leave college and play jazz."

My reply was an enthusiastic "OK."

I then went to a wonderful little college called Talladega in Alabama, north of Tuskegee and 60 miles south-east of Birmingham. There I continued my music studies, majoring in music theory, ear-training, sight-singing, the beginnings of counterpoint, harmonizing melody, building up four-voice harmony from a figured bass: in short, learning all the rules and regulations that the great composers grew up by in the conservatories of Europe.

Incidentally, I would recommend music theory education to any musician, no matter what instrument he plays or whether he's a jazz or classical player. I found it absolutely invaluable to get appreciation of voice leadings and the inner structure of music to refine my playing. I think even classical concert performers sound a shade better when they have had such a musical training in addition to the intensive study of a particular instrument. So I majored in theory and throughly enjoyed it. Nevertheless, I still did not want to continue my studies and did not go back on my decision to play jazz professionally. My views were shared luckily by both my mother and my brother Gus.

When Gus and I left home mother gave us 50 dollars apiece, and we made tracks for Detroit, which was naturally the likeliest place for us to go. We were both familiar with the city and our aunt was living there. However, we did not plan to live with her, and neither did we. We shared rented rooms with a bandleader called Bob Cruset. He had no organized band on the road and did not make recordings. He just lived in Detroit and worked mostly on weekends. The result was that there were many small groups playing around the suburbs of Detroit on weekends under the name of the Bob Cruset Orchestra, although it was difficult to tell which was supposed to be *the* Bob Cruset Orchestra. Perhaps none of them!

Bob himself did a kind of musical quick-change act, leaping in and out of his car, standing maybe fifteen minutes in front of one band, before rushing off again to the next with which he was working. He was what we called a "club-date bandleader." The work we did for him was in the fall of 1929, around the time the school year would begin. That's how we started work, mostly on the weekends, with Bob Cruset and other leaders in various bands around Detroit. We got to know many jazz-orientated musicians there around that time, and also went to the Graystone Ballroom when we could scrape together the one-dollar admission to hear the big bands. These included clarinetist Jimmie Noone's band, which had a fine pianist called Zinky Cohn, who I had never heard of but who was playing in a style strongly reminiscent of Earl Hines. Anyway, Gus and I managed to get enough money for our food and lodging in this way until we encountered the Speed Webb band and went on tour with them.

Speed Webb's full name was S. Lawrence Webb and he was born in Indiana. He was well known as a bandleader in the late twenties and early thirties in ballrooms throughout the country, and many former members of his band considered it to be one of the best of its day. He featured a number of side-men who became famous, such as Vic Dickenson on trom-bone, Roy and Joe Eldridge (Roy, of course, on trumpet and his elder brother Joe on violin and alto), Eli Robinson on trombone and Reunald Jones on trumpet, and of course my older brother Gus on trombone, and myself. Speed had also been in an early talkie movie called *On With the Show* with singer Ethel Waters. Ethel was a great star in those days and sang a song in the film called *Am I Blue*, which became very popular in its day.

As a result of the movie publicity, Speed Webb went on tour with a show band. We toured the Middle West: Indiana, sometimes Minneapolis or Ohio, Boston, Massachusetts, Wisconsin, Nebraska. We played mostly one-night stands for dancers but nothing really steady. The band made no record-ings. It had standard instrumentation: three saxes, four (and later five) brass, and a four-strong rhythm section of bass, guitar, piano and drums.

I joined the Milt Senior band in 1930. Previously, Art Tatum had been playing with the band, but Art wanted to take the offer of a five-days-a-week half-hour solo radio program in Toledo, Ohio, the same city the band was playing in. The group was small, a quartet, in which I replaced Art Tatum at the piano.

Milton Senior had been an alto saxophone player with McKinney's Cotton Pickers. I heard him in that band long before I met him, because they were based in Detroit, as their home base. They'd play along with several other good bands at the Graystone Ballroom. A man called Jean Goldkette would rotate them in and out of the Graystone, and they'd go on the road, come back into the Graystone and broadcast in a well-organized succession. These bands were the Casa Loma (in those days under Hank Biagini's leadership just before Glen Gray took over), Freddy Bergen's Vagabonds, the Billy Minor band, and Big Teddy Buckner (Milt Buckner's older brother, who was a lead alto player in Detroit in those days).

In the succession, the McKinney's Cotton Pickers were, I think, the best jazz band. Of course, Goldkette had his own band, too, which at one time had Bix Beiderbecke and people like that in it. Although Goldkette was not a jazz musician, (he was a concert pianist, originally from Russia,) he organized the musical life of Detroit. He put the symphony on a paying basis there, and organized this tremendously successful jazz operation centered round the Graystone Ballroom as the home base for all these bands.

Meeting Art Tatum was the third big and decisive influence on my life as a jazz pianist, after Waller and Hines. He really had a tremendous influence on my style. He was so unlike Waller and Hines, and I had the great advantage of being around him a lot in person, so I learned a great deal from him. Art and I would get together every night after I'd finished my job. Art's own radio program started around 5 p.m. and was through at 5.30. I would usually be finished by midnight and then we would get together and go around the various speakeasies, as this was during Prohibition. Alberta's was one of our favorite speakeasies. Or we would go to various people's homes, where they had a piano, and have a session. On the way we would sometimes pick up a pianist or two from around town or who were passing through.

These marathon piano sessions sometimes lasted until daylight, and so I learned a great deal from Art. He was extremely helpful and kind to me, encouraging me to ask any questions I wanted to and responding warmly to the way I appreciated him. I shall deal with Art as a giant of jazz piano when I discuss jazz pianists in a later chapter. The Milton Senior band went to Chicago from Toledo, and the job we went on there didn't last. It went on for about six weeks, and at the end of that I decided that rather than go back with Milton Senior, I'd try to make roots in Chicago, because I felt it was a much better jazz town as a home base than Toledo, Ohio.

Meanwhile, I had lost track of my brother Gus. He stayed with the Speed Webb band for a while but later joined the Alphonso Trent band, based I believe, in Dallas, Texas. The members included jazz violinist Stuff Smith, who would front the band. Gus went to St. Louis with a number of players from Trent's band, under co-leaders Jeter and Pillars, where I believe they played a steady job at the Plantation Club. By that time Gus was getting into arranging, in continuation of what he had been doing at high school. His arrangement of *Clementine* was very highly thought of and his work is greatly admired by fellow orchestrator Sy Oliver.

I played in Chicago between 1931 and 1933 with Louis Armstrong, Erskine Tate (who played violin but was better known as a bandleader), Jimmie Noone, and an excellent band headed by trumpet player Eddie Mallory. Louis had a ten-piece orchestra including Keg Johnson on trombone, with Scoville Brown and Budd Johnson on saxophones. The band recorded about a dozen titles, perhaps the best of which were *I've Gotta Right to Sing the Blues* and *I Got the World on a String*. Of course, in any list of jazz names, his must stand out as that of a giant. As I recall, I first met Louis at a rehearsal after I had been hired by his agent. At that time Louis was doing strictly one-night stands on the road. I knew his work so well from recordings that I heard exactly what I expected to hear. I felt then, as I still feel today, that Louis Armstrong was the most important single soloist in the whole jazz world. He had an extraordinarily powerful influence on the path taken by jazz as a whole. It is a plain fact that jazz would not be what it is today if it hadn't been for Armstrong's trumpet back in the late twenties and early thirties. Louis was a genius, and I say that in full realization of the meaning of that much-abused word.

There are stories that Armstrong couldn't read music, but I know personally they are untrue because I *saw* him read when I played with him. Besides, he learned to play trumpet at a home for boys where they had a marching band, and you had to be able to read music for that. Neither should it be forgotten that he was in the brass section of Fletcher Henderson's band before he became a leader himself, and he was a member of King Oliver's brass section, where he played from written arrangements. I myself saw Armstrong read music when we did recording sessions. I did a three-day recording session with him in Chicago, and we recorded twelve tunes, all of them brand-new music.

It was a tremendous experience being able to work with Armstrong after hearing him so much on recordings. I was with him night after night on the road for about three months or so, I guess. We were based in Chicago and we toured Texas, the Middle West, most of the southern states: Louisiana, Mississippi, Arkansas, Indiana, Iowa, Nebraska. I used to marvel at this man's tremendous talent. His great influence started in the 1920s. His contemporary Bix Beiderbecke unfortunately died very young, so Bix's influence on the jazz trumpet rather got lost in the end. But those two were undoubtedly the most imitated of all jazz players in the late twenties and early thirties.

Working with Armstrong and hearing him take a popular song and bring it to life and make a masterpiece out of it, night after night without fail, was one of the most marvellous things I've ever heard. The quality of the band behind him was no good at all, although we had some good soloists: the Johnson brothers were outstanding. But that was not too important as we played mainly background behind Armstrong. He would play a chorus on his trumpet to start an arrangement, and sing a chorus mostly. Then he'd come back for a finish, and maybe there would be a little room for members of the band to play a few measures of solo improvisation, but it was mostly all Armstrong. So I got a good chance to listen to him: the beautiful tone he got on his trumpet, his infallible sense of rhythm, (I've never heard anyone surpass him at inspiring a drummer,) and the purity of his tone. His improvisational ideas were just so beautiful that every note he created was a melodic note – Armstrong never once wasted one. Each had a tremendous meaning all on its own and said exactly what he wanted to say – not too much, not too little – before he sounded the next one. His tone was like a thread of pure gold.

Off the bandstand Armstrong was nice and quiet. After one-night stands he would invite the whole band into his hotel room. There'd be lots of ice-cold Coca-Cola, a favorite drink in hot weather, and something else for those who wanted it. Then we'd be off to bed so we could get up in time to catch the bus the next morning. While we were on the bus Louis would spend a good deal of the time at the typewriter. He answered all of his fan mail personally and got to be quite an expert on his portable typewriter. On and on he would go, typing replies to the cards and letters from his fans. He was a tremendous success, and at the time, as a member of his band, I was earning 40 dollars a week. Armstrong had made a deal with his manager under which he was earning 1500 dollars a week. That was during the Depression, when I could live pretty well on 40 dollars a week on the road, as well as pay for hotels and food. Armstrong was earning that money long before he was making a big hit with tunes like *Hello Dolly* in the early sixties.

But even in those days he had one hit after another – every song he recorded. That was in the period after the Hot Five recordings which became so famous. They were no longer being made when I was with Armstrong. He gave up his big band just after the Second World War to form the All Stars. I think it was just about the best little band that was ever put together: Earl Hines on piano, Barney Bigard on clarinet, Arvell Shaw on bass, Jack Teagarden on trombone and Sid Catlett on drums – three horns and rhythm: just the best there were.

1933 was a very busy year for me in my career. A lot of important things happened. To start with, I met my first wife, Irene Armstrong, who had been married to a man named Edie, and was using the name Irene Edie. She was an excellent pianist and was playing at the time at the Vogue Club on Cottage Grove. I would go there some nights and sit in with her group. She was also a very good songwriter and wrote one of Billie Holiday's most successful recordings called *Some Other Spring*. Jazz musicians are still playing it today. I recorded it myself with my big band for Columbia and had Jean Eldridge sing the vocal.

After Irene and I got married we stayed in Chicago for a

while and I worked with Jimmie Noone, and also subbed for Earl Hines at the Grand Terrace with the Eddie Moore band, when Earl was on tour. In September 1933, I moved to New York to join the Benny Carter band, where I met John Hammond, undoubtedly one of the most important non-performing personalities in the jazz world of those days. I met Billie Holiday through him. Later, I joined the Willie Bryant band and also did accompaniments for the then-famous group the Charioteers.

In the thirties the Chicago gangsters and racketeers were in their heyday and they were great patrons of jazz music. It is perhaps paradoxical that these grim men, who carried guns and held sway over life and death, were always kind and generous to musicians and entertainers. So when I moved to Chicago I worked for the mobsters, with Al Capone as King of the Underworld at their head. I hasten to correct any impression that, in addition to my work at the keyboard, I was also toting a Thompson sub-machinegun in a violin case! The fact of the matter was a lot of mobster money went into entertainment and nightclubs, and that gave employment to musicians and other artists alike.

When I got a job at the Gold Coast Club in Chicago it was not long before I discovered that it was owned by Capone. It was one of his favorite clubs, with a private membership fee of 250 dollars – a lot of money in those days. The membership card was solid eighteen-carat gold, the size of a credit card with the member's name on it. Capone's guests did not know that he owned the club, of course. Often, after the regular guests had left, the doors would be locked and Capone himself would come in, accompanied by a fifteen-strong armed bodyguard. In addition he would take along a party of about twenty to see the whole show, eat, drink, and dance, and generally make merry until daylight. To our amazement Capone would come over to the bandstand every few minutes or so and give each member of the band a twenty-dollar bill, and then return to his table to sit beaming and smoking fat cigars, playing the part of the genial host and generally seeing to it that his guests were having a good time. When we had a break and went down to the bar on the first floor we would see Capone's fifteen bodyguards there waiting for him to leave in a convoy of three bullet-proof Cadillacs.

It was quite an experience hearing these professional gunmen talking so knowledgeably, not about the crime scene, but about their favorite jazz stars: the comparative merits of Johnny Hodges and Benny Carter as alto sax players. They would get excited talking about Louis Armstrong and Jabbo Smith. They knew all about Earl Hines playing at the Grand Terrace and what was available on recordings. They knew about Bix Beiderbecke, Eddie Lang's guitar playing and Joe Venuti's skill with the violin. None of them looked like the typical Hollywood-type gangster: to me they looked rather like bank clerks, young professors, or businessmen!

We usually worked from ten in the evening until whenever they closed, because there was gambling in the house too. Despite these irregular hours it was well worth it financially. You would sometimes make a whole week's salary in one night in tips, especially when the Capone party came in. That was in the early days of the Depression in America. With Jimmie Noone (1932-3) I was making twenty-five dollars a week. I was able to buy an old used car for 175 dollars and at one time I had a Chrysler Imperial which was three years old and cost me 275 dollars.

In a way I found Al Capone an intriguing person. Of course he was king of the racketeers and his image was that of a bloodthirsty killer who wiped out other gangs and ruled Chicago, operating in bootleg whiskey, gambling, vice, dope and prostitution, but he operated it so slickly and in such a businesslike way that working for him was like working for a bank. You never had a moment's worry about your money: his offices were just packed with bookkeepers, stenographers and clerks!

One thing, I think, Al Capone has to have credit for, even if it may seem negative. In America the first Negro millionaires were a family named Spalding, who founded an insurance company in North Carolina. The Spalding descendants are still running that insurance company today. The second group of Negro millionaires were the Chicago racketeers who were allowed to operate despite the fact that Capone wiped out all other rival operators. It is easy to understand why Capone was popular on the South Side of Chicago among the Negro poplulation. A name that springs to mind in this connection is that of the Jones brothers, who became millionaires in the numbers racket. Capone let the Negro racketeers handle all the bootleg whiskey, although he didn't allow any white racketeers to operate in Chicago except himself.

In the racial hierarchy in those days in America you could say that the Negroes were at the bottom of the ladder, then came the Italians, then the Jews, then the Irish, and finally the Americans without any of these associations.

It has been suggested that Capone perhaps let the Negroes in Chicago handle his whiskey business without interference out of some kind of sympathy with the underdog. Perhaps that is the explaination, I just don't know.

I joined Benny Carter through the efforts of the ubiquitous John Hammond. I first met Benny Carter, I think, in Toledo. I heard him with Fletcher Henderson's band. Also, when he was with Horace Henderson's band, he came through Detroit at the Graystone, but my first real memory of him was when he was conductor of McKinney's Cotton Pickers after Don Redman left. Don went back to New York and formed his own band and McKinney's brought in Benny Carter. They were doing some rehearsals in Toledo when I was living there, and that's when I met Benny.

When the Milt Senior band went back to Toledo in 1931 and I stayed in Chicago, I was hired, as I said, to sub at the Grand Terrace Cafe on South Parkway with a group called Eddie Moore's Band, when Earl Hines, who usually worked there, went out on the road. We would broadcast every night at midnight, the same as Earl had done when he was home. The Grand Terrace was Earl's home base for a long time, and I got to know him well there and sit in with his band, playing. I had been interested in arranging since my studies of music theory at school, and as I had gotten into writing, he asked me to write some arrangements for him, which I did.

Benny Carter, of course, was my favorite arranger.

John Hammond first heard me when he was listening late one night to the radio in New York. At that time the Chicago radio stations went on with their programs longer than the New York stations – well after midnight – and a lot of New York people were in the habit of switching over for more music. Hammond happened to hear me and he decided to draw me to the attention of Benny Carter, who came out to Chicago to hear me. he came up to Chicago with a friend of his, a man named George Rich, not a musician, but just a good friend of Benny's. They stopped to hear me playing, when I was with Jimmie Noone. Well, the upshot was that Benny liked my piano and wanted me to join his band. So Irene and I moved to New York.

Benny's friend, George Rich, a wealthy New Yorker, was such a Benny Carter fanatic that he bought a nightclub to keep Benny in a job. Rich had made a lot of money in gambling and he bought the legendary Connie's Inn and renamed it the Harlem Club. I remember that Benny also brought in Keg Johnson on trombone from Chicago at the same time. It was a tremendous thing for me to be able to work with Benny Carter because he too, like Louis Armstrong and Art Tatum, is unique. I believe that Benny Carter has got to be put in the genius category and, unlike a lot of other geniuses, he has done well in his own lifetime. Only recently I was driving in a brand-new Rolls Royce which Benny had just bought and which he well deserves. Another of his prize pieces is a 25,000-dollar piano, an Austrian Bösendorfer.

The extraordinary thing about Benny Carter is that, fine and versatile musician though he is, he never took a music lesson in his life! He is still probably the greatest living saxophone player in the world; he plays wonderful trumpet and clarinet and he plays piano too. He doesn't play a lot of notes on the piano, but he sounds better than a lot of professional piano players and he arranges for all the top singers. He has produced some wonderfully original material for the Basie band, for which he wrote the *Kansas City Suite*, a musical monument to Kansas City Jazz as it was in the twenties and thirties.

I should also mention that Benny Carter has been a musical director to Peggy Lee and Ella Fitzgerald and made the arrangements for a lot of their recordings. He composes for movies a lot too, makes soundtracks and TV background music for dramatic plays which have nothing to do with music as such, and even composes music for police and gangster films.

Benny Carter does just about everything in contemporary music and I would say he, too, is in that phenomenal class in which I put Art Tatum. Yet, as I say, he never studied: not a single lesson. He taught himself to read music; he's an expert player in a big band and probably the best saxophone improviser there is. When he can take time off he does seminars at some of the leading American universities and talks to the pupils about music as well as playing at festivals. Generally, he leads an extremely dynamic and busy life.

In the Benny Carter period I would say the most important recordings I did were in the small group Chocolate Dandies series, for it was the first group in which I was featured sufficiently to get criticism in magazines. This was a small band. Armstrong's had been a full band and there was no piano featured to amount to anything in the Armstrong records, but Benny Carter with his sextet had plenty of spots to feature the piano. I started getting reviews in the English *Melody Maker* jazz newspaper, because these recordings were issued under the English Parlophone label. At that time the American equivalent, *Downbeat*, had not yet been founded.

We played the Harlem Club and that lasted for a while. Then Benny moved the band downtown to a dancehall called the Empire Ballroom, and when that finished, that was about the end of the big band. I took a job with Willie Bryant, and subsequently some of Benny's men and Benny himself also joined. Benny became musical director. Then he really raised the musical level of Willie's band to great heights. He had Ben Webster in there on tenor saxophone, along with Johnny Russell, and Glyn Paque on one of the altos. Benny played lead alto himself. Willie Bryant was an excellent showman to front the band. He sang a little, told jokes, was an excellent dancer, beautiful rhythm, and a good master of ceremonies, a neat, crowd-pleasing entertainer.

It is perhaps convenient here for me to devote some words of great appreciation and gratitude to John Hammond, whom I have already referred to as "the ubiquitous." Well, he was. John seemed to be everywhere where things that were worthwhile were happening in the jazz world, and his great quality was perhaps this unfailing acumen and discernment in things musical. After Benny Carter he introduced me to Benny Goodman and after Goodman to Billie Holiday, and all these key contacts proved to be of decisive importance to my life and career as a musician. But, aside from jazz, John Hammond also got me acquainted with a lot of other aspects of New York life and – almost inevitably – my first contact with fine classical music was through him. He took me to hear the New York Philharmonic, where the immortal Toscanini was the resident conductor, and I heard pianist Rudolf Serkin when he made his first appearance in America. John also took me to hear the great classical French pianist Robert Casadesus when he became one of the giants on Columbia records. Later, he became a personal friend. Others I got to hear through John Hammond were Zino Francescatti the Italian violinist, and the German classical pianist Walter Gieseking.

Well, there I was in 1934 with the Willie Bryant band, a young man of 21, soaking up the scene in New York and meeting interesting and important people through John Hammond.

3

Lady Day

At that time John Hammond knew every bar in New York where there was any good music. He introduced me to Billie Holiday – Lady Day as she later got to be known – when she was still obscure and was singing in Harlem. John said to me: "Teddy, there's a young lady I want you to hear sing. Her name is Billie Holiday and she's singing in a club called Jerry's in Harlem." So off we went and listened to Billie singing by turns with another girl called Beverley "Baby" White, and a piano accompanist named Bobby Henderson. The two girls were both singing. That was the whole show. "Baby" did a lovely job of the ballads, and Billie was just incomparable with her rhythm singing. Later, when Bobby Henderson left, Garnet Clark was the accompanist.

When Billie and I were introduced we hit it off extremely well and Hammond decided to set up the recording series which I did with Billie for Brunswick, beginning in 1935, and which later made jazz history and is now so famous. I organized the bands – mostly seven-piece – and helped Billie select the songs she was to sing. I would do sketch orchestrations that could be easily geared to the three-minute duration of the 78 rpm records of those days. I would sketch the main body of the music, leaving the rest to be improvised, aside from the vocal chorus. By the time the Brunswick contract was over in 1939 I reckon we must have made some 200 sides together.

Billie was in her prime then: you only have to think of such numbers as *What a Little Moonlight Can Do* and *Miss Brown to You*, with Benny Goodman on Clarinet, Ben Webster on tenor sax, Roy Eldridge on trumpet, John Kirby on bass, and Cozy Cole on drums. Later it was tenor sax player Lester Young who accompanied Billie over the years, although Johnny Hodges, Duke Ellington's star alto player, did a lot too. I think those were among the first recordings Johnny ever made outside the Ellington band. We were recording about four tunes a month for Brunswick, which later became Columbia.

People have often asked me how I ever managed to get together such a collection of star musicians to accompany Billie Holiday on those records. In retrospect I suppose it is astonishing that I succeeded in getting together that quantity of top-flight talent! They were all big names and it was natural to think it must have cost a fortune to get them together. Looking back I realize that, great as they were, no recording company would have put up the money for such a dazzling show of talent on a purely commercial basis. What actually happened was that I would just get on the phone and call whoever was in town, and I was extremely lucky to hit the jackpot so often. Johnny Hodges did a lot on alto sax, Benny Carter did a lot, Ben Webster did a lot on tenor, also Chu Berry and Bud Freeman, but Lester Young did most of the tenor. On one or two dates we had Prince Robinson from the old McKinney's Cotton Pickers band playing clarinet or tenor sax. Our trumpets were Buck Clayton and Roy Eldridge, Charlie Shavers, Bobby Hackett and Jonah Jones. Benny Goodman himself did quite a few, and a lot of men from his band are on those records, people like Gene Krupa and Harry James. On clarinet, aside from Benny, we had some with Pee Wee Russell. We had some of the men from the Basie and Ellington outfits, and some from Chick Webb's band. The cream of the crop, just the best in New York I could get. Moreover, I succeeded in getting them on the recordings at rates which, to put it mildly, were only a pittance compared with what they were earning outside.

I can only explain the mystery by saying that it was only in those sessions that those artists could only play with a group which was at their own level. In their own bands they were the number one soloist, but at my recording sessions they themselves were one of seven top soloists. You simply could not pay these groups to keep them together on a steady basis; imagine trying to get together a reed section line-up like Johnny Hodges, Lester Young, Ben Webster, Benny Carter and Benny Goodman on an economic basis! The series was named "Teddy Wilson and his Orchestra." Besides Billie Holiday, vocalists included Ella Fitzgerald, Midge Williams and Frances Hunt.

So the Teddy Wilson small group sessions were the only chance these men had to play with their peers instead of being the best in the whole band. The result was that nobody really cared about the money they were getting; they were more interested in the excitement of playing with seven men who were all as good as they were. The music that was pro-duced was a rare monthly event – art for art's sake, if you want to use a high-sounding term. Many sides featured the musicians alone with no vocals at all.

In these sessions Benny Goodman, for example, made four tunes for twenty dollars – five dollars a side. Can you imag-ine Benny Goodman recording for five dollars a tune? I guess it would be 5000, or 10,000 dollars a tune now. Johnny Hodges and Gene Krupa did the same, and so did the others. So you can truly say it was a band of "All Stars", a frequently abused term.

As far as Billie Holiday herself was concerned, she was very popular with the musicians. You might might call her a musicians' singer, and she was in the company of soloists who were on par with herself.

The two girl singers in those days who were giants of the jazz scene were Billie Holiday and Ella Fitzgerald. Ella did one of those dates I am talking about because Billie couldn't make it. If I remember rightly, I got Ella, who wasn't famous then, to sing *All My Life* and *Melancholy Baby*. Those two girls dominated the jazz scene in Harlem before they were really known among the white population of America. Never-theless, there were records of Billie Holiday and of Ella Fitzgerald with Chick Webb's band in all the juke boxes in the Negro ghettoes. Billie was singing well then, with no trouble with narcotics, as there was later. She was very good to work with, extremely cooperative, and no trouble at all.

At our sessions we did four songs in three hours. The musicians had no rehearsal – they were such fine artists they didn't need it. Most of the songs the musicians never saw before we recorded them. They'd just run over the tune once to get the balance. I'd have the sketch arrangements with me for those tunes they'd never seen before. My little sketches would be to the length of a 78 rpm record, three minutes, and I would plan the tempo and give each man a part so he would know what was to happen: when he would solo, when Billie was to sing, whether one of the players was to improvise softly in the background behind her, or when he would be featured in the foreground. They would read the melody I'd written for them and they would improvise in between on the chord tones I had put down for them. This was because, when you improvise, you throw the melody out and make your own melody based on the chord structure underneath the original melody. You might compare it to a guitar part: there's a chord line and a melody line. All this made it easy to say: "Lester (Young), you take the first sixteen bars of this chorus and we'll do three choruses all together, and then partition it all out easily."

Billie Holiday had to do her own rehearsing and had to get familiar with the lyric and the music. But most of the time she was singing with the sheet music in front of her, although she had been over the tunes several times between dates with me – just the two of us at the piano.

When you are talking about Billie Holiday it's impossible not to talk about all those stories about Billie's breakup. To judge by the reports it was all very tragic indeed. I can't really make any useful comment on them myself because I was only around Billie for the recordings. We never played together in public, except for a short period at the old Famous Door.

In June 1959, before Billie Holiday died, I played with a small band at Newport, in the Jazz Festival series there, with people like Gerry Mulligan, Lester Young, Jo Jones, Buck Clayton and Milt Hinton. This was in the days before they moved the whole thing to New York. There might have been some odd occasions when Billie and I were on the same session, but I can't speak of steady work with Billie at that time, so I was removed a lot from her personal life and was not on the scene when the use of drugs and excessive drinking occurred.

Another story that has gone the rounds was that there was a romantic association between Billie and tenor sax player Lester Young. Personally, I never saw any evidence of it, although Lester was credited with having given her her famous nickname "Lady Day". A lot of musicians in those days were good at inventing words: you can see it in the slang they made up. Louis Armstrong himself invented a lot of slang words, like "dippermouth" and "cats," during the late twenties and early thirties. They seeped out from the jazz world and were taken up by young people who wanted to be hip and use jazz expressions as if they had invented them themselves. A lot of hippie and beatnik elements are now using jazz slang which musicians discarded over thirty years ago. They say "Do you dig, man" and that kind of thing. Jazz musicians were saying that during the Second World War.

Many people who were true Billie Holiday fans found the film *Lady Sings the Blues* with Diana Ross nauseating. It was supposed to be based on Billie's book, which I personally have not read. I was pleasantly surprised when I heard Diana Ross's recording of the song *Good Morning Heartache*. I did not know that she could sing like that and was very impressed, because I had previously only thought of her as a rock'n'roll shouter, shouting, yelling and screaming. But in *Good Morning Heartache* she really did some beautiful singing.

I was in Europe at the time the film came out and I happened to see it reviewed in *Time* magazine. I ought to say, and I may shock a lot of people by saying so, that magazines like *Time* and *Newsweek* are not my idea of first-class journalism. I regard them as a gimmick journalism, just as *Hollywood Hotel* as a film featuring Benny Goodman was a gimmick. However, even the critic of *Time* magazine described the film as a sorry memorial to a great artist. It shows how phoney and tinsel Hollywood can be when you consider that, although Billie Holiday was associated with the most famous artists in the jazz world of the last forty years, not one of them is in the movie. It's like doing a movie about Louis Armstrong with no musicians in it. No Johnny Hodges in the Ellington story and no Ellington in the Johnny Hodges story! All the same, the Billie Holiday movie was a commercial success, and to people who don't know the difference it was evidently well done as entertainment.

Although I made so many hundreds of recordings with Billie and in fact made her first important recording with her when she was fifteen, I wasn't ever consulted about the Diana Ross film, nor was any other musician associated with her.

Of course, I knew from my own experience with movies that they could make a commercially successful production without us if they wrote it interestingly enough. Actually, there was more in the movie adout dope than about music! You might say it was really a dope movie rather than a music movie. You could compare it in this respect to the *Benny Goodman Story*, where the truth was watered down into a phoney love story rather than an interesting musical documentary on one of the most important eras of music native to America. After all, what's so special about dope? Edgar Allen Poe used dope, but that is not what he is remembered for. To make narcotics the central point to the life story of an artist like Billie Holiday, who influenced so many other fellow artists, is simply absurd. Even today, I've heard girl singers in their twenties all over the world who have been influenced by Billie Holiday. The same goes for Goodman, who to this day is a tremendous force around the world with clarinet players. These things happen because people generally know nothing about jazz.

Typical of the Hollywood attitude was when the producer of the *Benny Goodman Story*, Aaron Rosenburg, and his writer and director, Valentine Davis, met the whole band at Davis's for drinks and supper after the day's shooting. They had already had a tremendous success with the *Glenn Miller Story* and they were riding the crest at Universal Studios. Davis played over the day's soundtrack on his home movie machine, and boys weren't satisfied with the way the band sounded and thought it should be done over again. Davis said, "You boys don't know what you're talking about; that soundtrack is first class and doesn't need doing again. We're not making a movie for Benny Goodman fans, or even for jazz fans, or even for Americans: we're making it for the whole world!"

Of course, I was aware of Billie's tragic end, although I wasn't around her at the time. Billie lay dying in hospital the night I went to hear Ella Fitzgerald's opening performance at the Waldorf Astoria – one of her great personal triumphs in New York. It crossed my mind, as I was sitting in the audience listening to Ella at this high point in her career, that these two girls started out at the same time. When I played with Ella she wasn't as tall as she is and weighed only about ninety pounds, a skinny little kid. Ella would always win the amateur contests in theaters in Harlem at the time when I was with Willie Bryant and Benny Carter. Finally, the drummer and bandleader Chick Webb hired her. As she was under age for working in a place where they sold beer (and of course they sold beer at the Savoy Ballroom, where Chick was playing), Chick had to assume some kind of legal guardianship over Ella to enable her to perform with his band. Ella was a complete orphan and was just as disadvantaged as Billie Holiday.

I knew Billie's parents. Her father, Clarence Holiday, was an excellent guitar player with Fletcher Henderson's orchestra. He worked with Coleman Hawkins, Benny Carter, Walter Johnson, drummer Kaiser Marshall and bass player, John Kirby. Billie lived at home with her mother. I'd go down and collect her and at my home we'd select new songs for her to record. So I was around her quite a bit in those days. But Ella had no father or mother at all; she was just an orphan.

Misfortunes never come singly, they say. Billie died a few days after that Ella Fitzgerald performance at the Savoy which was so successful, and Lester Young died shortly after Billie. But, as I say, I'll never know whether there was any connection, because I wasn't aware there was any love

relationship between them, although I suppose the occur-
rences of those times will continue to give rise to jazz legends.

I did a recording session with Lester, in January 1956 I
believe, when he'd just come out of a month's stay in hospital, drying out from drink. He hadn't had a drop in a month
– and you should have heard him play! There were two
albums for Verve: one called *Prez and Teddy* (Lester was
known as "The President," or "Prez" for short,) and the other
called *Giants of Jazz*. This was the same quartet, augmented
by Roy Eldridge on trumpet and Vic Dickenson on trombone.
In *Prez and Teddy* the quartet was Lester on tenor, myself on
piano, Jo Jones on drums and Gene Ramey on bass. You
should hear Lester on those recordings, the tone he was then
getting. He was getting the big sound and he had regained
the facility he had before the Second World War and on the
dates with Billie Holiday. There was tremendous vitality in
his playing again, just after one month of not drinking.

When Lester drank heavily his tone would take on a
despairing sound; it had no life in it and it was too languid. If
you listen to those records you'll hear the old Lester come
back to life again as if it was back in the thirties. Not a drop
to drink for a whole month, and the way he was playing that
tenor! When he was discharged from hospital he wasn't supposed to touch a drop of liquor for the rest of his life, but,
sadly enough, he went back to drinking. I remember when I
was in Milwaukee in 1958, during a Jazz At The
Philharmonic concert, Sonny Stitt came by to play with my
trio and he told us then he thought Lester Young was going
to die. He'd been drinking again and he thought it was
Lester's last day on earth. But he recovered, although he
didn't live for very long after. As I say, I don't know whether
any kind of emotional attachment to Billie Holiday was
responsible for this.

As for me, I'm not allowed to drink because the doctor
thinks it's bad for me. But I can say one thing: no woman ever
drove me to drink! To me it's just a pleasantly social thing,
indulged in after work – having a drink and a chat with
fellow musicians.

4

The Music Goes Round

The public sees only certain segments of an artist's life; like peering at a scene through a tiny hole in the wall, you see only patches of the whole panorama. I have been fortunate enough to receive a certain amount of recognition and acclaim in my lifetime, and of course recordings have played a big part in laying foundations for an enduring reputation and establishing for me a niche in jazz history. Naturally, I was not aware of this at the time it was all happening. The endless recordings one makes whizz off into the unknown and, through the magic of modern commercial distribution, arrive at the most widespread and unexpected destinations, creating an invisible audience all over the world and gaining you friends you have never met. On a tour, you do sometimes meet them, and it is then surprisingly encouraging and stimulating and at the same time humbling to discover what you have been doing has been so appreciated.

Only gradually does the sense of having a reputation dawn upon you. The loyalty and affection of jazz fans all over the world has encouraged me to record my experiences and impressions in the more durable form of a book, in the hope that it may contribute something to the general history and documentation of jazz music that has been growing up.

I can well imagine that most people picture me as the jazz pianist who made a name in the so-called Swing Era playing with the Benny Goodman organization and appearing in a successful film about Goodman. There is also probably a vague notion that I had something to do with being a big influence in the rise to fame of Billie Holiday, and that's about it.

So when you come to look at it you see that there are

inevitably a lot of gaps in public knowledge. Much of my day-to-day active work in music went unnoticed by a large mass of the public and perhaps left the impression that I had disappeared from view, had perhaps retired, and might even be dead. This was very far from the case, and in 1976 is still so.

I digressed a little just now, (and shall do so again when the occasion warrants it), to deal with Billie Holiday, but now I'll return to the 1933 period when I had stayed in Chicago after leaving the Milt Senior band and first joined Benny Carter and later Willie Bryant.

As I said, Benny Carter eventually gave up his big band and joined me in the Willie Bryant band, an all-Negro outfit. Willie had some very good players. Benny was the musical director of the band and Willie himself was a very talented Master of Ceremonies, dancer and humorist. He was a singer as well, and composer of some very nice songs which the band played, some of which were recorded on Victor records.

Our mainstay at that time was the Savoy Ballroom in New York, where we shared the stand with the Chick Webb band. Chick then had one of the greatest dance bands of all time.

Later, after I had joined Benny Goodman, we went back to the Savoy and again played opposite Chick Webb who, as I have said, was a mentor to the up and coming Ella Fitzgerald.Public enthusiasm was so great that the ballroom was just not big enough for the crowd. That whole area of Harlem was roped off and traffic was stopped. All the windows of the Savoy were open and the people in the streets were listening to the two bands. The ballroom itself was completely sold out. Everything was fine, but a turning point came when Chick Webb played his theme song, *Get Together*, one of his great numbers. After he played that I think the crowd liked Chick Webb even better than the Benny Goodman band. It was usual for the crowd to pick their favorite of the two – all in good fun, of course.

Chick was one of the great drummers at that time and Benny Carter, I believe, told me that Chick was his favorite. I was very fond of drummers Big Sid Catlett and Cozy Cole, both of whom played for Benny Carter when I was with him. Of the two, Cozy Cole played most regularly with Carter.

In the Goodman period at the Savoy (the tune *Stompin' at the Savoy* originated then) the Goodman band was in fine fettle. Jess Stacy was on piano with the big band while I was playing in the quartet with Lionel Hampton, Gene Krupa and Benny. It was all very exciting.

After playing with Willie Bryant for a while I got a job with a very popular singing group called the Charioteers. They sang with piano accompaniment only and I was their accompanist for a while and also played during intermission, as well as doing some work in between at the Famous Door in New York.

I remember Bunny Berigan's small group was playing too at the same time. Bunny had a quartet and that is when I met Joe Bushkin, the famous jazz pianist. Joe wasn't playing much in those days, but had an obvious talent which Bunny Berigan recognized. He has a bubbly quality in his playing: it just effervesces; Joe was a bright young man, full of fun, and his piano playing was like him: light and sparkling.

Berigan was then playing some of the most beautiful trumpet I had ever heard, although I had already heard him briefly in the Paul Whiteman band in Chicago, before he formed his own band. He was very successful as a studio player around New York and later had his own show *The Saturday Night Swing Session* on CBS radio. But then I got to hear him every night at the Famous Door and met other good musicians like Stuff Smith the jazz violinist and trumpeter Jonah Jones.

I have mentioned that the Willie Bryant band was an all-Negro outfit. In those days there was no racial integration in jazz orchestras in public, although there was on jazz recordings, where it didn't matter. The first public integration of black and white musicians was in 1936, when I joined the Benny Goodman band. It was an amusing thought that the Chocolate Dandies band I recorded with when I was with Benny Carter consisted of both black and white musicians, while the word "chocolate" in the title was supposed to indicate that the musicians were all Negroes.

It was around this period that I first heard Count Basie at the Savoy Ballroom in Chicago. Basie was there at the time with Benny Moten's band, a great outfit from Kansas City. He was then playing a very full piano, quite different from the style he later developed and became famous for. Basie's own band came to New York around 1937. In 1936 he had a small band at the Reno Club in Kansas City. He later played at the Grand Terrace Cafe in Chicago with an augmented orchestra. I actually met Basie when they came East and started playing in New York at the Famous Door, which didn't seat more than 100 people. Still, musicians flocked to hear his refreshing music.

The Basie rhythm section was a completely new sound at the time. They added something quite new to the New York jazz scene. The sound was produced by Walter Page on bass, Jo Jones on drums and Freddie Green on guitar, together with Basie's high single notes on the keyboard, spliced into the rhythm. Musicians took a great deal of notice of it. Page was doing the 4/4 in the bass, Jo Jones was playing with open cymbals, and not choking them like other drummers, plus a very light bass drum and his particular use of the sock cymbal. All this was a refreshing new addition to the jazz repertoire in New York then. From then on, until this day, Basie has been a giant in the jazz movement, with his own distinctive sound. He often reminds me of Duke Ellington in a way: both can make introductions on the piano in such a way that, when the band is ready to come in, it attacks as one man and starts to swing from the very first note. Before the band starts both men give a clear indication in their intro-duction of the kind of pulse they want in any particular arrangement, and there is never any doubt in the musicians' minds precisely where either Duke or Basie want their attack.

All these great musicians whom I got to know, people like Louis Armstrong, Benny Carter and Bunny Berigan, were very congenial people and were very plain and modest off-stage. They were not arrogant by any means; they simply made great use of their God-given talent, and for the rest they were just nice, ordinary people. Some had other talents as well, such as cooking or painting, or had interesting hobbies. But one thing they all shared alike: their passionate love of jazz music.

You would never hear any of these leading musicians saying anything derogatory about a fellow jazz musician; if they hadn't anything good to say, they just didn't say anything at all. Gene Krupa, a drummer of genius, was one of the most generous musicians I ever knew with his praise. At one time he was one of the most popular jazz musicians in the world, especially in the heyday of his appearances with Benny Goodman. Gene could hardly come out of a theater without a large escort, because the fans would tear his clothes off his body, rip them apart for souvenirs, grasp at a button or whatever, and he was often literally in danger of being physically hurt by the adoration of his fans. But Gene never got conceited about it and always gave other drummers tremendous credit, and never got things out of balance. Most of the others I was around were like that – true giants. They never lost their sense of proportion and saw themselves as they really were, not as their fans saw them.

Just by the way: it's a curious thing about a person who's on top that when you're riding the crest you can make mistakes and it's fine, because people who idolize you think you made the mistakes on purpose and they even imitate your mistakes, although they are perhaps things you yourself are trying to get away from! You can, in fact, do no wrong. But the artists themselves know only too well what they are doing, what is good and what isn't.

It was around 1936 that I did a number of concerts at the Town Hall in New York. The Town Hall was a privately owned concert hall which could seat about 1000 and was famous for its excellent acoustics. You could say it was the leading small concert hall of New York, as opposed to Carnegie Hall, which was much bigger. The Town Hall, by the way, was a favorite with Segovia, the world-famous Spanish guitarist.

No mention of the Carnegie Hall would, of course, be complete without recalling the historic concert given there on 16 January 1938 by the Benny Goodman band, of which I was then a member. I shall be dealing with the whole Goodman interlude later, but I could just anticipate here and say we are all extremely lucky that we have a recording of it which, incidentally, is still selling well, even today.

Actually, there were three groups of musicians at that concert: the big Goodman band, then the small groups, starting with the trio, augmented to a quartet after a few numbers by Lionel Hampton, and finally what you might call the jam session group, which had Count Basie on piano. Goodman and John Hammond decided who was to be invited to play. There's no doubt the concert did a tremendous lot to improve the status of jazz in the eyes of the listening public.

As I say, this period altogether was a very formative one in my life and all the great players I met helped to form my own ideas about music. When I went to New York to play with Benny Carter's big band I met jazz singer Mildred Bailey and her famous vibraphone player husband, Red Norvo, and played on quite an number of recordings with a band of hired musicians and some other small groups which included trombonist Jack Teagarden (whom I previously met in Chicago, but never actually worked with until New York), his trumpet playing brother Charlie Teagarden, Gene Krupa, of course, and the small groups with Benny Goodman, tenor sax player Ben Webster, trumpeter Bill Coleman, tenor sax player Chu Berry and so on. Chu, sadly enough, was killed in a car accident when he was still young.

At that time there was a young piano player, still very active today, named Claude Hopkins, who was bandleader at the Roseland Ballroom, where Fletcher Henderson's band had played for many years.

Don Redman was also around New York then and, after being the director of McKinney's Cotton Pickers in Detroit and Ohio, formed his own big band at the Connie's Inn Club, later to become the Harlem Club, where I first worked with Benny Carter in 1933.

The Cotton Club, too, was going strong in Harlem in those

days, and there was a whole bunch of nightclubs, all with a large line of chorus girls, singers, comedians and dancers. Theater life was in full swing, and so was the Harlem Opera House, a theater that, along with the Lafayette and the Apollo, presented jazz bands.

Whilst I was with Benny Carter's band I had the privilege of playing with the great Bessie Smith before she died. We were the house band at the Apollo Theater at the time and Bessie appeared there once for a two-week run and it was really a pleasure to play behind her. I was always impressed by her tremendous power; she had the dynamic range of an opera singer and the same control and power of voice, from the softest pianissimo, and a tremendous pulse in her singing. She certainly was "The Queen of the Blues" and it was a pleasure to hear her four times a day, every day, for a couple of weeks.

5

Swing Is King

I now want to deal with what was undoubtedly one of the most important phases of my life as a jazz musician: my association with Benny Goodman, and its coincidence with the rise of what jazz critics like to call the Swing Era, although, frankly, I use all such terms with great reluctance.

Let me say first that it was not jazz musicians but jazz critics who stuck these labels onto various currents in jazz and, although I can appreciate their usefulness as a kind of *lingua franca* which enables us to talk intelligibly about jazz, I am often very much in doubt about their accuracy. Admittedly, I haven't an acceptable alternative for all my scruples, although I think I would prefer some kind of chronological division instead.

In my opinion, there isn't such a thing as a Swing Era because jazz had "swing" long before the so-called Swing Era ever dawned. Just think, for example, of that famous Ellington tune *It Don't Mean A Thing If It Ain't Got That Swing*, recorded so well by Ivie Anderson with Duke's orchestra as long ago as 1932.

The dictionary says the word comes from the Middle English *swinger*, meaning to beat, fling, hurl or rush. So it's a Germanic-language expression and I am perhaps correct in thinking there is some kind of association with the German word *schwung* – something to do with drive? However, that's for the pedants, and here we are stuck with all these labels, so I suppose we shall have to learn to live with them. To me "swing" is not a noun but a verb: "to swing": it denotes that compelling quality in music which gives it a "life." I could play a piece and it would swing, and I could play it five minutes later and it wouldn't swing.

All I can say is that music either swings or it doesn't.

When people talk talk about swing music they are really talking about jazz as it evolved in the 1930s. The word really originated in this context among jazz musicians in the 1920s and I see no reason why you shouldn't talk about classical music in the same way. A movement from a symphony undoubtedly "swings" better under one conductor than under another. The word "swing" has got to do with the rhythm or the pulse of the music, when it begins to take on a "motion" kind of feeling, if you like: when the music comes alive. And that's the way musicians use the term, not as a noun. So any music can swing, even a march played by a military band.

When they called Benny Goodman "the King of Swing" the publicity men just stuck a tag on him in the same way they stuck one on Paul Whiteman by calling him "the King of Jazz." In fact, Whiteman's band wasn't a jazz band at all. Of course, he had some mighty good jazz players in it, people like Bix Beiderbecke, Tommy Dorsey and Frankie Trumbauer. You'd get some good jazz when Whiteman let Bix improvise and the rest of the band was quiet, and the same goes for Jack Teagarden, Tommy Dorsey and Bunny Berigan when they were with Whiteman.

So Whiteman had a lot of good jazz players, but the general style of his band was not that of a jazz band in the sense that other bands of the time were: bands like the Casa Loma Orchestra and, of course, Ellington. While we're talking about these categories, it's hard to classify a man like Scott Joplin, who is now so popular, despite the fact that he was composing in the 1890s.

We also tend to forget that there was a lot more to the so-called Swing Era than Goodman's band. Just take the orchestrations: a lot of Goodman's most successful performances, which set the style of the band, were written by Fletcher Henderson and Edgar Sampson – things like *Stompin' At The Savoy* and *Don't Be That Way*. Fletcher Henderson wrote *Down South Camp Meetin'*, and the Goodman band orchestrations of pieces like *St. Louis Blues* and *Sometimes I'm Happy*.

There was, then, really no such thing as "the Goodman Era"; it was a general development in jazz of which Goodman was a part. Goodman himself was often bewildered by the sudden switch in taste to his kind of music. I remember once, in Philadelphia, after a performance with the Goodman band, there were the usual wild demonstrations with people jumping up and down and tearing up seats, eating the lunches they had brought with them. And people in line outside because they couldn't get in. The manager was tearing his hair and the kids in the audience were giving a bigger performance than the band on the stage! Backstage, after one of the sessions at the Earl Theater in about 1939, Benny said to me: "Teddy, do you understand what's happening?"

I replied: "I just don't, Benny, the whole thing's a mystery to me. Here we are, the toast of the country, playing exactly the same music we played a few years ago, when nobody paid any attention to us."

I first joined Benny Goodman as a regular member in 1936. In those days a lot of musicians met and kept in touch with each other during concerts at the Congress Hotel in Chicago, organized by the jazz critic Helen Oakley. The first-ever performance of the Benny Goodman Trio was at a concert organized by Helen Oakley and sponsored by the Chicago Rhythm Club. Its success was such that Benny Goodman asked me to join him on a permanent basis.

But the very first origins of the Benny Goodman Trio go back to a house party organized in 1935 by Mildred Bailey, the jazz singer, then married to Red Norvo, the vibraphone and xylophone player. At that time I had been doing a lot of recordings for Red and Mildred in small groups, providing backing for Mildred, who was a very successful star singer then, having left Paul Whiteman's band and started off on her own. Both Goodman and I were at the party and Benny brought along his clarinet. Gene Krupa, who joined the trio later, was not there, so we had no percussion. Mildred's cousin, Carl Bellinger, a keen jazz fan and test pilot for a big aircraft company, whose unrealized ambition was to be a jazz drummer, started to give some simple time on a chair with a couple of whisk brooms while Goodman and I played.

John Hammond was also at the party and was so taken by the sound that he immediately arranged a recording session with Victor. John wanted just the same sound: no bass player – just Goodman and me and a drummer.

As Carl Bellinger wasn't a professional drummer, John Hammond and Benny Goodman decided to get Gene Krupa. I didn't know Krupa at the time, although I might have met him somewhere before, but that recording session would in any case have been the first time I ever played with Krupa, despite the fact that both Benny and Krupa were Chicagoans and I had been playing a lot in Chicago. Bud Freeman was another well-known Chicagoan I never met in Chicago. I first met him, and others like Eddie Condon and Dave Tough, in New York.

Getting back to my hobbyhorse about labels in jazz, "Chicago Jazz" is another of them. If you ask me what are the characteristics of Chicago jazz I would say they are applicable to certain Chicago musicians but certainly not to all of them. To take another example: two clarinet players like Ed Hall and Barney Bigard. Both come from New Orleans but their styles are about as alike as chalk and cheese: both good but different.

To me a player is either good or not: a good sense of rhythm, a good sound, a good tone on his instrument, a good technique and an original way of playing that is creative and is saying something. These are the factors I would look for, rather than think in terms of categories.

I soon got to know Gene Krupa for the great jazz drummer he was: his perfect control of his drums, his sense of rhythm, and his touch especially, which was beautiful. No matter how loudly Gene played he never broke a drumhead, a tom-tom, a bass drum or a snare drum. Many other drummers would frequently break drumheads, but never Gene. He played with a beautiful touch even when he was playing with plenty of volume. His drumming sounded equally well on recordings and in person, and I always found him a very inspiring musician.

Krupa and Goodman had grown up together in Chicago and it was very sad that he died of leukemia. He suffered a lot from poor health later in life. As I have said, he was very well known but had some negative publicity when he became one of the first famous personalities to be arrested in the United States for smoking marijuana. Nowadays nobody would think anything of it, but in those days it caused quite a stir and wrongly gave Gene the reputation of being a drug addict. In actual fact he was the victim of new legislation making the use of marijuana illegal. It had not previously been on the narcotics list and was, I think, put on around 1938 or 1939. So Krupa was one of the first people to be arrested for smoking it after it was legally banned. People have often asked me whether Krupa was a drug addict, and I always said no, because he wasn't. Some people even said to me, almost triumphantly, "No wonder he played the drums like that if he took drugs!" Nothing could be further from the truth. Drugs, like alcohol, do not improve your playing, they make it worse, and the fact that Krupa played the drums so well proves he *wasn't* a drug addict.

In my early days as a professional musician hard drugs were not being used by jazz artists. Alcohol was the main stimulant. In those days there was prohibition in the US. There was illegal corn whiskey, especially in the South. You could get it of good quality, sometimes in charcoal barrels, and it would be a very good drink. In the Northern states they were making a lot of bad bootleg liquor which was making people sick, causing damage to eyesight. It was called all sorts of names like "lightning" or "white lightning."

The drink "top and bottom" was used quite a bit when I was around on the road because it was much better than "white lightning." It was home-made wine with gin, and it could be drunk safely because gin could be made without being too dangerous. It was plain alcohol cut with distilled water and then mixed with some of the delicious fruit wines then available. It was a good thing and seemed to me less dangerous than some of the bootleg liquor then around, although there was some excellent whiskey being smuggled in from

Canada, where the consumption of alcohol was still legal.

Very few musicians could afford Canadian whiskey. There was the stock market crash in 1929 and the Depression was just starting. I started around the time when people were saying how good times *had been* in jazz!

Coming from alcohol to drugs, I can say that marijuana was used, although under various names: Louis Armstrong called it "weed" in that song *The Peanut Vendor* and he did a trumpet number called *Muggles*. I think that was an old nickname for marijuana. But the hard dope was not used in those days. Maybe that began during the Second World War. I think its popularity has died down today, in the seventies, among young musicians. I disagree with people who associate jazz with dope. I think research and a check with clinics would show that jazz musicians are not more represented than any other group among drug users, and maybe a lot less.

It may be that this impression prevails because jazz musicians have always got bad publicity out of drugs. When Gene Krupa got arrested for possessing marijuana, word went out that he was a dope fiend. Well, as I've said, Gene Krupa was never a dope fiend. We know from official publications today that marijuana is less harmful than alcohol or even ordinary cigarettes. Marijuana is not addictive, like morphine or heroin. Gene Krupa never used these.

The last job I played with Gene Krupa was in New York, at the Saratoga Performing Arts Center in a beautiful outdoor setting. It was the summer home of the Philadelphia Symphony Orchestra, with whom Goodman played some classical music in the first half of the program. The final half was by the original Benny Goodman Quartet. That would be the last date I played with Krupa, in August 1973, and he died in October that year. I was supposed to play with Gene the week after Saratoga in Indianapolis, Indiana, but his doctors wouldn't let him play.

Of course I've played with other excellent drummers. I've not played better than with Cozy Cole or Jo Jones and, if I may for a moment indulge in a little family pride, my own son Teddy Jr. plays perfectly for me.

So thanks again to the moving spirit of John Hammond, the trio, in the composition that made it famous, got together again on Easter Sunday 1936, when the Goodman band presented its third concert at the Congress Hotel in Chicago and I became part of the Goodman organization. Before I joined the organization, the trio (with me in it) had recorded the sides *After You've Gone, Body And Soul, Who?* and *Someday Sweetheart.*

In the mid-summer of 1936 the quartet was born, when Goodman, Krupa and I met Lionel Hampton at the Paradise Café in Los Angeles and had a jam session. The first Goodman quartet session for Victor, the one that produced *Moonglow*, was held a few days later, and Lionel Hampton, too, became a member of the Goodman organization.

Contrary to popular belief, Benny Goodman was not the first to introduce small groups to jazz. Even when I was at school I had recordings of Jelly Roll Morton's trio with drums, piano and clarinet. There was Louis Armstrong's Hot Five, and Bix Beiderbecke, Frankie Trumbauer and Red Nichols also had small groups – remember the Five Pennies? But what I think can be said from a historical point of view is that credit must go to Goodman for having introduced for the first time public performances by an interracial small jazz group.

I have had occasion previously to refer to racial relationships an America and that is why the Goodman innovation was significant. It should be remembered that, in those days, Negro people were excluded from practically every area of white activity in the higher income levels, except in show business. I am not talking now, of course, about the privileges extended by Al Capone to the Negroes in Chicago, who were certainly in the higher income bracket! Before Benny Goodman broke through the colour bar with the Trio in public performances, there were plenty of Negro stars earning good money. There was Ethel Waters, for instance, earning about 7000 dollars a week, a great deal of money in those days of the early thirties. Today this would be equivalent to between 40,000 and 50,000 dollars a week, which they earn in

Las Vegas and places like that. Others who come to mind in this context are Bill Robinson and the Mills Brothers, who were experiencing a resurgence in popularity and were certainly in the higher income bracket. And Ellington, of course, was going strong. Also Cab Calloway was very popular.

But we all had to face the fact that in every category, and not only in entertainment, Negroes were not welcome in the majority of white hotels in America, even in the northern cities, like New York. I remember, as late as after the Second World War, that a very good friend of mine, the noted Negro actor, Canada Lee, was refused service in a Swiss-style restaurant in New York. However he sued the restaurant and got awarded considerable damages.

America is literally the whole world, and yet all the people from different racial backgrounds, Negroes, Jews, Italians, Irish, never came together. When I first went to this big city of New York, everybody would stay in his own particular area of town: all the Negro people were to be found in Harlem; Little Italy was where the Italians were; German people were to be found around East 86th Street, called "Yorkville"; while the Puerto Ricans were in East Harlem. At that time the Goodman band was one big happy family and we were a small version of the whole world: Benny himself was Jewish, Lionel and I were Negroes, Vido Musso had an Italian background and Red Ballard I think was Irish. It was, in fact, an all-American band. As for Harry James in the trumpet section, he claimed to be descended from Jesse James, the notorious "baddest man in the West"!

People much older than I am have told me that in New York many years ago you simply had to be together with your own group to get home safely after school because you'd get beaten up if you got into the wrong group. You wouldn't get killed, but you'd get a beating up on the way home with fists and shoes. It was not only like that with the Negro people, it was among whites too. If you were Irish you had to get with the Irish kids to get home safely to your neighborhood, and if you were Jewish you had to get with the Jewish kids to get home safely.

When Lionel Hampton and I first joined the Benny Goodman organization we would have to stay in different hotels from the rest of the band. When the whole band got into town for a one-night stand, instead of putting everyone to the inconvience of trying to find a hotel where all twenty could stay, Lionel and I would get into our cars and drive straight away to the Negro ghetto in the town and find a Negro hotel, or some professional rooming house. When you did one-night stands like that you simply had to do everything you could to make things easier for everybody. All you were thinking about was getting some sleep and some food, playing a dance and getting off to the next town. Then it was simply a question of the time not being ripe to make demands; the whole band would have been tied down by us and couldn't have moved on the road at all if Lionel and I had demanded equality with the rest of the boys.

Humiliating? I suppose so, to a certain extent, but it was considered so normal in those days. People today should not forget that it had been like that since we were born. Such conditions were a small step forward from slavery. After all, our grandfathers actually were slaves. They had been brought to America in chains and had worked for nothing, doing hard manual labor for nothing in return. They had no rights whatsoever as human beings. They could be killed. There was no justice for them in the courts because they had no ability to sue. They had literally nothing, and that was especially true in the South.

Of course vast changes have come about in America since then, and the country is gradually becoming what it is really supposed to be: the fusion of the whole world. America is now so far along this path that I would not have believed that I would live to see it. American community life has come much further than I ever expected. If you had asked me some thirty years ago, I would have said it would take at least a century to get to where we are now.

Of course, the old situation is not entirely dead, but it's vastly different from when Lionel Hampton and I first joined the Benny Goodman organization. Historically, then, this period is much more important – stepping, for a moment, outside the context of this book – than the advent of the Benny Goodman band. It's all related to the social pattern of American life in those days.

Even today Jews are excluded from many categories of society, although their position has greatly improved. I very well remember the "restricted clientèle" advertisements relating to Jews – country clubs, social organizations, different types of membership and so on. There was also subtle discrimination against Italians in those days.

But now, as I have said, America is the whole world: a big cauldron from which a shape is gradually beginning to emerge, more in accordance with the original conception formed following the Declaration of Independence.

So it is to Benny Goodman that the credit must go to for hiring me, a Negro, against the advice of his booking agents. By doing so he in fact took a gamble on his career. You see, in taking me on, Goodman was torn between two forces: on the one side there was John Hammond , a wealthy young patron of the arts who probably did more for jazz than anybody else outside the players themselves, pressing Benny to hire me and, on the other side, show business people, who were saying to Benny:"You're a bright young man, you're a very talented clarinet player and you're going to block your career at its very beginning. You're only in your twenties and you'll never be successful if you hire a Negro player."

But Benny's feeling was that music was more important than race. Benny decided to make the gamble and it turned out to be a great success for him. And when he hired another Negro, Lionel Hampton, a year later, there was no doubt as to whether it would work. Lionel's addition to the group made it much stronger with the public.

Of course there were incidents, and I know Benny had to put his foot down many times on this issue when it came to bookings, often without either Lionel or I knowing. Goodman always insisted that the agent should take the band in its entirety or not at all, and we played all the jobs.

There is one particular incident that occured when the

Goodman band was on the road which has been circulated in various versions, so perhaps this is the right place to get the record straight. It is said that Lionel and I got roughed up by the police on one occasion. The true facts are that the incident took place when the Goodman band played its first engagement in the southern part of the USA, in Dallas, Texas, in about 1937 or 1938.

At that time Texas was celebrating some kind of anniversary and the Goodman band was there as part of a big program of entertainment, featuring artists from all over the United States of America. It was our first engagement in the South and a professor from the University of Texas, who was a keen jazz fan, was at the concert. He had a bottle of champagne sent backstage for Lionel Hampton and myself with his compliments and a request to be allowed to drink a glass with us.

The Police intervened and said he would not be allowed to do so. This story, of course, got around and so the next day the Dallas Chief of Police came to investigate personally. When he heard the story he gave the whole police department a bawling out and instructed them to give us the greatest consideration. That was very rare in those days. He told Lionel and me that, should there be any further trouble, we were to let him know immediately and personally. He said: "I'm the baddest man here: any trouble at all and you let me know."

I have said that the Benny Goodman Trio was not original in jazz because of its smallness; it was original because it was interracial and played publicly as such. The question remains: what was musically new about it? I think the instant success of the trio recordings was due to the refreshing quality they had. The bass was absent and you got a good chance to hear the way I was using the left hand on the piano, coordinating it with Krupa's bass drum. The simple answer is, I think, that there was no sound like it on records then.

The other obvious parallel that comes to mind is the Jelly Roll Morton Trio, but that was ten years earlier. Jelly was using a very different style from mine, to start with, and his clarinet player, Omer Simeon, had quite a different style from Benny Goodman. Of course, there was Gene Krupa's sound on drums, and there was a big difference there, because Jelly's drummer wasn't even using a sock cymbol, a very important instrument in the jazz drummer's armament. The Benny Goodman Trio therefore represented a very new sound. That's what made it unique and in that sense I suppose you could say it was a first in its own way.

A lot of people called it jazz chamber music. I think it was John Hammond who first used that expression. He used to liken us to a combination in the classical world of Walter Gieseking and Joseph Szigeti.

Interracial musical collaboration went an important step further when Benny got Fletcher Henderson in to do his arrangements, and it was these arrangements that gave a new refreshing sound to the big band. Previously, I'd never heard of Fletcher orchestrating for anybody but his own band. In a way he was parallel to Duke Ellington: he had a big jazz band at the time, although he never achieved Duke's popularity. Duke just left everybody behind. Even Benny Carter, talented as he was, couldn't keep up with Duke, who notably succeeded in being good musically *and* financially – a very important combination!

Goodman was never able to make arrangements himself, so he hired arrangers from the beginning. First the style of the band was set by Fletcher Henderson, and later Goodman had some very effective originals composed for him by Edgar Sampson: *Stompin' At The Savoy, Don't Be That Way* and arrangements of current tunes and standards. A man who did so much for Goodman, but never seems to have got the credit, was Jimmy Mundy who had been Earl Hines's arranger when Hines had a fine big band. At one time Mundy was turning out something like five arrangements a week for Goodman and they were all excellent. He was extremely talented, but he never got the recognition and publicity that Fletcher Henderson did, although Henderson was a well-established bandleader when Goodman hired him to arrange and compose for him. Glenn Miller was a great arranger and composer for his own band, and of course Duke Ellington remains the shining example of the leader who did that.

When Fletcher Henderson took up writing for Benny Goodman in 1939, he gave up his own band for a long while and helped to give the Goodman band its own distinctive sound. Goodman at the time even outstripped Ellington in popularity, despite the fact that Duke had been established for so many years. However, Goodman, in his turn, was over-taken by Glenn Miller, who came in with that new reed section sound. I don't think Glenn Miller was as jazz orientated as Benny Goodman's band because Miller made more use of the ballad sound with the flowing legato reeds: the doubled reed melody with the clarinet on top.

I should say here that jazz players generally did not at that time neglect the tremendous institution of the jam session. There has been some talk of jazz musicians "fleeing" to the jam session to get away from the strait-jacket, the regimentation and high precision work of big band playing. Personally, I don't believe a word of it. It was simply that the jam session, as an institution in its own right, was an ideal stamping ground for musicians to keep their hand in at playing spontaneously and creatively. The sessions would run all night long in Harlem and Greenwich Village and all over New York.

Sometimes they would start at four in the morning. Musicians would leave a nightclub and go to an after-hours club and play until nine in the morning. Many times I've been with Art Tatum at jazz piano sessions which would wind up at noon the next day. That's the best way for young musicians to get their apprenticeship as jazz improvisors, just playing for fun.

The jam sessions were so popular and spread so much that the unions in the end clamped down on them because a lot of nightclub owners started taking advantage of the fact that they could hire a trio or a piano player, and before the night was out there would be ten men on the bandstand, all clamoring for a chance to play, both for their own pleasure and that of the audience! The musicians themselves were getting tremendous practice at improvising. Don Byas, the leading tenor sax player, is an example. He was a great jam-session player in New York years ago. When I listen to his records I always think that the perfection you hear stems from all those jam sessions Don attended way back in the 1930s in New York. He was playing alongside Lester Young, hour after hour, and alongside Ben Webster and many others.

Goodman's great strength as a musician was to recognize the qualities of other players. He was excellent at running a jam session. He would call out :"You take the next chorus," "Now, we're going out," "Drum solo, or "All right! Piano break, four bars!"

In that way, Goodman was a very good leader. All those intricate trio, quartet and sextet arrangements were put together by the whole group, but it was Goodman who would put everybody's ideas together to form the final product, and only then would we record. It was Goodman who decided whose idea would be used for the introduction, whose idea would go into the interlude, and whose idea to change the key at a certain point would be used, and of course he contributed ideas himself. So all three of us in the beginning contributed ideas and we were joined later in this by Lionel Hampton and Red Norvo. These latter two contributed a lot of ideas to the sextet recordings. But it was always Goodman who was the final arbiter. He would say: "We need an introduction," or "We need an interlude," or he would decide when a particular instrument was to be featured, Goodman's talent for this kind of coordination made him a great leader.

Goodman has frequently been depicted as a stern taskmaster for his fellow musicians. In an interview with George T. Simon in 1946 (quoted in his book *The Big Bands*,) Goodman admitted that he was a perfectionist and that musicians' mistakes bugged him. "I'll never be satisfied with any band. I guess I expect too much from my musicians, and when they do things wrong I get brought down."

I think we should remember that all bandleaders have to be disciplinarians to have an orchestra like Benny

Goodman's, Artie Shaw's, Glenn Miller's or Tommy Dorsey's.

I was listening to a recording of the Tommy Dorsey band only the other day, made in the days before Frank Sinatra, who was with Dorsey, became a professional singer. I thought as I listened that Dorsey's band was as perfect as a little symphony orchestra, certainly as perfect as the studio orchestras of today.

In those days, forty years ago, to get that effect you'd have to rehearse and rehearse and rehearse. Only then would you get seventeen or eighteen men playing like one man. When the reed section played, everybody would breathe and phrase in exactly the same way as the lead alto. The same applied to the brass, and you would have to get the ensemble to phrase like the lead trumpet. All this took a lot of dedication and hard work at rehearsal. So a leader simply had to be a stern taskmaster; if he wasn't, he'd have a sloppy-sounding band.

All those bands were just about perfect. Listen to some of Artie Shaw's things, even after the war, before he got out of the business and added strings. His recordings in the middle forties had symphony-orchestra perfection and in musical terms were on a par with a classical performance.

Neither will you hear any sloppiness in a good symphony orchestra or, for example, in the Budapest String Quartet, a great favorite with music lovers in America in those days. That quartet was perfection itself and simply gorgeous to hear, and showed the results of hard work done by extremely talented musicians.

Goodman may have been unique in the sense that, although he may not have known how to handle his men as some leaders did, he got results. Some men like Woody Herman knew how to drive a band hard and get the best out of it without hurting anybody's feelings. Tommy Dorsey could do that too, but his own way of relieving tension was to tell a good joke in between and get everybody laughing. Toscanini got perfection out of the NBC Symphony Orchestra, a technical perfection that today may be common to symphony orchestras around the world. But it was certainly an achievement in those days to get a hundred men playing as one. I have heard that Toscanini used to tear his clothes to shreds during rehearsals: and then perhaps he would tear his shirt off! All the same, he got that NBC Orchestra playing perfectly and there was nothing to compare to it. It was pure magic to get a hundred men to achieve that precision, feeling and concentration and it takes hard taskmasters to get that.

Duke Ellington is another example of how somebody goes about getting what he wants out of an orchestra. I'll give you an example of Duke's subtle methods of getting the results he wanted. At one time Duke had a drinking problem in his band. So he tackled it by writing a feature solo piece for each of his star musicians. When he caught a man too drunk on the stage, the Duke would say: "And now, ladies and gentlemen, we will feature our first trumpet player (or whomever) in a solo in such-and-such a song." And the fellow would try to play it after he had had too much to drink – with what results you can best imagine!

So each leader has his own methods of extracting what he needs musically out of his men, and the Duke's were perhaps among the most original.

As for Goodman, he became famous (or notorious) for staring at a player he didn't like. It was called "the ray" by his men. You might perhaps call it "the death ray." This was a special kind of glare at a player who wasn't doing what he wanted him to do. Personally, I'm not sure whether that's true or not. After all, it's very possible that he might have just been staring into space, or thinking about the tempo of the next tune he was going to play. However, a lot of players thought he was annoyed with them because he was glaring at them in that special way. All the same, you can stare at someone and yet not see them; you might be thinking of something 1000 miles away. I'll probably never know the truth of the matter.

So if you ask me whether Benny was a hard taskmaster I would say, yes he was, but so were the others, and they had to be. I remember doing a recording session with Tommy Dorsey once. Dorsey had a large band at the time – fifteen or eighteen pieces – and he came over to me where I was at one side playing the piano and whispered in my ear: "Teddy, don't use the sustaining pedal on the piano."

So you can see Tommy Dorsey's ear was sharp enough to hear, with all those trombones, trumpets, saxophones, guitar and drums playing, that I was using the sustaining pedal on the piano! But he wanted it "drier"; he wanted "crisp" piano. Now some leaders would have told me across the room, so the whole band could hear it, but Tommy was more discreet. But when Benny Goodman was at work there was no levity or humour in him; he had a way of correcting someone in front of the others, in a way that to some did not seem tactful or diplomatic. He would be right, but his method of getting what he wanted sometimes dented the egos of the various players. So he wasn't always skilful in handling his men.

In the classical field the same sort of thing apples. I have said that Toscanini got perfection out of the NBC Symphony Orchestra by showing his displeasure only too clearly when it wasn't playing as he wanted it to. But, by the time the rehearsal was over, the NBC Symphony would be playing as one man, and it was absolute perfection.

I remember when I was at school we had a bandmaster who could take high school boys and make them sound almost like a first-class military marching band. He would scream at the musicians and use four-letter words, all mixed up with jokes, and would have some seventy-five young musicians laughing just like Tommy Dorsey did, but he would get what he wanted in the end.

In the Goodman band you can hear that perfection, the blend of all the horns. When the reeds play, they all phrase together, they all breathe together, and the same applies to brass. When the whole ensemble plays, everyone plays with the same expression; all the horns play like one man. There's lots of rehearsal, lots of discussion, lots of running over certain passages time and again, but what comes out is great music.

Of course, in small improvising groups you don't have

that. In the trio, quartet and sextet Goodman was just one of the boys; we weren't playing written and ensemble music which calls for such perfection in coordination. The emphasis in the small groups, as distinct from the large orchestra, lies in not repeating the same thing, but saying it differently each time. So you have quite a different type of rehearsal for a small improvising jazz group to the rehearsal needed for a big band playing written music. So Goodman was much more relaxed then, because everyone in the small jazz group was on an equal footing, and he didn't have to play the stern taskmaster.

When you're recording in a small group you all know when you have to do it over. You could have a take of a number which could be just right, then you could move on to the next one. But when it's not right everybody knows it. The leader has to decide whether a recording is good enough for the public. The same goes for actors, even for stars: they don't argue with the director when he says: "You've got to do that over again." Personally, I've never seen any temperament on the movie set and I've worked with people like Mary Martin and Ethel Merman, who were big musical stars in America, and I've seen Ethel Merman work like any extra you'd never heard of. It was simply "Do it over 'til it's right." If you belittle people, it's easy to get a negative reaction from them. If someone's temper gets the better of him and everything gets blown apart you might just as well cool down for a while, otherwise the whole thing gets lost.

6

Into Films

"Teddy, do you understand what's happening?" Benny Goodman had said to me after that 1939 concert in Philadelphia, when people went wild at the sound of the band, tore up the theater seats and were jumping up and down and dancing in the aisles

Well, I didn't understand and told Benny so, and I cannot explain it to this day. I suppose you might compare the whims and fancies of the public, the "thousand-headed monster" as it has been called, to the migration of birds and the spawning of the salmon: there are mysterious forces at work which we cannot fathom.

Why *did* jazz get so big in the Benny Goodman period? There was no logic in it really. Duke Ellington had been big before that, of course, in his own way; there had been Cab Calloway and Jimmie Lunceford and then, suddenly, the whole thing came to a tremendous climax with the Benny Goodman band, the Quartet and the Trio. This is all the more astonishing when you consider that, in 1937, the economy was on the downgrade. Yet people still apparently found money to hear and dance to the big bands. Those bands obviously filled a big need at the time.

All this hullabaloo had not gone unnoticed in Hollywood, where the film moguls saw financial opportunities in jumping on the bandwagon and getting carried along by the wave of popular enthusiasm.

The first Hollywood excursions into the jazz scene were modest and cautious. Some of the films Goodman featured in before *The Benny Goodman Story* was made were *Stage Door Canteen*, *A Song is Born*, *Powers Girl*, *The Big Broadcast of 1937*, *Hollywood Hotel*, *Sweet and Lowdown* and a soundtrack for

Walt Disney's *Make Mine Music*. It was clear from the start that Hollywood was going for the popular public entertainment angle. The film producers were not interested in giving the public an accurately documented account of the jazz scene, or even in pleasing the jazz fans. They cast their nets wider and wanted to take in all the various categories of the public at once. So the result, in jazz terms at any rate, was a watering down of the original: usually a phoney and rather syrupy love plot was woven around the factual material by scriptwriters, as was done in *The Benny Goodman Story*. In *Hollywood Hotel*, which contained some excellent and exciting but all too brief camera shots and close-ups of the Trio and Quartet, the main jazz characters were portrayed more or less as buffoons rather than skilled musicians. In a way, I suppose the myth Hollywood wove around jazz did it more harm than good in terms of presentation, but on the other hand it did a lot of good keeping jazz and good jazz players before the public eye through the powerful medium of film.

Of course the impact of jazz and film produced a lot of surprises on both sides. The Hollywood people were grappling with what was for them completely new material and they were trying to fit it into a popular success formula. The jazz musicians, serious about their business, had never looked upon themselves as popular entertainers, least of all as actors! So there were the necessary remonstrances on both sides: the musicians thought the Hollywood approach was superficial and the Hollywood producers thought the musicians would never get the requirements of modern entertainment through their thick heads. Still, I suppose both parties learned something from each other.

For me personally the jazz film interlude was a very interesting experience.

In the early films the old bogey of race relations reared its ugly head, and concessions had to be made to the movies of the time. In the very first movie the Goodman band ever made, they wanted me to make the soundtrack but not appear on the screen. They wanted a white person to be filmed at the keyboard. So I was not in that film, the argument being that, since it was the first chance for the band in films, it could lead to others where this concession could be dropped. So I did appear on the screen in *Hollywood Hotel*, made the following year.

All that was okay with me. It was more important in this case for the Goodman band to get into their first movie and then get Lionel Hampton and me in later.

Of course in the 1955 film *The Benny Goodman Story* I did the whole soundtrack on tape and the whole film too. In a sense this was historically incorrect, because it was Jess Stacy who always played with the big band and in *The Benny Goodman Story* I was filmed all through with both the small groups and the big band. I guess that was because, for some reason, Benny and Stacy didn't come to terms on the business arrangement, so Stacy was not in the movie, although he should have been.

As for the film itself, it was a Hollywood product and from an historical point of view, was only about fifty percent accurate, I should say. The chief thing wrong with it was the love story they wove into it. That was just phoney. The movie ends in 1938 and I'm not sure Goodman was even associated with his wife at that time. However, that didn't bother the scenario writers and they wrote her in all through his career. Benny might have known Alice by the end of the movie, but he didn't get married to her for years after that. The whole love story was a true example of Hollywood make believe, just as the Billie Holiday film was.

The Hollywood technique of building the actual film onto a previously recorded soundtrack had its problems. When we were on the set I would have to be very much on the alert when the cameras gave a close-up of my hands; the soundtrack would be blaring away and I would have to make sure as best I could that my fingers were not hitting the bass notes when the sound was in high register! So we spent no end of time memorizing the improvisations we had made originally on the soundtrack to make sure we could get a plausible picture going. Of course, the synchronization was very rarely perfect, but if the producer said it was OK, we went on to the next scene.

I have to smile when I recall that I personally got quite a lot of fan mail for my *acting* in the picture. That goes to show you the kind of phoney situations you can get into. All the same, I enjoyed making those films, in spite of everything. Movie-making is a fascinating business: one single film can shoot you straight from obscurity to world fame. You also get to appreciate the skill of professional actors. Once the director has called out "Roll 'em!" everything becomes difficult, instead of easy, as it appears on the screen. It even becomes a problem to walk three feet from one chair to another – to do it easily and naturally. They gave you marks on the floor where you had to step.

Then there is the problem of the expressions on your face when the camera's on top of you. When I saw myself in the Benny Goodman film I wasn't too happy, especially having to say lines which weren't natural. You were a parrot for the Hollywood scriptwriters. Imagine my aversion at having to say another man's lines about how *he* thinks jazz musicians talk, while he himself hasn't the slightest knowledge of jazz.

In *The Benny Goodman Story*, for instance, I had to say to another musician: "Hot bands are cold turkey in this town." That may have been the scriptwriter's idea of the style of con-versation of jazz musicians, but in fact it was just silly. Any self-respecting jazz musician would rather be found dead than caught saying a thing like that. All this can be very embarrassing, especially to me, because I loathe creep slang, even jazz slang. I personally would never think of using such expressions as "I dig, man."

While on the subject of the distortion of true facts, I can quote the stories in circulation about how Lionel Hampton came to join the Benny Goodman Trio. The version in the movie, where Benny, Krupa and I were having coffee in a roadside café and Lionel was supposed to be a waiter, was simply a figment of the imagination of the scriptwriters. By some Hollywood miracle Lionel happened to have his vibra-phone with him!

The truth of the matter, as I have already said, was that Goodman and I went to hear Lionel first at the Paradise Club, where he was Master of Ceremonies, a bandleader being featured on vibraphone, drums and piano. It was almost a one-man show.

Lionel was, and still is, a tremendous talent who pioneered the vibraphone as a solo instrument, changing it from a one-note-per-arrangement novelty into a solo instrument in its own right. In so doing, Lionel brought about tremendous technical changes in the construction of the instrument, and manufacturers started adapting it to the new possibilities he opened up, to make it suitable for continuous playing: stronger chords, more attention to tone, adjustment of the resonating columns, construction of the bars, and so on. Lionel pioneered all that.

In the *Benny Goodman Story* Benny himself was not on camera, since his part in the film was played by actor Steve Allen. However Benny was around the set every day to see how the film was progressing. Our call was perhaps from seven in the morning until seven in the evening, but we would actually be on camera for only part of that time. The rest of the time was taken in up fixing lighting, the shifting of stage scenery by stage crews and so on, Sometimes there were days when we did nothing but sit around, waiting to be called.

Steve Allen had a piano on the set during these in-between periods we would have jam sessions. Steve was a good piano player himself and he and I took turns at the keyboard and the other players did, too. The horn players had a lot of fun. Steve always had a long table with a lot of refreshments on it, so the musicians were constantly supplied.

I had quit my work with CBS in 1955 to work in the Benny Goodman film. My Hollywood contract called for two months of continuous appearance at the Universal Studios and the CBS contract could not guarantee me a steady job with CBS in New York if I took two months off. So I thought it would be wise to take the plunge for two reasons: the film would get me back into the public spotlight, since I was playing in the movie myself, and, secondly, the move would get me back into touring around and performing to live audiences again, rather than playing to just a microphone on radio, or making studio recordings.

I don't regret that decision, looking back on it from my 1970s vantage point. I am convinced that jazz should be performed to live audiences. It is not good for jazz musicians to stay behind the scenes, playing to microphones behind singers, and all sorts of other jobs just for the sake of financial security, although I must say that, in all the staff jobs I had, there was always room for me to be featured. I was never at any time simply used as a utility pianist, and I always had my own program.

Through the media of records and films, jazz had spread far beyond the national borders and had gone round the world. It had even penetrated what the politicians liked to call "the Iron Curtain," and eventually the mighty Soviet Union beckoned the Benny Goodman band to go and show the Russians what jazz was all about.

7

To Russia With Jazz

In 1962 the first American jazz tour of the Soviet Union was arranged for the Benny Goodman band in exchange for a visit to the United States of a group of Ukrainian dancers. The tour was of six weeks' duration.

This tour was of particular interest to me since it was the first time that I had ever been in any of the socialist countries, and we had an excellent band at the time.

We broke in the band before the Soviet tour by playing a series of one-night stands throughout the United States for a couple weeks, winding up at the Seattle World's Fair for a week. From Seattle we went to Moscow under the auspices of the State Department. Before our departure, however, I had met President Kennedy at a Sheraton Park Hotel Banquet sponsored by the White House press photographers. Mr Harold Macmillan, then Prime Minister of Great Britain, was one of the guests of honor.

I was there with the Benny Goodman Quartet, but there were also entertainers and comedians, including some from Britain. Among them, I believe, was Peter Sellers. There was a lot of fun, and an American comedian gave an imitation of President Kennedy, while I believe it was Sellers who gave a take-off of Prime Minister Macmillan.

After the show all the artists formed a circle, and Kennedy and Macmillan went around and shook hands and thanked everybody for their performance. Even before I was introduced, President Kennedy singled me out and said: "Hello, Wilson, I hear you're going to Russia."

I replied "Yes, Sir."

He said: "Well, do a good job," and I said: "We'll try."

I was introduced to Mr Macmillan, too. At the Russian end

I was to meet Nikita Kruschev, so in that short time I met three world leaders: Kennedy, Macmillan, and Kruschev. I had already met a lot of politicians and diplomats when I played the jazz clubs in Washington, DC, and I found many of them were jazz fans and, in some cases, amateur musicians themselves.

Apart from Moscow, the Goodman band played to wildly enthusiastic Russian audiences in four or five Soviet republics, visiting Leningrad, Kiev in the Ukraine, Sochi on the Black Sea, Tbilisi (Tiflis), capital of the old Georgian Republic, and fabulous Tashkent.

Benny Goodman had originally thought of having a book of modern pieces and arrangements for the Russians, but it was soon apparent that what I might call the "classic" Goodman repertoire of the thirties, when the band first became famous, went down best with Soviet audiences. There was criticism from some of the musicians of this choice of repertoire for the tour, but Benny was proved right in the end by the tremendous response he got. The US State Department was well pleased by the tour's reception.

We got lots of visits backstage from fans. It's a curious thing that, despite all the censorship of information, all the radio sets I saw in the stores had short-wave bands on them, so the public could not be prevented from listening to foreign broadcasts. So a lot of jazz was listened to in the Soviet Union, particularly on the Voice of America and BBC broadcasts. It was typical that Goodman got the biggest Russian response for Ellington's *Take The A Train*, which was the signature tune of the Voice of America Jazz Hour.

We had been briefed beforehand by the State Department about moves in the Soviet Union and about what we should and shouldn't do. We were told, for example, that the Russians frown on public drunkenness, especially on the part of foreign visitors. They did not want us to take any photographs in their airports or from the upper floors of buildings where we stayed. They have many skyscraper-type buildings, and photographs from the upper floors were out, as well as shots of bridges.

We were also warned that the Russians do not allow sexual fraternization between their people and foreigners and we should not mix with Russian girls. In particular we were cautioned by State Department officials about selling anything to the Russians. It was regarded as a serious crime in the Soviet Union to trade privately without the knowledge of the State. The warning was certainly not untimely because we were in fact approached on occasion by Russian fans who wanted to buy some article of clothing, a shirt for instance, especially something made of nylon.

There were police checks on this, although the police were fair, if efficient. I remember somebody in the band had given a young Russian boy a discography of Benny Goodman. The police swooped right down on the lad and detained him. He was hustled into a car and whisked off to the police station within seconds, although he was released, because we saw him again later. I suppose they wanted to know what was in the book he had been given and just let him go when they saw it was harmless. Nevertheless, I noticed a general fear of being seen around foreigners and accepting articles. Older people tended to stay away from us.

My own experience of the customs officials in the Soviet Union and Eastern Europe has always been very good: going in and out of the US, I have all too frequently had my bags examined, but not in Russia. They just went straight through.

So there we were: eighteen musicians and a girl singer, Joya Sherrill, an American and a Russian manager, two Russian girl interpreters and one man interpreter, plus a man from the US State Department, for a six-week tour, to do between thirty and thirty-five performances. Our crowd took me back to the height of the 1930s.

Premier Nikita Kruschev turned up at the Fourth of July Independence party given at the end of the tour by the American Ambassador, and he also came to the Moscow concert. His comment was typical: "I don't understand the music, but I certainly understand the girl singer!" No wonder. At the time, Goodman's girl singer Joya Sherrill had brought with her a fantastic entertainer's wardrobe complete with sequins, silks and satins, and she was a stunning sight on the stage. Apparently that had not escaped Kruschev's notice! Joya, I remember, was a Duke Ellington discovery, but she settled down to domestic life eventually after marrying a successful architect.

July 4th was a beautiful day in Moscow. The embassy had a beautiful lawn, where a temporary bar was set up, and the band did a continous jam session, without arrangements. There was quite a stir when Kruschev suddenly turned up with his Defence Minister, in a convey of three big Zis cars, but without a body guard as far as we could see. There were of course endless toasts to Soviet-American friendship and a lot of joking and laughing. We had an interpreter there and Benny Goodman was chaffing and kidding around with Kruschev and I shook his hand. Quite a lot of drink was circulating and some of the guests, including the Russians, could really pour it down!

That Vodka! Simply delicious! It seemed to have more body than the vodka we have in the States. It was not so thin, was actually very smooth, and did not burn going down. The Russians themselves just pour it down straight. They'll pour half a tumblerful straight down the hatch. One of the fellows in the band said the reason why Americans get drunk quicker on vodka is because they sip it, whereas it should go straight down, the Russian way. The Scandinavians, I found, down their Aquavit in one, but then the glasses are much smaller than in the Soviet Union.

There was some very excellent Czechoslovakian beer in the Soviet Union, much to the delight of the beer drinkers in the band, and it was a pleasant surprise to find that the wines were excellent there, too. There was one sparkling wine in particular that was like champagne.

It was in Tbilisi, the capital of the old Georgian Republic, that I had my first experience of what seemed to me a very nice way to entertain. The band were the guests of the mayor after the concert there and we had a vast variety of food: roast pig, caviar, and every kind of drink. I thought it was a nice custom that no one took a drink without a toast being made.

Everybody had a variety of drinks in front of him, from alcoholic to soft drinks, and when the toast was said it was bottoms up and you just had to drink it all the way down. At first the toasts were serious, but got considerably lighter in vein as the drinking proceeded. This contrasted with my socializing in Sweden, where they used to sing a song before taking a drink instead of proposing a toast.

Many of the concert halls we played in were beautiful, and in Moscow we played in a stereo concert hall. At the rehearsal of the Goodman band (well attended by a lively audience) it was a great experience to hear the reeds coming out of one set of loudspeakers and the brass out of another. The amplification made the band sound like a symphony orchestra. We had not forgotten to bring along some recording equipment with us, and records of the concerts were marketed after we got back to the USA. The LP album issued was called *Benny Goodman in Moscow*.

As I say, during this very successful tour, Goodman wound up programming the concerts with the old repertoire of the original band he became famous with. When the Russian trip was first planned he had a wealth of new compositions and arrangements done by some of the leading contemporary American jazz composers and arrangers, but the Russians seemed to go mostly for the older things, so Benny ended up playing about ninety per cent of the older music and perhaps ten per cent of the new. The State Department were extremely pleased. All the performances were sold out and the enthusiasm was tremendous. I would say the Russian tour was quite comparable with American enthusiasm way back in the 1930s, when the Goodman band was at the height of its popularity.

With the big band was an excellent pianist named John Bunch, and he was also in one of the two small groups. In the concert program I would play one trio set and Goodman would join me for some quartet numbers, while John Bunch would play the sextet segment and all of the big-band numbers. At the American Embassy jam session John Bunch and I would take turns at the piano, but other members of the band would also sit in on the keyboard. I shall always remember it as a very happy afternoon.

I found out when I visited Eastern Europe that jazz was very much alive in the socialist countries and there was tremendous interest in it. However, I think the Soviet Union would have been the last of those countries to have jazz, although it became well developed there. I understand jazz was officially sponsored under the government five-year plans, and an income provided for jazz musicians, which was not the case when I was there. At that time the Russian players had to practise jazz on their own and there was no government appropriation for them. I saw many musicians working there, however, possibly as many as the US. Every restaurant, every hotel, had its musicians, and there were many bands and orchestras for the circus and the ballet, also there were symphony and opera orchestras. The whole field of music was represented. Actually, I would be rather interested to know what some of the Russians are doing with jazz today, because it is a wonderful idiom for musicians to express themselves without being carbon copies of the Americans. They are probably coming through with some very interesting sounds and ideas and I would very much like to hear some of them.

When I was in the Soviet Union with Goodman we were the first American jazz group to tour the country, so a lot has changed since then.

When I got back home I was, of course, asked a lot of questions by my family and friends about my impressions of the Soviet Union and its inhabitants. There are a few things that stand out in my memory. One of them is certainly the beauty of Tashkent: the men and women in their multi-coloured garments alongside people in European-style dress. The people,too, I noticed, were very varied in their physical appearance: there was almost every type – from European to dark-skinned people who looked like Indians and African-type people. Judged by its people alone, I would say that Tashkent was the most colorful city we were in on the Goodman tour. Moscow fashions were drab by comparison.

It was an unforgettable experience to live for six weeks in a socialist country like that. Apart from the restrictions I have mentioned we had a great deal of freedom. We were able to roam about where we wanted in the Russian cities and we could engage taxis at taxi stands.

Talking of taxis, the Russian cab drivers were quite an experience, I found. My belief is that they are the fastest in the world. Taxis in Rome are an exciting enough experience, but I think the Russians outmatch them. Those Russians get on those broad boulevards in Moscow – there are no traffic lights – and they belt along at 60 mph. If a car were to come across there's no way they could stop without a tremendous smash. They drove like cowboys! Russian cars were very flimsy by our standards in the West in 1962. The buses then went at about 30 mph and had a very uncomfortable vibration, and the doors on cars and taxis rattled very often.

Then, as I have said, theft is an extremely serious offence in the Soviet Union and property, conversely, is sacred. I remember one of the members of the Goodman band took a clothes hanger from a hotel by mistake. We were all in the bus, packed and ready to leave for the airport, when somebody from the hotel came running out – almost as if there was some sort of crisis on – just to collect the missing hanger! I had a personal experience of this kind myself. Again, we had checked out and were ready to go to the airport and somebody came running out of the hotel and stopped the bus, and we all wondered what dreadful tidings had broken upon the world. There was a loud buzz as the word was spread: somebody had forgotten their handkerchief! As it turned out it was my handkerchief, and I couldn't have cared less, but they insisted on my having it. You would never have to worry about people stealing from you, as it was a serious crime.

Speaking generally, I would say the standard of living in Soviet Russia was much lower than in the USA, as far as the comforts of life were concerned. The clothes and the quality of the buildings were not up to American or Western European standards. Unfortunately, many of the Russian architectural masterpieces have been allowed to decay and it was a sorry sight to see gorgeous old churches just crumbling. On the other hand, to draw an artistic comparison, the ballet was excellent. We saw Tschaikovsky's *Swan Lake* done in Leningrad and both the prima ballerinas and the *corps de ballet* were uniformly excellent. I've never seen anything more impressive or thrilling.

Our long-distance travelling in the Soviet Union was done in very good aircraft, although such niceties as oxygen piped in from the ceiling, as in Western planes, were absent. Instead, each passenger had an oxygen tank next to his seat, and you felt rather as if you were in hospital. The food on the aircraft, too, was not up to our standards. Generally, you could say that Russian food was good but plain and not particularly distinguished. There was plenty of bread, butter, eggs, chicken, fish, cucumbers, potato and cabbage, but very little meat and leaf vegetables. The band did not eat casually in restaurants. A table would be reserved for the whole band of eighteen and our girl singer. We never sat at tables at random. We did not have a menu to choose from and just ate what they brought us.

After the Russian tour I tacked on a couple of days in Poland, just for experience. It was not for the money, because you couldn't take the money you earned out of the country. The same applied to the Soviet Union although, in our particular case, I think through the good offices of the State Department, we were paid in dollars – and well paid at that. The Polish engagements were paid for in Polish money which had to be spent in Poland. So I bought Soviet and Polish watches and some beautiful crystal ware and porcelain, which I gave to my wife and children.

It was nice being in Poland and I played with a young bass player and a drummer who played as if they'd been with me for twenty years! The Poles take their jazz very seriously, as many European musicians do, and they're familiar with American recordings, so when they played with me they immediately did an excellent job.

The same went for Yugoslavia, although I had an Austrian rhythm section there from Graz. In Yugoslavia I met two very good musicians who had a jazz school modelled on the lines of the Berklee College of Music in Boston and were doing very well with it. Yugoslavia went back some years in jazz experience, in contrast to the Soviet Union. I attended a jazz festival there, too, where many international musicians were playing, and it was there that I got to know a Japanese group, a contact which later led to my making several visits to Japan to play professionally. The Yugoslavs were playing mostly avant-garde jazz.

Looking back on my association with the Benny Goodman organization, that is to say the big band and all it represented in that period when it swept all before it in America, I must say that even today I am impressed with that band. There was, for example, the tremendous brass section of five, which had the power and volume of a brass section of seven or eight today. They specialized in blending big tones together to get that very special sound the Goodman brass section had. Red Ballard and Vernon Brown were on trombones, and Chris Griffin, Ziggy Elman and Harry James on trumpets. As far as piano was concerned, Jess Stacy played with the big band and I played with the small groups.

Jess, by the way, is still very active at the time of writing, and I've heard him playing just as well as ever, if not better. Once, years ago, in one of our many discussions about piano playing, Jess humorously remarked the eighty-eight keys sometimes turn into eighty-eight teeth.

As to my own relationship with Benny Goodman, I could perhaps best describe it as one of mutual respect. As I have recounted, our association started in a very pleasant way with the original trio recording with Krupa for RCA. You might say it was "a pleasure project." It should not be forgotten that Benny and I had made records together before he became a bandleader. There had simply been small groups under his name and small groups under my name. The Billie Holiday series, for example, was all under my name and Benny Goodman was on clarinet on some of them.

We have often talked about classical music together at his home, where he had music for clarinet and piano and I would frequently try out the piano part with him. He had some excellent Brahms pieces he had a special weakness for. Now, I must admit that I am not such an expert sight-reader for classical music and of course I'd hit a few wrong notes occasionally when I was skimming through them. Sometimes Benny would play classical music with a symphony orchestra in the first half of a concert, which I would hear, and in the second half we would be playing jazz together.

Benny was especially fond of the Mozart Clarinet Concerto. We all know Mozart pioneered the clarinet in symphony writing, and he worked wonders with it. Other favorites in Benny's music library were a beautiful Debussy Rhapsody for clarinet and orchestra as well as a Weber Concertina for clarinet and orchestra. After playing things like that in the first half of the concert he would often be playing jazz in the second half, either with the trio or sometimes with a seven or eight-piece combination.

8

A Band Of My Own

I suppose it is the ambition of every successful musician to
have a band of his own, preferably a sizable band he can do
something with, in the way of composing and arranging, so
it can have its own character and special "sound" distin-
guishable from other bands. Of course, I had made records
which went out under my name. But, as I have already
recounted, these were pick-up bands, however high the quality of the individual musicians playing in then. What I had in
mind was a regular band which, by sticking together, would
become a homogeneous unit and thus build its own character.

In telling the story of my close association with Benny
Goodman I have necessarily had to play hop-scotch with
chronology, because that association was spread over so
many years. Yet I have thought it would better serve overall
clarity if I kept the Goodman experiences together, although
I would give a wrong impression if I presented that association with Goodman as being one continuous collaboration in
time.

Let me then note here that the whole Benny Goodman
association was spread out intermittently over the years from
1935 to 1962, and I stress the word intermittently. My first
contacts with Goodman were in New York in 1933, and in
1935 my important association with Billie Holiday, which
also involved Goodman, started off. That was also the year in
which the Benny Goodman Trio was formed. Then in 1939,
the year in which Fletcher Henderson gave up his own band
to start arranging for Goodman, I left Benny and formed my
own fifteen-piece big band.

That was a period when many big new jazz and dance

bands were formed. Gene Krupa, for example, had already left the Benny Goodman organization and formed a group of his own, which was very successful, and I too left after an engagement at the Fox Theatre in Detroit.

I went to New York and started rehearsals with my band, in which I had on trumpet, Karl George from Detroit, Harold "Shorty" Baker from St. Louis, who had previously been playing in New York with the Don Redman band, and Doc Cheatham from Nashville, who at one time had played with the Cab Calloway band. I had Jake Wiley, an excellent trombonist from Detroit, and a very old friend on the other trombone, Floyd Brady, originally from Pittsburgh, although I had known him in the Midwest before I ever came to New York.

My reed section had Rudy Powell of New York on lead alto, whom I featured with clarinet solos, Pete Clarke on third alto, who also doubled on clarinet and baritone, for which we we did arrangements inspired by the Duke Ellington orchestrations, George Irish on tenor sax and finally Ben Webster, who was the featured star on tenor. I might add that I think that Ben did some of his best-ever tenor sax playing in my big band.

In the rhythm section, I had J.C. Heard on drums, whom I had found in Detroit, Al Hall from New York, whom I knew from Philadelphia, on bass, and Al Casey on guitar. Al, by the way, was an old friend of mine and played on many of the Billie Holiday sessions with the small groups. In Buster Harding I had a very valuable collaborator who helped me with arrangements and also played piano. He did many excellent original numbers for the band, in addition to arrangements of standard and popular tunes . We used two pianos and Buster and I would take turns at playing, and very often I would be out in front of the band. This isn't really necessary with a jazz band but it was customary in those days.

My own arranging was confined mainly to standard ballads and current pop tunes (youthful readers please note: the "pop" of those days was short for "popular" and is not to be confused with what is now known as pop). Buster did strictly jazz-orientated arrangements. Edgar Sampson did some arrangements for us, too. Then I had another talented arranger, Danny Mendelsohn.

The four of us formed the main body of the arranging staff, while Ben Webster also contributed original numbers and arrangements of his own. Ben wrote a very swinging tune called *71*, named after its number in our book of arrangements. Rudy Powell, our lead alto player, also wrote a very successful number called *Coconut Groove*.

It's very exciting to front a big band, especially when you're writing for it, because it's different from just playing the piano. As a matter of fact, I was getting so interested in writing, I think I made a couple of arrangements where I forgot to put a piano solo in! Just so I could stand in front of the band and hear my writing. I can understand how Ellington thrived for so many years by writing. It's a wonderful thing to put the sounds on paper and have them brought to life by good musicians.

The band started off by doing some road work. We had a singer called Thelma Carpenter doing the vocals and later got Jean Eldridge, who was discovered by Duke Ellington and had already made a recording with the Ellington band of the lovely Billy Strayhorn tune called *I Want Something to Live For*. Except for two with Thelma Carpenter, Jean was on all the recordings with vocals we made for Columbia.

Altogether, I think we made about twenty sides during the lifetime of that big band. We played as far west as Detroit, and in Michigan, New England and Pennsylvania, and finally settled with a steady job at the New Golden Gate Ballroom in Harlem, just a block or two away from the Savoy. We stayed there for a long while, but in the meantime I was learning that big bands were expensive to run, and I was losing quite a bit of money. I had financed it myself from my savings from the time I had worked with Benny Goodman.

In those days you could either finance a band yourself or borrow the money at very high rates of interest, mostly in the ratio of 60:40, meaning you would get 60 per cent of the profits and the financier 40 per cent, as soon as the band showed a profit. The original investment would have to be paid off first and then the investor would share.

In the event, I decided to finance my own band and lost, because I had to pay the salaries and expenses of my men, while not enough was coming in. The music world, like any business, is a game of chance, and you have to run the risk of losing. So in the end I had to give up the big band to stop the financial rot. We never got off the ground economically. It wasn't an immediately popular band because we were working with a lot of musical values and we didn't have a big repertoire of exciting tunes. We had a lot of arrangements and things that were appreciated by musicians, but we didn't have a lot of what you'd call good head arrangements. We didn't last long enough to develop a good repertoire of hits like the Basie band, or like Goodman had with his *Sing, Sing, Sing*, those arrangements that you can't put on paper. They were the lifeblood of a big band, those head arrangements. A lot of the old Fletcher Henderson things were basically head arrangements, too.

After a year and a half of running the big band I was offered a long and steady engagement with the Café Society Downtown in New York, which I accepted with a small six-piece group. I took the offer because it gave the opportunity of a steady income so I could pay off some of the debts I had incurred with the big band.

Ben Webster managed to get a job with Duke Ellington, with whom he made some very famous and memorable recordings. I think Harold Baker joined Ellington, too, and Karl George joined Stan Kenton. Doc Cheatham is still going great guns to this day as a successful trumpet player around New York, and is in great demand at jazz festivals and concerts.

Rudy Powell is still very active on alto, although he is featured mainly on clarinet with a group called Saints and Sinners. I've lost track of Pete Clarke, and George Irish has passed away, as has Ben Webster after becoming a household name in jazz around the world. Ben lived in Amsterdam, Holland for a while, like Don Byas, and then moved to

Copenhagen. He died eventually in an Amsterdam hospital in 1973 at the age of 64. Drummer J.C. Heard is still doing well with his own group in Detroit, and Al Hall is active in New York, dividing his time between jazz bands and pit orchestras in Broadway shows. Al Casey is still very much in evidence – in fact I made some recordings with him fairly recently and expect to do some more work with him in the near future.

Buster Harding passed away several years ago, although after my big band broke up he did quite a bit of composing and arranging for Count Basie.

So in 1940 I went to the Café Society after the big band folded. I should mention that the theme song of the band was a tune I composed myself called *Little Things Mean So Much*. It was originally written as a piano solo but Harold Adamson wrote a vocal chorus which Jean Eldridge sang and Edgar Sampson and myself did an orchestration. I wrote another song when I cut down the fifteen-piece band to eight pieces called *Sunny Morning*. I haven't thought of going in for song-writing seriously. Frankly, I don't think I have too much talent for it and, besides, I was always traveling too much.

The Café Society job proved to be very interesting. So many people who were unknown when they appeared there later became famous: Adolph Greene, Betty Comden, Judy Holiday, Zero Mostel (who started as a zany comedian and later became a world-famous actor), Lena Horne, who became world-famous as a singer and movie actress, Hazel Scott, the singer, who abandoned the night clubs to do concert work exclusively and later married Congressman Adam Clayton Powell.

There were some quite famous people in the audience, too. Peggy Lee was a regular visitor, as were Congressman Powell, actress Lana Turner, writer Quentin Reynolds , singer-actor Paul Robeson, Carol Bruce and Virginia Bruce, both actresses, John Steinbeck, the novelist, Mrs Franklin D. Roosevelt and Franklin Roosevelt Junior, as well as Bing Crosby and Arturo Toscanini, who was conducting the NBC Symphony at the time.

I shall always remember the night Toscanini attended as very exciting for me and the other musicians: just the thought that the great man himself was in the audience was enough. But it was all ruined by the house photographer who flashed a light in his eyes and he got up and walked out. Toscanini had been having a lot of trouble with his eyes and was obviously afraid of more flash bulbs popping, so he never got to hear us play a single note! People shouldn't try to capitalize on a great artist when he's simply out for an evening.

Another great musician who came to the Café Society and paid me a high compliment was the famous French classical pianist Robert Casadesus, who was teaching piano at Princeton, New Jersey, and performing on tour. He used to call me "the Mozart of the piano".

It was when I was working at the Café Society that the Japanese bombed Pearl Harbor, on 7 December, 1941. We all had to register for the draft after America was at war, and I shall never forget the day I went down. We all had to strip down and were handed a bunch of papers. With these we had to go from one examiner to another, and the papers had to be filled in. At the end of the line was a psychiatrist. Well, I was known as a 4F classification. I was about 29 or 30 at the time and 4F meant several categories would be called up before me, the most immediate category being 1A. However, the war ended before I got called up so I was playing all that time at the Café Society, which was a very popular recreation spot for the armed forces.

I played a lot, too, at hospitals for soldiers and at the Stage Door Canteen on Times Square and the Lighthouse in Manhattan, a home for the blind, although this was not connected with the war effort.

There was one interesting experience at that time. Benny Goodman took a small group down to New Orleans for a couple of days, where we played for American servicemen and also at a German prisoner-of-war camp. The group consisted of Benny, Red Norvo, Morey Feld on drums, Sid Weiss on bass and myself. However, by the time the war ended and Harry Truman was president I had not seen any active service.

The personnel of the band I had at the Café Society engagements did change from time to time. The original line-up was Bill Coleman on trumpet, Benny Morton on trombone, Jimmy Hamilton on clarinet, Al Hall on bass and Yank Porter, an excellent drummer who had worked years before in the Middle West with Louis Armstrong. My other drummers after Yank Porter were Sid Catlett and J.C Heard. After Bill Coleman left for Europe, I had Joe Thomas in the trumpet section as well as Emmett Berry. Jimmy Hamilton was offered a job with Duke Ellington, and his place was taken by Edmond Hall, who stayed with me until the end of my small-band days with the Café Society. Ed was a great clarinetist, although he had a completely different style from Jimmy Hamilton. He had some dates of his own that I played on, Commodore dates, too. Benny Morton on trombone stayed with me right through from the beginning to the end (1940-44). Benny had played with Don Redman and Fletcher Henderson and was regarded in those days, with Jack Teagarden and Jimmy Harrison, as one of the "big three." I still do work with Benny to this day.

We had a happy time at the Café Society. We were the house band and we played for the various acts that needed musical backing, for dancing and to open the show. The show at times consisted of Hazel Scott, Albert Ammons and Meade "Lux" Lewis, all three playing boogie-woogie style piano, while Joe Turner and Lena Horne were singing. Lena wasn't famous in those days. Art Tatum also played the Café Society as a featured soloist.

That year at the Café Society proved so successful that the owners opened a second nightclub called Café Society Uptown. The original club, Café Society Downtown, was at Sheridan Square in the Greenwich Village area. The new nightclub was on East 58th Street in a very expensive residential district, and proved very successful too. It was a very special nightclub. There was nothing in New York like the Café Societies. There were little jazz bands besides mine that worked there. One would have been Red Allen's band, with J.C. Higginbotham, because Ed Hall had been with that band before he came with mine. Kenny Kersey played piano with Red. Henry Red Allen and then Eddie Heywood were with the Café Society for a long time. Then John Kirby came in with Charlie Shavers, Russell Procope, Buster Bailey and Billy Kyle. Eddie South, a great violinist and a very popular jazz and classical musician worked there with his trio. The Café Societies had so many acts and singers who were initially unknown and then became household names in America. Billie Holiday was known, but not as widely as she became later. She really opened the Café Society. She was the first attraction they had Downtown, working with Frankie Newton's Band. I stayed with that club for about a year and then, in 1944, I rejoined Benny Goodman and played in a show called   *The Seven Lively Arts*. My place in the Café Society as bandleader was taken over by the New Orleans clarinetist Ed Hall.

The Seven Lively Arts was a Broadway stage show featuring people like actress Beatrice Lillie and comedian Bert Lahr and was produced by showman Billy Rose. Stravinsky wrote the ballet music for two of America's greatest dancers, Alicia Markova and Anton Dolin. Goodman had a Quintet in there with Sid Weiss on bass, Red Norvo on vibes, Morey Feld on drums and myself.

That lasted quite a while and after that Goodman organized a big band, went into the Paramount Theater, toured some, and played the 400 Restaurant on Fifth Avenue, New York. I stayed on as a member of what became a Sextet. He brought in Slam Stewart on bass, Mike Bryan on guitar, Red Norvo stayed on vibes, and there were Goodman, myself and Morey Feld. Charlie Queener was playing piano with the big band, just like the old days, when Jess Stacy played piano with the big band and I was with the small group.

I should explain that, in the middle and late forties, I was doing all sorts of things which were out of the public spotlight. This led many people at the time to believe I had retired, whereas, in actual fact, I was very active indeed around the New York area with radio and other work. I was hardly on the road at all: I might have gone to New England at a weekend, for instance, to play at a college or something like that, but would go straight back to New York again. In short, there was no extensive travelling as there was when I was with Benny Goodman. Then we travelled from one end of the country to the other throughout the year: California in the summer, New York in the winter and all points in between. One-night stands, theaters, in places like Pittsburgh, Cleveland, Chicago, Dallas and so on.

So there again, after the *Seven Lively Arts* show I had a steady job at WNEW, the new radio station in New York, which lasted until about 1952. I always had my own trio show, bass, piano and drums, on WNEW five days a week. Then I changed to a staff job with Columbia Broadcasting, and did a Saturday afternoon show with my own trio.

It was through working with the *Seven Lively Arts* show that I got to know a man named William Schuman. He had written the overture to the second act of the show and was slated to be the new President of the Juilliard Music Conservatory in New York. During rehearsals I got quite friendly with Schuman and he asked me whether I would care to join the faculty at Juilliard teaching jazz piano. He was familiar with my work at first hand through being around at the *Seven Lively Arts* rehearsals. His proposal appealed to me very much and he explained to me that so many students came out of Juilliard who were not really equipped to teach and were perhaps not fortunate enough to make a full-time living as concert pianists. His thinking was that, if they could learn something about jazz, they could perhaps do work outside the concert stage, such as recordings or commercial work, including radio, where the ability to play jazz piano might be necessary. He proposed hiring me to join the Juilliard staff for this purpose.

Well, the upshot was that I stayed there in the Summer School from 1945 to 1952. I had twenty private students weekly, each term, and there were two weekly classes which additional students could attend. I am very proud to say that many of my pupils from those days are now doing very well. With one of them, John Phillips, I have recently played on the same programme, in Washington, DC, when we shared the piano at the Blues Alley Club.

Then there is a recording I have of which I am very proud: two of my students collaborated on it. One is Dick Hyman, who wrote a piano concerto a few years ago, and he plays the piano part, while another pupil of mine, Nick Perito, conducted the symphony orchestra. To think that both these men studied with me some twenty or twenty-five years ago, when they were only teenagers!

Dick Hyman not only studied with me, he also worked with Tony Scott, Red Norvo and Benny Goodman and was also on the staff of NBC in New York. Worth mentioning also are his recordings with singer Maxine Sullivan, who was John Kirby's wife from 1937 to 1941. Also on the recordings were Buster Bailey (clarinet), Hilton Jefferson (alto sax), Oscar Pettiford (bass and cello), Milt Hinton (bass) and Osie Johnson (drums).

Another student I should mention is Roger Williams, who became very succcssful in America over the years and is probably one of the highest paid in the popular jazz field. It is with great pride that I keep track of such pupils from those teaching years.

I should say that, at each radio job I had, I had my own show. I didn't just do a lot of routine staff work, where you sit as an anonymous person in a band. I had my own trio show for years on station WNEW, following a very popular programme called the *Make Believe Ballroom*, with Martin Block, one of the first-ever disc jockeys in America. Block was a supporter of the big bands in putting together his program, and I had a live trio – myself on piano, Walter Josten on bass and Phil Krauss in drums – to give a fifteen-minute show after the *Make Believe Ballroom*.

During that period I got into studying the piano some more too. I went to some fine teachers during that period when I was off the road. I had several get-togethers with Leonard Bernstein, who was the up and coming young classical pianist in America when he was about twenty-one years old. I got a lot of sessions with him and another friend of his called Sol Caplin, and a lot of help from an excellent teacher named Richard McLanaham, who had been trained in London, and Tobias Matte, who was very important in the development of piano teaching in the early part of this century, and then later with an excellent Russian pianist who had moved to America, Nadia Reisenberg.

At CBS, round about 1952, I had a Saturday afternoon trio show, with Jo Jones on drums and Milt Hinton on bass, and two jazz guests at each show, people like Roy Eldridge and Dizzy Gillespie, whoever was available, in the same way that I put together some of the Billie Holiday sessions.

All this was out of the public spotlight – teaching at Juilliard and working with a radio station. The only public playing I did would be a special occasional jazz program. In this connection I remember doing the Esquire Award Winners' concert at the Metropolitan Opera House in New York and Esquire Award-winning recording sessions and many post-war recording sessions around 1946 to 1948, some with Coleman Hawkins, Roy Eldridge, Charlie Shavers, Charlie Parker, and a Red Norvo session with Dizzy Gillespie, Flip Phillips, J.C. Heard, Specs Powell and Slam Stewart.

Talking of Slam Stewart, I should say that Slam must have a great deal of credit for being one of the first important soloists on the bass. Before him the bass was strictly a rhythm section instrument, and Slam was an innovator in bowing the bass for solo work. Later, another important development was introduced by Jimmy Blanton, who was discovered by Duke Ellington, and who evolved a special solo plucking technique, new and original.

Another pioneer developing from rhythm section playing into solo playing was drummer Gene Krupa, especially in his rendition of the Benny Goodman version of *Sing, Sing, Sing*. Krupa's drums were featured in that and, I think, made the jazz world more drum conscious than it had ever been before.

Before that, one of the great rhythm section bass players was John Kirby, who had been with the Chick Webb band and was a bandleader in his own right. Then, of course, there was

Walter Page. When Page came to New York with Count Basie he created quite a stir among the bass players with his use of the G string – the high string on the bass violin – in a 4/4 rhythm, playing very high notes with some very unique drum sounds from Jo Jones and sparkling crisp chime-like notes from Basie's piano. While on the topic of the rhythm section, the pioneers of the guitar should be mentioned, for example Charlie Christian. All these men were very important. Also, along with Charlie Christian, for single-string solo work, Django Reinhardt must be remembered. I recall first hearing his creative use of the jazz idiom on Hot Club of France recordings in the 1930s.

Jazz has certainly come a long way and some of the bass players nowadays play with a technique and fluency that was the prerogative of guitar players many years ago. This is all handed down from one player to another – ideas and discoveries getting improved upon, like a tree sprouting branches. That's why I think you have such a profusion of skill nowadays around the world, while years ago there was only a handful of these great technicians, really true innovators.

Well, that was just an aside. To return to my activities in those days I should also mention some recording dates with Sarah Vaughan on Musicraft Records before Sarah became famous. Then it was Teddy Wilson and his Orchestra or Teddy Wilson and his Quartet with vocals by Sarah Vaughan. She sang beautifully in those days – there wasn't so much improvisation, just beautiful refreshing singing. When she desires, Sarah can make the simplest phrase as exciting as others' most complex improvisations. Charlie Ventura did some of those dates on tenor, Remo Palmieri was on guitar in some of the groups, and Billy Taylor Jr. on bass. I also did some ten- piece band dates with Benny Carter doing the arrangements.

In those days, too, there was a radio program which did quite a bit of good for me. It was called *Casey, Crime Photographer*, and I was always the pianist in one concluding scene where the crime photographer of the newspaper and his girlfriend would come to the Blue Note Club and master-mind the solution of the crime before the Chief of Police could. I was supposed to be the pianist of the Blue Note and I would be playing the piano in the background while they put all the pieces of the puzzle together to find out who the murderer was. I got a lot of fans who liked listening to me on that program and became a popular part of it.

Before me a wonderful pianist named Herman Chittison had done that role. He really created the Blue Note pianist and I came in when he left CBS. Chittison, who came from Ohio, was a great disciple of Art Tatum and started out as a professional player at the same time that I did. He was with the Zack White band around Ohio, based in Cincinnati when I was with the Speed Webb band, along with Reunald Jones, Roy Eldridge, Vic Dickenson, my brother Gus on trombone, and also doing arrangements, Sy Oliver. Sy was later a Jimmie Lunceford trumpet player and arranger and later still, he was with Tommy Dorsey, for whom he wrote so many hits. Now, I hear, he's back again in business with his own band, playing his trumpet again for the first time in thirty-odd years. It's a small but very good band – not a combo – and I think he uses between eight and ten men with written arrangements.

So quite a few of us started out at the same time. I should also mention trombonist Quentin Jackson, who was later with Duke Ellington and Count Basie, as being in the Zack White band, which was a very good outfit, playing Sy Oliver's charts.

No review of jazz developments in the 1940s would be complete without a mention of bebop jazz. In that period the whole jazz stream evolved into more complex harmonies and more intricate rhythms and this laid the foundation for later jazz and the jazz of today. Nevertheless, it should all be seen as one continuous path of evolution. Actually it all goes back to the 1920s, and I have sometimes demonstrated this with recordings. Take the *Maple Leaf Rag*, which Scott Joplin wrote so many years ago, and you'll find a consistency right down to what jazz players are playing today. You'll find little snatches and patterns that have lasted through all of this century in the evolution of the jazz piano.

I would say that the imposition by the US government of a tax on dancing (due to the strain on the war economy resulting from lend lease) played a part in the rise of bebop. A 20 per cent entertainment tax was introduced, and that hit the jazz world in a special way. It knocked out dancing, so musicians had to play music that was interesting enough for people to spend their money just to sit and listen to, and not dance.

The type of musicians this produced included people like Thelonious Monk, Bud Powell, Dizzy Gillespie, Charlie Christian and Charlie Parker. In my opinion Charlie Parker was one of the truly creative giants of jazz. He found himself without destroying the foundation. Many who have changed the foundation have found nothing.

Then there were the famous sessions at Minton's Playhouse in Harlem and on 52nd Street, where the music really blossomed during the Second World War, but they introduced quite a few changes in what we had been doing in the thirties – changes in the harmonies of jazz. They were resting on the solid foundations of the jazz of the thirties but they made some additions and alterations to traditional chord tunes, producing some refreshing new sounds harmonically and introducing more intricate rhythm in with the steady dance pulse. Since dancing was at a low ebb it was no longer necessary to have such a pronounced dance rhythm, and this freed a lot of rhythm instruments from restrictions, so the drums began to play more complex rhythms behind the soloist, nobody having to be sustained by a drum to dance. All the same, bebop was grounded in the older music because they were improvising and playing to great extent on the same songs we'd been playing in the thirties.

I have said that this is all part of a gradual evolution, and so I really speak about "bebop" or "swing" with reluctance, at least if these terms are used to indicate some completely new and self-contained jazz developments unrelated to what had gone before.

Teddy at the piano. (*Downbeat*)

Teddy's father,
James Augustus Wilson Sr.
(Teddy Wilson Collection)

Teddy (left) with his mother and brother James in 1927, not long after his father's death
the previous year. (Teddy Wilson Collection)

The Speed Webb Band 1929: Teddy
Wilson (piano), Melvin Bowles
(Sousaphone), William Warfield (guitar),
Samuel Scott (drums), Vic Dickenson and
Gus Wilson (trombones), Chuck Wallace,
Leonard Gay and Ben Richardson (saxes),
Roy Eldridge, Reunald Jones and Steve
Dunn (trumpets). Speed Webb is in front.
(*Downbeat*)

detail

Teddy and Billie Holiday.
(Teddy Wilson Collection)

Billie Holiday with critic, pianist and songwriter
Leonard Feather. (Wouter Van Gool)

The Benny Goodman Quartet: (left to right) Gene Krupa, Lionel Hampton, Benny, Teddy Wilson. (*Downbeat*)

Recording session (probably 4 October 1940) with Yank Porter (drums), Charlie Christian (guitar), Billy Taylor Sr. (bass) and Teddy Wilson (piano). (*Downbeat*)

Pianists' get-together during Earl Hines' residency at the Embers, New York: (left to right)
Teddy Wilson, Eddie Heywood, Errol Garner and Earl Hines. (*Downbeat*)

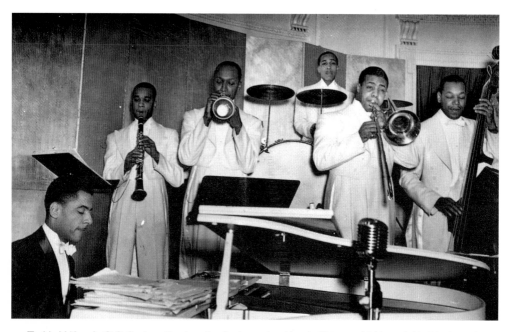

Teddy Wilson's Café Society Band at the Ambassador Hotel, Chicago, 1941, with Teddy (piano),
Jimmy Hamilton (clarinet), Bill Coleman (trumpet), J.C. Heard (drums), Benny Morton (trombone) and
Al Hall (bass). (*Downbeat*)

European travels (1): Teddy and Dutch Swing College Band leader Peter Schilperoort celebrate the award of a Gold Disc for their recording together, Rotterdam, 1974. (DSC Record Productions)

European travels (2): Teddy with singer Marlene Widmark and saxophonist Lars Gullin.

Teddy receives his honorary Doctorate in Music from Berklee College of Music President Berk. (Teddy Wilson Collection)

Theodore   Teddy   Steven

TEDDY WILSON AND SONS

Teddy Wilson and Sons – the trio he formed in the last years of his life with Theodore (bass) and Steven (drums). (Teddy Wilson Collection)

If you attach names and tags to jazz, such as "bebop" and "swing" and "progressive" it makes it difficult for people to understand, because not everybody interprets the terms in the same way. What some people call "mainstream" for example, others wouldn't. Lots of people say that "swing music" is not the same as "jazz music," so I personally find all these categories very misleading. I prefer to think of jazz chronologically, in terms of a certain year or years, such as the 1920s, and in terms of some of the giants of that period and some of the lesser lights who didn't quite reach the same heights. Louis Armstrong, for example, has imitators round the world; he was perhaps the most imitated musician in the whole of jazz. But, later on, along came Charlie Parker and Lester Young, who also got imitated all over the world.

These men were highly creative and contributed so much to the existing storehouse of jazz, one might compare them to the peak of a pyramid with a whole host of imitators below the peak. Some of those lower down emerge and become peaks themselves and they, in turn, have a host of disciples. But I think it should all be taken historically, in terms of years – the twenties, the thirties, the forties, the sixties and so on. Or you might talk in terms of categories like pre-First World War, post-First World War, pre-Second World War, or preferably some other classification, because we all hope of course that there will not be a Third World War, which will probably be the last anyway! In any case we want a classification which is much more accurate than vague labels like "swing" or "progressive"

Today, jazz is part of the curriculum at many major universities in America. Many schools are hiring first-class people to head their jazz department, like a good friend of mine, Larry Ridley, an excellent bass player who is head of jazz studies at Rutgers University. Yale University has a wonderful man in Willie Ruff, one of the finest french horn players in America. He is also a fine bass player, a musicologist and a great classical player.

So nowadays, in spite of pop and rock, jazz is coming into its own again with the young people of America. In a way, the

Juilliard School pioneered this many years ago in New York, but unfortunately, and ironically, Juilliard has no jazz department at all now. At a time when jazz tuition is spreading all over America, Juilliard has cut it out, which is rather disappointing. But I think the others more than make up for it.

One of my sons has a high school jazz band, playing the same tunes that I'm playing, and this would not have been possible even six years ago.

9

Europe, Here I Come

In the summer of 1952, my teaching job at Juilliard ended after eight years and that fall I made my first trip abroad, to Europe, and went to Scandinavia through a promotor named Nils Helström in Stockholm.

The first currents of jazz trickled through to Europe from America and began to make their impact there and, as the years went by, there was a sort of fermentation process which later developed into an interaction on both sides of the Atlantic, although America continued to be recognized as the "cradle" of this typically American music.

It is always a fascinating experience for an American jazz musician to make his first acquaintance with the European jazz scene and I know I was often amazed how smooth the liaison frequently was. That is particularly true of Scandinavia, which I regard as one of the finest jazz "regions" in Europe.

You cannot discount the enormous influence of recordings in Europe. I have already described how the early records of people like Fats Waller, Earl Hines and Louis Armstrong had a big influence in molding my own jazz beginnings and it is obvious that recordings played a major role in spreading the jazz idiom throughout the world, setting off a chain reaction among musically perceptive people who were seized with enthusiasm for the music and in many cases wanted to emulate the performances of the American originators.

Lots of European jazz talent gravitated towards the home of jazz in America for its further development, George Shearing as an Englishman springs to mind as an example, while in other cases, such as the Quintet of the Hot Club of France, with Stephane Grappelly and Django Reinhardt, a new and original contribution to the jazz idiom was made in Europe itself. This is leaving out of account the influence of jazz on some European classical composers, Stravinsky being a striking example.

In the wake of the vast "invisible" phonograph audience came the very natural desire to see and hear the original greats in the flesh, and modern air travel certainly greatly facilitated all this to-ing and fro-ing and stimulated contacts on both sides.

So in Scandinavia I did a tour with bassist Simon Brehm's small band in Sweden, Denmark and Finland and I did a trio album for Swedish Metronome Records. On the tour I would play with the rhythm section, after the band had played several numbers, and end with an all-in number with me playing with the whole band. They were excellent, and I really enjoyed that first tour of Europe.

In the following year, 1953, I went over to England and Scotland. As I did when I went to Scandinavia, I went alone, doing most of my playing with the Freddy Randall band. That was when I ran into some slight trouble with the British Musicians' Union, as so many American musicians have. They felt that, under the terms on which foreign musicians played in England, my status was not quite legal. They took the view that my visit was not quite above board because I had come in as a "variety concert artist" and I was not doing the variety halls but performing mainly in concert halls. That, they said, was against the rules and added that, though they would not stop my tour, they would forbid English musicians to play with me at the same time on the stage. In practice that didn't work out because at every town the English artists didn't hesitate to invite themselves to play with me and I even played at the Albert Hall in London with drummer Lennie Hastings! So the union ban didn't really hamper the tour in any way and it was very successful.

At that night at the Albert Hall, with an audience of 7,000 people, there were some first class groups on the programme, including Johnny Dankworth's small group. He was working at that time on the repertoire of his big band. Later in the tour, in Glasgow in Scotland, I played with the six-piece Freddy Randall band to an audience of 5,000. I mention this to show how popular jazz was in Britain in the early 1950s. Ted Heath was going strong at the time and others I met were Kenny Ball and Kenny Baker and an excellent pianist named Alan Clare. There were some American friends too, including Mary Lou Williams, who was living in London at the time.

I thoroughly enjoyed my tour in Britain, which was done through the auspices of a magazine called *New Musical Express*. I was very impressed by Scotland as well as England and the beautiful scenery I saw. The stone fences there up north and the greenest grass I'd ever seen in my life – startlingly green. As for the famous London rain and fog – I didn't have a single day of it. It must have been September or October when I was there and nearly every day was equally beautiful. I saw it all at its best because we were riding in a new Rolls Royce, a four-door sedan, with the sunroof open, and we did so much of the tour with the roof open at highway speeds.

English jazz has improved tremendously in the past twenty-five years or so since I was first there, when I found it rather spotty. There were a few good drummers but there weren't many musicians of the Johnny Dankworth class with the true jazz feeling. It was all a bit stilted and stiff to the best of my recollection and still well within the confines of what they had learned from American recordings. Today it is different and English players, and for that matter players all over Europe, have got into the expression of jazz in a creative way of their own. That goes for Sweden in particular. They are not just carbon copies of the Americans. By comparison British jazz was very seriously behind Scandinavian jazz in those days.

I have already mentioned Stephane Grappelly and Django Reinhardt and I would say Grappelly is one of the handful of great living jazz violinists: people like Joe Venuti, Svend Asmussen and Jean-Luc Ponty who today, in the 1970s, I would regard as outstanding.

We were able to get the records of the Hot Club de France

in America way back in the 1930s, when Grappelly was teaming with Django Reinhardt, to me the finest example of two Europeans who took American jazz and used it in a creative way, rather than make carbon copies. As far as I know they were the first European jazz musicians to do that.

A European jazz band I have a particularly soft spot for is the Dutch Swing College Band of Holland, headed by its versatile leader, Peter Schilperoort and I would say that, man for man, it's one of the greatest seven-piece jazz bands I've ever heard, and in a way I think it's the greatest small concert jazz band around today. By that I mean that their programme for a concert is so varied and interesting. They play the early New Orleans music; they use the banjo when it's necessary and the guitar when appropriate, they play early and late Ellington and all the tunes that were popular with musicians like myself to improvise on, including the Benny Goodman recordings of the Trio, the Quartet and Sextet. Altogether, they combine so much jazz history in their concerts and it's all so expertly done.

As it has turned out I have had quite a long and close association with the Dutch Swing College Band and what started out as just another business relationship has developed in the course of time into a series of friendships which have been very enjoyable and refreshing, as I shall recount, because the association was not without its humorous and even comical aspects at times!

A prime mover in my association with the Dutch Swing College Band was Arie Ligthart, the banjo and guitar-playing manager of the band, who is something of a legend in his own country. Arie is a cheerful and lovable character and a fine jazz musician and he tells me that the Dutch Swing College Band promoter in West Germany, Gerd Mayer, thought it would be a good idea to add some American attractions to the band to give an extra spice to their concerts in Germany, where they were, and still are, very successful and have a big following, bigger in many ways than in their native Holland. It was all a matter of finding the right combination. Modern, avant garde musicians would not have fitted in with the Dutch Swing College Band, so it had to be known American jazz musicians who played in the Dutch Swing College Band idiom. So they played and recorded with blues singer Jimmy Witherspoon, New Orleans clarinet player, Albert Nicholas, trumpet player Billy Butterfield and trumpet player Nelson Williams, who was in the Ellington band from 1949 to 1951. After Nelson left Ellington he was in Paris for a time and later went to Holland, where he married a Dutch girl and lived in The Hague. Sadly he died in 1973.

The band also did some European tours with soprano sax player Sidney Bechet and trumpet player Bill Coleman. With most of these American musicians the band made recordings on their own record label, DSC Record Productions. Arie Ligthart has told me that, when German promotor Gerd Mayer suggested that the Dutch Swing College Band team up with me, members of the band greeted the suggestion with enthusiasm.

So Gerd Mayer asked me to do the tour with the Dutch Swing College Band. I was not familiar with the band, although I had heard of them. I only heard later what their history was, how they had started out as a bunch of amateurs during the Nazi occupation of Holland and played all the jazz evergreens with the titles translated into Dutch so the Germans wouldn't be able to identify them. At that time the Nazis considered jazz as decadent and not in line with their ideology.

The band has been a going concern for more than thirty years now, quite an achievement in itself. The meeting clicked so well that I did repeated tours with the band and recorded an LP and a double album with them, both of which have sold and are still selling very well.

My first tour with the Dutch Swing College was in 1972 in Germany and at the time of writing we have just made our fourth tour of Germany, Holland and Switzerland.

The written music of the band is done by Peter Schilperoort, Bob Kaper the clarinetist and alto player, and Bert de Kort, cornet. The orchestrations are all excellent. It is perhaps unusual that they do not normally have a pianist in the rhythm section, but the way they are organized it is not really necessary. They have the three rhythm: guitar (doubling on banjo,) bass and drums, and they use four horns: two reeds and two brass. Peter Schilperoort and Bob Kaper both double on other instruments and Peter plays the whole sax family, (especially his favourite, soprano,) as well as guitar, piano and some exotic Latin American instruments.

Dicky Kaart, the trombonist, doubles on another baritone horn, a valve instrument. Guitarist Jaap van Kempen, who took over from Arie Ligthart when he decided to concentrate on managing the band, is very gifted and doubles on banjo.

Dutch Swing College Band drummer, Huub Janssen, I would regard as one of the greatest drummers of all time – he's probably the greatest European postwar drummer there is. For sheer perfection I think his drum solos are on a par with any other drummer in the world today you like to mention. He has a phenomenal command of his drums, delicacy and power and a tremendous sense of pacing. He knows just when to do what; when to really bear down and when to ease up; he has a great sense of structure of the arrangements and a great sense of humour, too, when he does his Louis Armstrong imitations. He likes to tell the story of Albert Nicholas being in the dressing room waiting to go on and getting the shock of his life at hearing what he thought was the voice of the great Louis's ghost floating in from the stage!

I must also mention bassist Henk Bosch van Drakestein for his wonderful rhythm section playing. When he gets a bass solo he does a wonderful job as a musician and is greatly appreciated by the audience too.

As I have said, the band does not use a pianist in its regular composition so when I turned a seven-piece group into an eight-piece group I would play some numbers with the whole band interspersed with a few numbers with just bass and drums.

The Dutch Swing College Band and I are very serious about our work together, but we have quite a bit of fun offstage, when we are on the road in our bus. I must say, some members of the DSC have invented ingenious ways of killing time on these long journeys. One, for instance, is called "pick-ling", and don't forget (at least you are not allowed to) there are rules to these games which you have to abide by or pay the penalty. In "pickling" you flick another fellow's ear from behind with tremendous force. You get so adept at it that you can steal up from behind and flick another fellow's ear with your thumb and second or third finger and release it with lightning speed behind his ear. But, beware if this is done out of turn because, then, the one who is at fault must submit to two or three penalty "pickles" according to the seriousness of the offence.

This same game has a variant with the flat of the foot against your rear end. You can come up behind the victim and give him a very hard kick in the *derrière* with the flat of the foot in the seat of his pants. But again if the kick is out of turn and against the rules, the one at fault has to bend over and let the innocent party deliver two or three penalty kicks!

Then there's the Dutch Swing College Band pistol game. You will be riding in the bus and all of a sudden you feel a trickle of cold water running down your neck and into your back under your clothes. This is a lovely little game called "water pickling". I might add that, if the game is played in hotel (as it often is) the walls are soon streaked with water. All this good clean fun by grown men and I suppose helps them to blow off steam.

Perhaps the most sensational game in all respects is played by the Dutch Swing College Band men with blank cartridge pistols which give a very loud and alarming report. They are very realistic and make a deep impression on people in the street when they are produced, as they often are, under most bizarre circumstances. The DSC men once caused a real sen-sation in Germany when they staged a riotous "gun battle" in the crowed lunchtime streets. Pretending they were gangsters the Dutch jazzmen fired from behind parked cars, took pot shots at each other from doorways, or while lying on the pavement, using their luggage as a "cover"against the "rival gang". Similar hair-raising scenes are staged in the crowded lobbies of hotels to the consternation of all and sundry. So, all in all, we have a lot of fun off stage as a comic relief from the serious business we do on stage.

I could not conclude any reference to Holland without mentioning that it was there that the idea of this book was born. Arie Ligthart and I had had so many relaxed chats and swopped so many anecdotes between shows that when I was at his house near The Hague, enjoying the hospitality of the Ligthart family, it seemed to crop up quite naturally that it might be worthwhile putting down in black and white my first-hand knowledge and experience of the developing jazz scene and its giants over the years, hopefully for the pleasure and entertainment of the millions of fans who have supported me so faithfully on records and at live concerts.

We decided to call in a friend of Arie's, Humphrey van Loo, an Englishman of Dutch parentage who graduated in newspaper journalism and for some 30 years was a correspondant for Reuters' news agency. As it happened, Humphrey was himself a keen jazz fan, had been so from his youth, and had more or less grown up with my music and the whole Goodman era. He took up the suggestion of collaborating in the scheme with enthusiasm and thus the new "Teddy Wilson Trio" was born that day in The Hague!

After the production of the *Benny Goodman Story* in 1955 the bulk of my work was playing in public with my trio. My first steady trio had Jo Jones on drums and Gene Ramey on bass. Later, I had Al Lucas on bass. When Jo went off on his own to form his own trio I got an excellent drummer from Sweden whose name was Nils Bertil Dahlander. I did several Columbia LP records with him. We shortened his name to Bert Dahlander because nicknames are popular in America. Then I had two very fine bass players, first Arvell Shaw from the Louis Armstrong All Stars and in the last stage of my steady trio I had a fine player named Major Holley.

I guess this would bring me up to the early 60s and, after that trio, I began to freelance the rhythm sections, not keeping a steady group together. I did a great deal of traveling and playing with good musicians in each town or country, and this is what I've been doing mostly since then. In that way it

became economically feasible because the rock'n roll movement did sidetrack quite a bit of interest in jazz. I was therefore able to do well just going on my own and hiring a good
bass player and drummer in different towns and countries
while keeping ahead of the picture economically myself. But
now the picture's improving, sufficiently to start thinking
again about one steady group to travel with me all the time,
so we can build arrangements and produce a situation where
one night's work leads to another and a lot of good new ideas
take shape, as they do when you keep the same men together
steadily.

In recent years I've recorded a solo tribute to Fats Waller
called *Striding After Fats* on Black Lion, and in America
there's a solo album tribute to Billie Holiday called *With Billie
In Mind*. We recorded a small band where we try to do a
three-minute version of each song with each player taking
eight bars or sixteen bars like we did years ago in the series
with Lester Young and the players. This time we did it with
Harry Edison and Bob Wilber, Vic Dickenson, Major Holley
and Oliver Jackson. This was done at the Chiaroscuro studios
in New York. As I said, I've done two albums with the DSC,
plus lots of records in Japan (both solo and small groups,
which include a couple of excellent clarinet players,) and then
there's solo albums from Stockholm, and with the singer
Marlene Widmark, Rolf Ericson on trumpet and Arne
Wilhelmsson on bass.

I think electric guitar has a place for solos in a band,
because you can't hear the acoustic guitar unless you've got
an excellent engineer to put the microphone on. At Nice this
past July, I heard the Basie band, and the engineer had turned
the mike off on Freddie Green's guitar, the mike was also off
on Basie's piano, off on the bass violin, but it seemed to be at
quadruple volume on the trumpets. This shows that you have
to cope with engineers, too, so you really do need an ampli-
fier for bass and guitar, it does perform a functional purpose.
I like the bass where the natural wooden bass is slightly
amplified by a very good speaker system, not the electric bass
guitar or that sort of stuff. There's some makes of electric

piano nowadays that when you strike the key it gets into the acoustic piano technique, but on some of them it doesn't matter if you press it with your finger or hit it, or even push it down with an umbrella, it's the same tone, and the volume's done with a pedal. On the best of them the volume's controlled with the finger tips, just like the real piano.

People often ask me what my views are on pop and rock. Before I give them, please do not think my reactions are dictated by a sour grapes philosophy because they have been so popular. I try to look at everything as objectively as I can, even the things I don't like. Well, all I can say about pop and rock is that I just don't understand them. The whole rock movement, to me, is not music at all; it's a sociological phenomenon. There's no doubt it's very important because it's saying something that has swept the whole earth. The twist and rock kind of dancing has caught on in all classes: it's done in the discothèques by maharajas and emperors, kings and queens and the people in the White House, as well as by the poorest people on earth; starving and underdeveloped people. So it's all over the earth, but it's not music, it's a sociological manifestation of something. Frankly, to me, it's like the whole earth vomiting at once. The whole earth is sick, and it vomits. That to me is rock'n'roll and discothèque dancing. You see these adults dancing around to the music and when I see they like it, I can only conclude they're mentally retarded! But it's not their fault: it's just a manifestation of our times around the world.

Actually, the whole rock movement has lost its folk roots, although it may have started out with them. Nowadays it's manufactured by businessmen in London and New York and other big centers. The Beatles and Rolling Stones are good examples of a cynical caricature of folk music. It's an absolute farce to hear intelligent Englishmen trying to imitate the vernacular of ignorant Southern Negroes in the US who haven't been to school.

I suppose you might say, in a distorted kind of way, that it's democratic: it has attacked both rich and poor. You can see either crowned heads or the presidents of states or little kids of seven all doing the twist.

In some places I've played I've seen people of sixty-five or seventy years of age jumping up and down like teenagers on a dance floor, twisting and jerking themselves around. It seems to put life into them and it's democratic, so I suppose that's a good thing. Perhaps I could best sum it up by saying that rock to me is like a red flag to a bull!

10
Handful Of Keys

I have chosen this as the title of this chapter not only as a tribute to one of the really great masters of the jazz piano, Fats
Waller, but also because it aptly sums up what I am going to
talk about. It is good to see that there is a growing number of
books about jazz these days, both biographical material and
excellent reference works, but all too few recognized exponents of the jazz idiom take the trouble to give the jazz lover
a deeper insight into the niceties of handling a particular
instrument, without at the same time becoming too technical
for the majority of readers.

As I have said earlier *Handful of Keys* was a Fats Waller solo
which I, as a young and aspiring jazz musician, carefully
studied note by note, played and committed entirely to
memory. It was, and remains, a classic of its kind.

Although Fats was my first favorite jazz pianist I wasn't
around him a great deal. I knew his work on recordings long
before I got to meet him in person in New York. I had heard
his recordings when I was at school, as well as recordings of
Earl Hines with Louis Armstrong's Hot Five. These two
pianists were the strongest influence on my own decision to
become a jazz pianist and they really helped me to make up
my mind that I didn't want to pursue a career in any other
field.

The strongest influence of all was Art Tatum, whom I met
in Toledo, Ohio, after I had left Speed Webb to join the Milt
Senior band which, after Toledo, played at the Gold Coast
Club in Chicago for Al Capone and his friends.

Art Tatum was the master of all of us in those days and we
were all awestruck when he sat down to play this most phenomenal piano. I think that, even to this day, he is probably

the most amazing keyboard talent I have ever had the privilege of hearing, either classical, jazz or any other style of music.

It was quite a thing to witness Art when he played in person: his perfect command of the keyboard; the flexibility of his hands. He did not have big hands, but they could go out to any distance he needed, almost as if they were made of rubber, he was so relaxed and fluid in his playing. There was nothing like him in those days and he was a very strong influence on me.

Now these three players who played such an important part in my musical life were all distinct. I think Art was at his best in the solo piano. Hines and Waller were both excellent soloists as well as rhythm section pianists, but for sheer astounding piano neither Hines nor Waller, James P. Johnson or any of the giants of those days you like to mention, or even for that matter anybody who has come up to this very day, has to my knowledge even remotely got the sheer skill and pianistic ability of Art Tatum. It even goes beyond any consideration of him as a jazz pianist. It's simply an astounding skill that is given to very few human beings. I could compare it to the man who can make a hole in one any time he picks up a golf club or a baseball player who can hit a home run every time he picks up a bat. Having this just phenomenal ability at the keyboard, jazz happened to be the medium Tatum chose to work with. Because his life coincided with that phase in the American popular music of his day, he chose it rather than classical music. I imagine he could have been a great player of Chopin, Beethoven or any of the classical European composers. It's certain that none of their music would have presented any technical problems to him, because he had greater dexterity and a greater command of the keyboard than any classical pianist I've ever heard.

So, you see, I can just go on raving about him. Such people are very rare. There was another phenomenon who comes to mind in this connection, a negro slave, I have read about, named simply "Blind Tom", way back in the 1840's, who could hear a Chopin *étude* or a most complex classical piece, and could reproduce it after one hearing, note for note, at the keyboard.

Then again, there was a young 13-year-old Spanish boy, Pepita Arriola, who is reputed to have memorized overnight Bach's *Well Tempered Clavier*, when his teacher had only assigned him one single prelude and fugue to work on for the next lesson! I repeat, Tatum belongs to this rare category of phenomenal people who occur every hundred years or so in various fields of human endeavour. Tatum studied music at a school for the blind and could read braille. He had the sight of one eye, however, contrary to popular belief that he was completely blind. Jazz improvisation on the piano would present no problem to anybody with impaired eyesight because it involves creating your own music from a given framework. It's done by ear and what knowledge you have of harmony and your command of the instrument. Most of the great blind pianists I know of (Shearing, Ray Charles) were born blind.

As to Fats Waller, I was hardly ever fortunate enough to see him away from the bandstand, for instance at house parties, or other social gatherings, where we would have had a chance to converse. I guess my time was taken up by the Benny Goodman band being on the road all the time and Fats himself was very popular and was traveling a good deal. I was able, altogether, to see Fats four or five times around New York city, where he would appear at the Yacht Club and at a little club owned by Adrian Rollini, the well-known baritone player. Sometimes I would see him in theaters.

There was, however, one occasion when I experienced Fats at first hand. That was in Washington, DC, and Fats had the night off. He came to visit the Benny Goodman band, which was then playing a dance at the Colonnades Ballroom in Washington. Fats came around and spent the evening with us and what an evening! I'll never forget the enjoyment he got out of our music. He didn't play himself at all that night and was, in fact, the official bartender! He brought two large pieces of luggage with him: one contained practically every bottled drink you could think of while the other suitcase was packed with paper cups, bottles of soda water, ginger ale,

coca-cola and so on: two full-sized suitcases and Fats the bartender to the Benny Goodman band!

He sat on the bandstand with us and the band played like
it had never played before – such fire, such enthusiasm! Fats
appreciated every note. With every solo he would roar out a
great fat laugh of appreciation and sheer enjoyment. The
audience caught the spirit of it all too and it was certainly one
of the happiest nights I ever had with the Benny Goodman
organization – with Fats Waller as our bartender at the
Colonnades Ballroom!

I was rather saddened, really, when Fats became a "great
entertainer", because I had originally known him as a musician and I did not appreciate his singing and all the humor he
was selling to the public, although of course I am glad he was
able to become so successful and earn a very good living
during the Depression, which was a hard time for a lot of
people. The original Fats Waller recordings which attracted
me to him as a musician were just piano alone, without
singing or comedy. What impressed me about Fats was the
fact that he had refined and added so much to the James P.
Johnson stride style of playing. Perhaps "refined" is the
wrong word to use, because James P.'s piano was in its own
way flawless and immaculate.

Technically, you could say Fats added a few things: using
the left hand "stride" bass or "swing" bass, where the bass
note alternates with an after-beat chord, Fats used the 10th as
his bass note: a span of ten notes in the scale between the little
finger of the left hand and the thumb. Very few players had a
reach to do that because on average they could only span the
octave (eight notes). James P., on the other hand, used mainly
the single note and the octave. The 10th bass gave an especially rich and full sound. Fats, and also Tatum, were tops in
using the 10th in the "stride" bass.

Fats of course had his own little ideas and nuances that
make each player different from another and these were
extremely attractive, making him very different from James
P. He also had flawless accuracy, just as James P. and Art
Tatum did. There was no such thing as hitting wrong notes

with Fats or with the others.

Speaking of Fats's big reach on the piano, spanning ten notes where most pianists have to be content with eight, people often ask me whether having large hands is not an advantage when playing the piano. I can say that the size of the hands is *not* a factor in the quality of the playing; the important thing is that a pianist is being creative and non-imitative. There are many very fine exponents of both jazz and classical music and you'll find both small and large hands among them.

Now let me turn to Earl Hines, the other great pianistic influence in my life. I first got to know his music through the recordings of the Louis Armstrong Hot Five when I was at school and, as in the case of Fats, I learned some of his solos from records. I was able to play accurately, note for note, for example, his piano solo part in the now famous *West End Blues*.

I later got to meet Earl Hines personally when I moved to Chicago from Toledo, Ohio, I think around 1931, and was able to meet him at the Grand Terrace Café there, where he had an excellent fifteen-piece band. I was down at the Grand Terrace on many nights when I wasn't working myself, listening to Earl in person. In the end I became friendly with him and, as I said earlier, he let me sit in with his band and play on many occasions. I also did some orchestrations and arrangements for him of jazz tunes which were popular with musicians at that time. I learned more about the Earl Hines style by actually being around him in person and listening to him a great deal, in the same way I had previously been around Art Tatum.

I have said that Hines was both a great soloist and a great rhythm player. For my taste I enjoy him in both roles. He has a beautifully powerful rhythmic approach to the keyboard and his rhythms are more eccentric than those or Art Tatum or Fats Waller. When I say eccentric, I mean getting away from straight 4/4 rhythm. He would play a lot of what we call accent on the "and" beat. This is the beat that comes *between* the 4/4 quarter note beats, and Hines accented it by starting a note between the 4/4 beats. He would do this with great authority and attack. It was a subtle use of syncopation, playing on the in-between beats or what I might call "and" beats: one-*and*-two-*and*-three-*and*-four-*and*. The "and" between "one-two-three-four" is implied. When counted in music, the "and" becomes what are called eighth notes. So you get eight notes to a bar instead of four, although they're spaced out in the time of four. Now Hines would come in on those "and" beats with the most eccentric patterns, that propelled the rhythm forward with such tremendous force that people felt an irresistible urge to dance or tap their feet, or otherwise react physically to the rhythm of the music. All great players have this, but Hines has a very marked gift for it.

I have seen him play solo at the Regal Theater in Chicago and, after only a few moments, he had the whole audience stamping their feet and clapping their hands in time to his music, and he was playing the piano alone on that vast stage with no rhythm section to help him. He had such a beautiful approach to playing rhythmic piano that he could easily move an audience.

Fats Waller had the same thing too, but it was different. There were of course similarities in everything people did, but each man had such a storehouse of originality that anyone familiar with jazz piano could easily tell them apart. When you heard one of them his name was just written all over his music after only a few moments of listening.

Hines is still a giant to this day. I had the pleasure of working with him on a tour of Latin America in 1974 and 1976. We played a programme together at the Nice Jazz Festival where we did a one-hour program in which I played during the first half-hour with bass and drums and then he would play the second half hour. Of course we reminisced about our days in Chicago. It is a real pleasure whenever I am associated with Earl nowadays, and he's just about my favorite living jazz pianist.

The main thing, I found, was to understand the rhythm of Earl Hines and the relationship between his improvisations and the basic chords of the piece he was playing. By listening to him so much, I was able to learn a great deal about what was happening and of course this was invaluable. As I have said, Hines is very intricate in his rhythm patterns: very unusual and original, and there is really nobody like him. This makes him a giant of originality. Naturally, he was playing a lot of things that are generally played: he could play a swing bass or a stride bass and so on, but the technique he used gave great force to the solo piano in the big band before the days of electrical amplification. Undoubtedly a great contribution to piano jazz was his melodic improvisation in the right hand, similar to the horns, and he evolved that style, a "heavy touch", before we had amplification. His octave technique was original, brilliant, and clear, even above full ensemble backgrounds.

When I first started playing, the microphone was beginning to be used on the piano and all one had to do was turn up the volume control to be heard. Using the octave, instead of the individual fingers involves utilizing hand touch and gives you much more power, so you can be heard in a hall where there is no amplification. By hand touch I mean the power of the whole hand behind the touch instead of just the individual finger. Hines pioneered and developed this technique and introduced it with tremendous dexterity so he could produce improvised piano solos which would cut through to perhaps 2,000 dancing people, just like a trumpet or a saxophone could.

Even though the octave has been used for centuries in keyboard playing it had not previously been employed in the way Hines used it. It was absolutely brand new and a trememdous contribution to jazz piano technique. Hines not only got his force in this way; he also had the speed to go with it, which entailed having a very fast hand and an exceedingly flexible wrist joint. Very few pianists ever develop absolute freedom of the wrist joint, and I am sure he was born with it, although practice and experience must have developed it still further. What always amazed me about Earl was that, no matter how loudly he played, he never lost his touch; he never really banged the piano. He would always come at that keyboard and play each note with complete control and intention, no matter how loud, whereas many players, when they get carried away with emotion, and want to achieve *fortissimo, crescendo* and high volume, stiffen and begin to hit the piano and consequently lose the rhythm. But Hines never did and never lost his touch, although he could carry the volume up to the point where he might break a string on the piano! Nevertheless he never had calluses on his hands or broken nails. His tone was just perfect in high volume because then your feelings are not inhibited, when you really want to cut loose and play with real force.

All music at times has to be *fortissimo*. In classical music you have *f* and *ff* up to the triple *fff*, which as loud as you ever play in an orchestra. But you need that volume at times to express certain feelings and it is a great asset to players to be able to rise into the higher volumes with complete freedom. You can get a lot of musical things off your chest in that way which you can't with low volume. So it's very exciting to hear Hines "stretch out" on the keyboard like that.

The so-called "trumpet piano" effect, for which Hines became famous, was not, as some people think, the result of pedal work. It was the hand; the hand behind the two fingers forming the octave – the little finger and the thumb. And don't be deceived by the fact that a pianist raises his hands to "strike" the notes. You can also "press" the keys from a distance! In other words, what happens when your fingers reach the keyboard is very different to what is happening in the air. Ellington, for instance, has a way of letting his right hand hang limp at his side and then swinging it up in the air before striking the notes, seeming to "hit" a chord from a distance. Actually, the motion itself means nothing: what happens when you actually contact the keys is quite different to what is happening in the air.

I used to stand beside Earl at the Grand Terrace and watch what he was doing with some of his favorite patterns and then he used to let me sit and play the piano for him to give him a rest at times.

Fats Waller, too, was able to get into the high volumes easily, as could his master, James P. Johnson. James P. and Fats played the "stride"style, which means the left hand playing low single bass notes on beats one and three, then the after-beat chord, round the middle of the keyboard, playing on the second and fourth beats of a four-beat measure. In that stride bass idiom James P. and Fats seem to have stood out head and shoulders above so many of their contemporaries.

I think it was John Hammond who told me the first influence of any kind in jazz music which he experienced was when he was a boy at prep school and he heard records of James P. It seems James P. had made recordings after the First World War, and John Hammond once played me some old 78s he had of him. These recordings were probably made around the early 20s and I believe some of his ideas in his right hand would sound just wonderful if they were orchestrated for the Count Basie Band today. James P.'s ideas in jazz could be perfectly executed by the Basie Band and sound very proper and in place over that number of years. He shared Fats's, Hines's and Tatum's flawless techniques: never a wrong note. His style was very powerful and I heard him play several times in person, in addition to hearing him on recordings.

One of the great unknowns in the James P. stride idiom, who did not achieve the fame of James P., Fats and Don Lambert (one of my favorites too) was a man called "The Beetle", who was brought to my attention by Ben Webster, the famous tenor sax player. Ben was a great fan of piano playing and, incidentally, played a very good stride piano himself.

Ben introduced me to the Beetle at someone's apartment in Harlem, where everone was taking a turn at the piano. There were a lot of those get-togethers like that in those days – late, after work was over. What amazed me was that the Beetle managed to play his "stride" style, in which his left hand would go down to the last octave on the keyboard – on the left down in the bass – with the long sweep up to the middle for his after-beat chords, based on one and three, the after-beat chords on two and four counts of the measure, *without looking*! I've seen him play flawlessly in this way, with this long sweep of the stride, where the left hand is covering maybe a span of two feet from the bassnote to the after-beat chord. I've seen him do this, and even carry on a conversation with someone who was standing beside his right hand. In other words: he was looking exactly away from his left hand, but still going down to the last octave on the keyboard with the little finger of his left hand and striking the right note with perfect precision every time! I keenly enjoyed the Beetle's playing.

And the touch too, that some of those players got on the piano! A nice full touch, with no banging or harshness. They all all had finesse and touch, those great players.

I have sometimes been asked how you develop a style of your own. Personally I don't think you can calculate a style: you develop into it because you're so intensely interested in keyboard music and in other instruments too. So when you finally emerge with your own style you might not even be aware of it. In actual fact you are influenced by a whole host of people: saxophonists, trumpet players, arrangers, written jazz – all sorts of ideas are flooding into you. An idea will enter your mind from someone else and that will inspire you to say: "If that can be done, this other thing can be done too".

There's no end to this constant flux of impressions and influences. Ideas came to me from all sorts of sources, although the keyboard players would be, of course, the primary influence. You might say style has been achieved if you add something someone else has not done. Hines's melodic approach to the right hand was a giant contribution to the development of the jazz piano and it had not been done before. Comparing Fats Waller with Hines we find that his was not so much a horn style as a pianistic one: lots of chords and small intervals such as right-hand thirds, two notes struck at once, the interval of a third apart. With Hines what was most important was the single line – a horn can only make one note at a time.

Art Tatum's feeling at the keyboard did not require very high volumes. He would build his intensity by making his harmonies much more complete. This does not mean to say that he never used extended volumes and accents too, but he never got into the high volumes of Fats Waller, James P. Johnson and Earl Hines. In my own playing too I keep within a narrow range; I don't get into the dynamic range of Hines and Fats – I play nearer the Tatum range. My playing is a sort of blend of the three: I use a finger technique inspired by listening to Tatum (whose finger technique was unsurpassed) and I combine that technique with the melodic ideas and touch of Hines's octave playing and, since I can stretch the 10th in the left hand, I use the stride bass I got from Fats Waller.

Those would be the main points I incorporated in my playing from each of these three masters. The reason I do not use the extremely high volume of Hines and Waller is that I seem to be able to express myself well within a much narrower dynamic range. I was in much closer personal contact with Hines and Tatum than with Fats and I would like to say here how grateful I am that both were very free and generous in teaching me anything I wanted to know. I was able to stand over Art Tatum and watch his hands as he played. From our earliest contact in Toledo, Art realized I understood and appreciated his genius.

I was one of the very few people who could interrupt Art Tatum while he was playing a particularly dazzling passage and ask him to repeat it slowly for me. If necessary, he would stop playing and show me exactly what he had done and then resume the piece. I was one of the very few he would do this for, because he had a very soft spot for me. He would demonstrate all his runs, ascending and descending, on the keyboard, utilizing a special pattern in one octave and then an octave higher, repeating the same pattern. He did this for me up and down the keyboard, slowly and patiently, teaching me how they were done.

Art was very famous in those days for those very original runs. There was no other piano player in the jazz world making runs like that from one end of the keyboard to the other and I am deeply grateful to Tatum for his willingness and patience in showing me all these things. I still play Tatum runs to this day!

As to another important element in jazz music, improvisation, I wouldn't say by any means that it comes naturally. It's like everything else: the more you do it the more proficient you get at it. Even today, if I don't do it – say for months – I become less proficient, I seem to lose something.

There is a common belief that improvisation is something that is typical of jazz music only. We tend to forget that improvisation was also a great feature of classical music but has somehow got lost today. Beethoven was a great improviser, so were Mozart and Bach. Beethoven, for example, left open opportunities for improvisation in his late piano concertos. In the fourth, the G major, at the end of the first movement, there is a long period for the piano to improvise a cadenza. Today, most concert pianists use cadenzas that were written out by the masters of the past – a case in point are Busoni's.

Jazz, on the other hand, relies heavily on improvisation in addition to written music.

I think once you have settled into a style you should stick to it. The French say *le style c'est l'homme*, the style is the man, and there's a lot in that. I was interested to see that Alfred Hitchcock, that fine old veteran film producer now in his seventies, said the same in his own amusing way. He recalled that he had been criticized for repeating himself and added: "To me style is imitating yourself".

When asked by the interviewer what he intended to do next, he replied slyly: "Oh, I shall just make another thriller so that people can say, 'There he goes again, the same old stuff.'" The same would apply to the great individual stylists of jazz. You can pick them out immediately: Armstrong, Johnny Hodges, Benny Carter, Earl Hines and of course Jack Teagarden, who found the secret of the way he thought he should play the trombone when he was a young man and never changed.

The same applies to my own playing. I have not tampered with my foundation, just refined it here and there over the years. My style is still basically the same as always.

The same applies to classical music: the music of Händel, Bach, Scarlatti, Couperin and so on. All of them have something so basically right that they have never been relegated to the museum. I have noticed the same thing in sculpture and painting, too, while wandering round the Villa Borghese Gallery in Rome. Michelangelo, Caravaggio, Bernini and Raphael: these men's paintings and sculptures are as alive today as they were the day they were created. And when you look at the work of some of the others, it's like looking at a calendar. You see the way everybody was doing it at that particular period in history. For each of those other paintings or sculptures its date is its chief value and it's not living and breathing canvas or stone like some of them. That's why it's ridiculous when people talk about a "revival" of jazz or about "nostalgia", as if it were something dug up out of a grave. The great works of genius in art are good by any standard and when you've said that, you've said everything! The reason it's alive today is because it was sincerely created and felt and is not "plastic". It's for real.

I might mention that some people, like all my children, have the gift of absolute pitch. I myself have relative pitch. If you strike a note on the piano keyboard someone with absolute pitch knows instantly what the note is without looking. I have to be told what the first note is and only then can I tell you what the second note is without looking.

I have done quite a bit of private teaching in my life, too, and the young people I've had as pupils have always been between sixteen and twenty years of age. At one time I had my own school in New York, "The Teddy Wilson School for Pianists", from 1936 to 1939, with three excellent partners, and we turned out some very good students. J.Lawrence Cook was my chief assistant there and he was great on the theoretical side of the jazz piano and shaped the printed courses we had, containing sheet music of my improvisations on popular melodies. They proved very successful in teaching by mail. However, I had to give it up in the end because costs just kept soaring. Advertising and copyright payments were heavy items, especially as the latter were always for very popular songs. The other partners in my school were Eve Ross and Teddy Cassola. Their contribution rounded out the work done by the Cook and me. My having to be away traveling and performing so much of time led some to believe I only "fronted" the school. Not so. I was completely involved.

I did my best to teach my students what I knew both by demonstrating technique myself at the keyboard and by playing illustrative recordings of successful pianists of all kinds. Sometimes I would have the student play the left hand accompaniment in the bass while I played two choruses in the right. Then we would switch without pause, the student taking over the right hand and I taking the bass part. Sometimes we would work over a song for ten minutes like that. I found it to be an excellent technique for developing improvisational facility and also facility in accompaniment or "back-up" piano. Later at Juilliard I used this technique extensively using two pianos.

I have dealt at some length with the three great pianistic influences in my jazz life: Fats Waller, Earl Hines and Art Tatum. After absorbing their influence I evolved my own style which, gratifyingly, found wide appreciation. I had a great following among jazz pianists in the late thirties after I had become well known all over the world through my recordings, the Columbia and Victor Records with Benny Goodman and the early Chocolate Dandies dates with Benny Carter, set up by John Hammond. Columbia and Victor were the two big recording companies that really meant something in those days in terms of worldwide circulation.

After I had come up in the piano world a young man appeared on the scene who had been working on much the same technical lines I had – Bud Powell. But his ideas were powerfully influenced by alto sax player Charlie Parker, who became the great innovator in jazz after the Second World War, along with Thelonious Monk and Dizzy Gillespie.

Talking about "keeping in the swing" and absorbing influences, night life in Harlem during the Second World War was musically very exciting. I would finish work at four o'clock in the morning at the Café Society, come uptown and have to stand in a line to get a table at Monroe's Uptown House or Minton's Playhouse, where jam sessions were just starting after the legitimate clubs had closed. Dicky Wells's club was still going strong in Harlem and, altogether, there was lots going on, sometimes until daylight. Some of the piano sessions would even go until noon the next day.

To get back to Bud Powell and Charlie Parker. Powell played a wonderful single-line improvisation finger style, of the kind which I had introduced to jazz. But you wouldn't confuse his style of playing with mine by any means because his ideas were entirely different and he had also been listening a great deal to Tatum's chords. His melodic ideas, I felt, were strongly influenced by Charlie Parker's alto sax.

Outstanding pianists who came into prominence in the early forties were Nat Cole and Al Haig. Nat soon became so famous as a singer that many never knew what a fine pianist he was. He was first heard to great advantage on some Lionel Hampton small group recordings.

Al Haig at that time was both a fine solo player and rhythm section man. He worked with Charlie Parker and many of the famous players of the 1940's. He is still active today, playing mostly solo jobs around New York. He doesn't seem to want to do much trio work or travel on the road, so a lot of his fans have wondered what happened to Al. I can assure them he is still very active around the New York and New Jersey area. I remember on one occasion, when he was playing in a restaurant, I heard him just toss off a flawless rendering of the Chopin Fantasy Impromptu. That will give you some idea of the pianistic ability he had achieved by study. One of the melodies in the Impromptu I am talking about is well known as *I'm Forever Blowing Bubbles*, but the original piano music calls for concert pianist stature to play it correctly, as Al did. George Shearing, too, can play European classical music at concert pianist level, not as a talented amateur but as a fully-fledged concert pianist.

Quite a few jazz players, although admittedly not many, can do this.

André Previn is of course the outstanding example. Not only has he mastered all the schools of jazz but he also plays classical music on a professional level and does symphony orchestra conducting.

Other names which spring to mind in this connection are Stan Freeman and Dick Hyman, and Frederick Goulde in Europe. Goulde played in the Birdland Club in New York and I hear from his friends he's one of the best Beethoven players of our time.

After I left Goodman to form my own band in 1939 a young pianist came into prominence named Mel Powell. Mel had a truly rare gift at the keyboard and got swift recognition from musicians and fans. He joined Benny Goodman, then later was in military service as a member of the Glenn Miller Army Airforce band. After the war he became a serious student of Paul Hindemith and became so interested in classical composition that he rarely performed jazz. He is at present dean of a conservatory in California. Mel had a thorough understanding of all previous styles before him, and in his own playing brought a light sparkling touch with perfect rhythm, and fresh harmonic ideas, shown in his writing as well as his playing.

I have been influenced by horn players too. I learned a great deal working with Louis Armstrong and also with Benny Carter, the way he played the alto sax. And I learned from listening to Duke Ellington's men, particularly Johnny Hodges on alto and especially from working with Johnny in the Billie Holiday series of recordings. So you can learn from horn players as well as from other pianists, although they may be the strongest influence.

I think everyone knows what you're talking about when you say that jazz took a certain direction round about the beginning of the Second World War and earned itself the nickname "bebop". Typical exponents of this style were Thelonious Monk on piano, Charlie Parker on alto sax, and Dizzy Gillespie on trumpet. Bud Powell could be said to be of that period too, although his style was quite different from that of Monk. Bud played a single-line right hand imitation of Charlie Parker's alto sax style. Every time I was able to hear him, I never heard what I considered Bud Powell's own style.

Thelonious Monk knew my playing very well, as well as that of Tatum, Hines and Waller. He was exceedingly well grounded in the piano players who preceded him, adding his own originality to a very sound foundation. He was musically very creative and did a wonderful little tune called *Round About Midnight* that might have been more singable and more popular in its appeal than a lot of his instrumentals.

I also had the privilege of hearing two other artists who are important to the jazz piano: Erroll Garner and George Shearing. Garner is an old friend of mine and one of the greatest talents there was. What a shame he died so young! I never asked him whether it was true that he didn't read music. If he didn't, that makes him, in my eyes, one of the greatest talents there was: to have developed the way he did on the jazz piano. His harmonies were as modern as tomorrow and his conception of jazz exquisite, as well as his sense of rhythm. He had everything going for him. He was wonderful in the rhythm section and he was a great solo player. There was no weak point. He was left-handed but his right hand had all the agility he ever needed, and no-one would ever realise he wasn't right-handed when you saw how he got around with his right hand. I suppose the true answer is that he was ambidextrous. His harmonies, his rhythm and his melodic ideas were all highly-developed and this is something we all try to achieve. This is the criterion that has been set over the centuries: that all the faculties of a great musician are equally developed and that there is no weak point in the harmonic, rhythmic or melodic parts. Garner certainly qualified by those standards.

Distinctive about Shearing is that he is has a beautiful "touch", often a characteristic of blind players, and so he has an exquisite sound. He is also extremely versatile. I remember when he came to New York, to play in the same club as Garner, that he was using block chords a great deal.

Nowadays this is a technique used by many pianists. As far as I know the first to use it was Milt Buckner, whom I heard with Lionel Hampton's band. Buckner was featured in that band with the tune *Nola*, a piano solo in block chords. The speed of the hand touch is carried to a height very few players ever achieve.

Earl Hines has that speed of hand touch, but using the octave in the right hand. But when Milt Buckner plays *Nola* he plays block chords using both the left and right hands, working in parallel motions simultaneously. George Shearing was using that technique when I heard him playing in the same programme as Erroll Garner at the Three Deuces Club. Shearing is very versatile: he could play almost exactly my own style and he did a wonderful job with the Art Tatum style as well as stride piano; in fact he could play the whole history of jazz as far as I could see. But he seemed to concentrate mainly on the block chord style first perfected by Milt Buckner. However, he applied different ideas to the technique and, I think, was very much influenced by the musical ideas of Charlie Parker and Dizzy Gillespie. It was a great treat for me to hear those two, Erroll Garner and George Shearing, taking turns at the piano night after night.

Today Oscar Peterson can be considered the pianist who has inherited the mantle of Art Tatum, for sheer keyboard dexterity and overall command of the instrument.

Ralph Sutton and another pianist named Dick Wellstood are to me both excellent solo and rhythm-section players with a rather classical approach to jazz. They can play all kinds of styles, including Willie "The Lion" Smith, Fats Waller and the piano music of Bix Beiderbecke. Both these players are prosperous today and do not just play music of their own time: they go right back to Scott Joplin and through all styles down to their own original improvisations today. Both have exceptional skill on the keyboard. Of the pianists who have come into prominence in the last thirty years, Oscar Peterson is doing that too, giving people an idea of the development of the jazz piano style.

I would also like to say a word about Joe Sullivan, who

used to play with Bing Crosby many years ago and later with Bing's brother, Bob Crosby. Joe went off on his own and did a lot of solo work, like Ralph Sutton, and was one of the outstanding jazz piano players of the last forty or fifty years. He overcame a serious illness back in the thirties and was out of commission for about a year, although he came back with his piano playing undiminished. I got to know Joe very well when I was playing with my band at the Café Society in New York during the Second World War.

A piano giant I should mention as one of the great pianists with small bands is Bob Zurke, who played with Bob Crosby at one time. He is very important from the point of view of jazz piano style, since he evolved a unique and original approach to the piano.

Of course the contribution some women jazz pianists have made to the development of jazz in my time should by no means be underestimated. Mary Lou Williams is one who immediately springs to mind. Even to this day she is outstanding. She never gets stale and has an ever-growing mind. She is another pianist who can play the whole range of jazz piano history with perfect ease. She played with Andy Kirk's band for many years in the 1930s and can also score excellently. She did some originals for Benny Goodman in the late thirties, such as *Roll 'Em* and *Camel Hop* and they are just as fresh now as they were then.

Then there is Marian McPartland, wife of Jimmy McPartland, the trumpet player, who is still an active professional pianist. We once did an album together in which we played four solos each and four duets, without bass and drums. Barbara Carroll I should also mention as a leading woman jazz pianist who has worked a lot around the New York area but has not been on the road much.

Many jazz pianists have also taken to the organ – Fats Waller, of course, Count Basie, Dick Hyman, Wild Bill Davis – but I never tried it myself. There is a lot of experimenting going on, but the tools we jazz pianists work with are still much the same as those used by classical composers.

Europe too has produced a fine crop of very talented jazz

pianists and I could go on mentioning names for ever, but will refrain, beyond saying it all indicates how lively the jazz scene today is. I ask forgiveness of all those talented people I have not mentioned and anyway this is not a jazz reference book. For the jazz enthusiast who is keen to track down his favorites there are plenty of well documented works available.

11

Whither Jazz?

Looking back on the eventful years I have spent on the jazz scene and seeing the changes that have taken place, the question inevitably arises: what of the future?

Looking around today and speaking from my own daily experience with audiences at jazz concerts, I am not at all inclined to be dismayed or doubtful about the viability of jazz. True, there have been moments when it looked as if jazz would be eclipsed in the public taste by such new upsurgings as pop music and there is no doubt that many fine jazz musicians felt the pinch from this new switch in public attention. But the sales of recordings of all kinds of jazz are there to prove that there is an abiding interest in this kind of music. In fact, the interest is so great that many record companies are now digging deep into their archives to unearth hitherto unreleased masters and these "new" releases are finding ready buyers.

On my travels, when I cast an eye at the shops and big stores, the windows are well filled with the attractive sleeves of new jazz recordings and reissues. Frequently, on my tours, I find time to answer a request for a local recording which later sells well and it is heartening to me to see young people, both in the concert halls and the record shops, who were certainly not even born when the great names of jazz were in their prime, rooting about in the jazz collections and discovering it all afresh for themselves. No, definitely, jazz is not just for old fogies. Like any good music it does not age and in my view there will always be a good public for it. Just compare the great jazz orchestras and soloists with the host of other forms of music that have come and gone as fads. How many orchestras that were household names to a previous generation are now completely forgotten? Not so Louis Armstrong, Duke Ellington, Benny Goodman, Glenn Miller, or Coleman Hawkins, Fats Waller, Earl Hines, Art Tatum, nor, fortunately, my own contributions.

It remains to be seen what of pop will survive. I make no bones about it; to me, seen from the point of view of a jazz musician, it is "anti-music". I am not saying you can just sweep it under the carpet, because you obviously cannot. It is a phenomenon, an unaccountable phenomenon, just like the sudden tremendous public enthusiasm in the thirties for the Benny Goodman type of jazz music, despite the fact that Goodman had been playing this music before without even being noticed by the great mass of the public. Perhaps we have to leave it to the sociologists to explain such phenomena. By any sort of valid measurement, Goodman played *music*. The opposite of music is the only way to define the rubbish, electronic or otherwise, that dominates the sales charts of today.

I have noticed a trend in some of today's jazz players to improvise for long periods of time on one single chord, or two chords, but I think that's a dead end and will get us nowhere. I had a piano teacher who had examples of European composers in the past who had tried to do that, and they are all forgotten today. All the great composers of classical music were masters of everything, not just two chords. I think jazz musicians today are just wasting their time experimenting with things like that. Of course, you have to consider that disc jockeys will welcome any new trend they think they can cash in on. A disc jockey cannot get famous playing Louis Armstrong records; he has to come in on the wave of a "new genius" and that is why a lot of them are playing one-chord music. After all, it is a great challenge to stay interesting on one chord for about ten or twenty minutes. But it is sheer torture to have to sit and listen to it, even if the performer himself is having fun. I would even like to do it myself; just to sit and improvise on one chord. If you run out of ideas, you just wait until you get some new ones.

The Benny Goodman arrangement in the 1930s of *Sing*,

Sing, Sing, was a good example of improvised jazz where the harmony wasn't important in one section, as each soloist was playing only with Gene Krupa's drums. The horn could play anything he wanted to: one chord, two chords, change the key. He couldn't play a wrong note. Anything he did was alright. I think it was okay as Goodman was doing it, but to do it by the hour is just too much!

When saxophonist Ornette Coleman came to New York he brought no chord instrument, no guitar and no piano. He had just the horns, bass violin and drums. That way you don't really have a wrong note because the horn is maybe playing two or three octaves higher than the bass violin, and then there's no such thing as a wrong note; there is no chord to relate to, and as long as they stay with the rhythm everything is alright. The bass sticks rhythmically with the drum and the soloist is not restricted in improvising by the chords of the piano and the guitar. So that created quite a bit of interest when Ornette Coleman came to New York in 1959 and 1960. All the jazz critics who were looking for new talent were talking about "a new find", so they could hang on to his coat tails and make a lot of money campaigning for him.

What a contrast, for example, when you see what black musicians in South Africa are doing with jazz! In 1975 I toured in South Africa with the English clarinet player Dave Shepherd, who is a friend of mine. We played in the principal cities, although we had a local rhythm section.

On one occasion we shared the bandstand with an African group in a township ten miles from Durban. In the daytime these people worked in Durban and returned to the township at night, because of racial restrictions in South Africa. I must say they were excellent jazz musicians. Personally, I was most impressed because I did not think they would be up to that standard. They used two reeds, trumpet, trombone, two saxes, alto and tenor, a wooden upright bass, a pianist and a drummer. A lot of credit must go to them for the way they played because they had not had the opportunity to hear any American jazz apart from recordings. Of course they had plenty of recordings of American rock'n'roll, in addition to their own African music, which everybody dances to. But these fellows had gone to the trouble to get their instruments from I don't know where, and they were quite good. The saxophone players, I remember, had real technique, as well as the brass players, the pianist and the drummer, who was particularly gifted.

They seemed to have been influenced chiefly by Count Basie and Ellington recordings and they were playing the standard jazz tunes, well-known to all American jazzmen, improvising on blues chord lines. We ended up with a jam session on *How High The Moon* in which the group I was with was joined by the local African group and we all had a wonderful time.

Most people have a picture of jazz musicians leading wild and woolly lives, full of drink, drugs and women in between jam sessions. Like all popular myths this is not a true picture, but a caricature.

I have already described what Hollywood did to jazz in the *Benny Goodman Story* and the quaint notions held by movie scriptwriters of how we lived and talked. I suppose a lot of wishful thinking goes into what the public thinks about us: they want us to be bizarre characters leading disordered, if not chaotic lives, and that probably accounts too for the way the Billie Holiday story was handled. Of course, nobody would pretend we live model "suburban" lives and the nature of the musical profession is such that "regularity", whether it be in the hours we keep, the times we eat, or where and how we sleep, is all too often absent. But perhaps people tend to forget that there are many other professions which entail such living conditions. Take, for example sailors, journalists, the police, writers, painters, taxi drivers, doctors, hospital workers: the list is endless. I suppose the jazz musician is surrounded by an aura of what people like to call "glamour", whatever that may mean, and they tend to project their own conceptions onto the scene. But behind all the color, the drama, the humor and the tragedy common to the human comedy there is a background of serious, solid hard work to earn a living.

As with everybody else, money keeps the jazz musician on the hop and he too, in addition to keeping his head financially above water, is just as preoccupied as anybody else with the apparently mundane business of making a career and having a home life, at least if he can, given the ups and downs of his profession.

I have been talking about my purely professional career, how I evolved as a musician, the people I met and what happened to me. But, in between times, plenty was happening in the personal field. My marriages and my children were of vital importance to me. Jazz music played an important part in my first marriage, which was to Irene Armstrong, whom I met in Chicago where she was appearing as Irene Edie, the name of her ex-husband. She was an excellent pianist and was playing at the Vogue Club on Cottage Grove. I would go there on off nights and sit in with her group.

Irene was also a very good songwriter and I have already recalled earlier that she wrote one of Billie Holiday's most successful recordings called *Some Other Spring*, which jazz musicians are still playing today. We had no children and later separated and divorced.

Then I married Janice Carati. She was from Brooklyn, New York and she bore my first child named Theodore Jan Wilson. He is known in the family as "Teddy Jr." but himself prefers to be "Ted" to distinguish himself from me.

Ted has come quite a distance in music. He plays excellent jazz drums with me when I have my own rhythm section and I'm freelancing. He gained a degree in classical percussion at the New York University music department and he has played sucessfully with a number of symphony orchestras. He is the official percussionist of the Billy Denison Orchestra at the Playboy Club in Great George, New Jersey, and teaches music history, both classical and jazz, at Kingsborough College, New York. He has also qualified for his master's degree as a student of the Music Department of Queens College, Long Island. Altogether he is doing extremely well.

Janice and I were together for quite a while but there, too, there was parting of the ways. I suppose many marriages suffer from the irregularities of a musician's life and we did not manage to make a go of things.

My third wife, Blanche Louth, was from Massachusetts and I met her in Chicago. We had a son named Steven, who is now living in France since Blanche and I separated and divorced. Steven also has a great liking for the drums, although he is still at school. He visits me now and again in New Jersey, where I live.

My fourth and present wife is Joanne Roberts. Our ménage consists of three children; a son from my previous marriage named William, James, aged ten, and a daughter Dune, aged nine. So altogether I have five children: four boys and a girl.

William is a good pianist and had a good classical training. Although he is still at school he has his own five-piece jazz band and also plays trumpet with the school marching band. He has written and arranged for the big band at school. Little James has studied quite a bit, plays good drums, and has gone on to do well with trumpet, the French horn and the bugle. Both James and daughter Dune are studying tap and acrobatic dancing and Dune, although only nine, has taken up piano, violin and E- flat alto sax.

My profession greatly influenced my family life and I am very proud of having such a musical family. Friends have joked that some day I may even form the Teddy Wilson family band! Steven, in France, will probably become a professional drummer, and William may go in for piano. Fortunately, the mothers of my children are all musical, too, although none, with the exception of Irene Edie, is a professional player.

People think it is natural for a musical father to teach his children but in actual fact I do not feel qualified to teach children. The young people I have had as pupils have always been between sixteen and twenty.

I am happy to say that all my children get on very well with each other, even though they have different mothers. It is also fortunate for me that my children understand my being away from them a lot when I'm on the road. They were born and raised with the knowledge of the necessities of a musician's life.

I have found a handy way of keeping in touch with my

children when I am on the road, thanks to the invention of the tape recorder cassette. I have a lively exchange of such tapes with them, and in off moments, "away from the bandstand", when I want to hear the family, I switch on and, as if by magic, there they are, saying hello, and often interspersing their news with musical interludes!

I would like to end on a philosophical note which comes from no less than Coleman Hawkins, who himself has known life in all its aspects. I once did a tour with Coleman in Canada in the 1940s with a excellent small group. We had Freddy Webster on trumpet, who was coming on very strongly in those days, although he unfortunately died very young. We also had Max Roach, in his early days as a drummer, and Hank Jones, who did solo piano, whereas I played with Coleman's group. Riding on the train I had a chance to talk to Coleman, with whose work I had been familiar for many years before I got to know him personally. He said his philosophy of life was that all good things that happen to you are completely accidental and unexpected. He said he never went after an objective: you work hard to achieve something and it turns out to be less satifying than you thought it would be. Looking back on his life he concluded that the things that had been good for him he couldn't possibly have forseen. An interesting observation coming from a man who was as successful as he was – both artistically and financially. In my opinion his *Body and Soul* is the best jazz three-minute solo ever recorded.

Well, that's my story. I've had a wonderful life as a jazz musician and I'm still enjoying it. If I had to do it all over again I would do it just the same way. Very often I am asked by my friends, who know I have been an itinerant musician since my early teens: "Don't you hate traveling?"

I reply politely: "I don't mind at all". But, if I really said what I thought, I should tell them I would go crazy if I had to live the lives they lead: working from nine to five, year in, year out, working at a treadmill in an office or a factory, doing uncreative work: that would be terrible!

I see the life of a jazz musician, making a living out of it, as something you enjoy. It is something all of us who are jazz musicians would be doing for nothing, if we weren't getting paid for it, because it is our hobby as well as our income. The jam sessions I have described make that very clear. Musicians went and played together after work right into the wee small hours just for nothing except the sheer pleasure of playing their instruments

So a life like that, and the touring that goes with it, is very fascinating and interesting. Wherever I go it is like coming home: Holland, Scandinavia, London, Paris, San Francisco, Los Angeles, Chicago, New York, Canada, Tokyo. Everywhere there are fellow musicians, friends and fans to greet me and to talk to. When's the next plane?

If I had a lot of money and could retire, I would certainly continue to live in the same way.

It is my hope that this book will help to correct the false image that jazz music had – and sometimes still has – among the broad mass of the public. In particular I hope it corrects the image in some people's minds of jazz musicians as either buffoons or debauchees. By and large, the men who built up this impressive body of American music over the years were serious and dedicated artists who, while bringing joy and relaxation to millions, gave their talents and their lives to the perfection of their craft, often without adequate reward.

The spokesman of them all is Don Byas, the star tenor saxophone player, who said with disgust after playing at an obscure club: "I've spent twenty years of my life perfecting my tone and style on this instrument, and look what it has got me. The pop and rock stars are millionaires"

Jazz musicians had to earn money to live and quite a number of them did very well financially. But even if they were unable to earn money or were hit by the Depression, they still went on playing. It is not for nothing that a famous jazz tune is called *Raisin' the Rent*.

I wish the best of luck to everyone – all the fans, the musicians and friends and, of course, those who have read this book.

THE END

Recording Chronology

compiled by Howard Rye

This discography is based on that originally compiled by Gerald Bielderman, amplified by reference to the sources listed in the bibliography below.

Scope: This discography includes all Teddy Wilson's recordings of which details have been discovered, though no attempt has been made to document private recordings made after the introduction of tape recording. For reasons of space, only original issues are included, except that where material originally recorded for sale to radio stations has subsequently been issued for commercial sale to the public, the first commercial issue is also listed.

Countries of origin: All records listed are of United States origin or for international distribution, unless coded after the label name, as follows:

(Au)	Australian	(F)	French	(Sd)	Swedish
(Da)	Danish	(G)	German	(Yu)	Yugoslavian
(Du)	Dutch	(It)	Italian		
(E)	British	(J)	Japanese		

Abbreviations (Instruments, etc.):

arr	arranger	g	guitar
as	alto saxophone	h	harmonica
b	double bass	p	piano
bars	baritone saxophone	ss	soprano saxophone
bcl	bass clarinet	tp	trumpet
bj	banjo	tb	trombone
bsx	bass saxophone	ts	tenor saxophone
c	cornet	vb	vibraphone
cl	clarinet	vn	violin
dr	drums	vo	vocal
elg	electric guitar	xyl	xylophone
fl	flute		

Acknowledgements: For assistance in compiling this discography thanks are due to BBC Written Archives (Jeff Walden), Derek Coller, John Holley, British Library National Sound Archive, Alyn Shipton.

Bibliography.

The following works have been consulted:

Walter Bruyninckx, *70 Years Of Recorded Jazz: 1917-1987*, Mechelen, Belgium, 1987- (in progress).

Walter Bruyninckx, *Swing Discography, Swing//1920-1985, Swing/Dance Bands & Combos* (12 vols), Mechelen, Belgium, 1986-1990.

Walter Bruyninckx, *Traditional Discography, Traditional Jazz//1897-1985, Origins/New Orleans/ Dixieland/Chicago Styles* (6 vols), Mechelen, Belgium, 1987-1990.

Walter Bruyninckx, *Vocalists Discography, The Vocalists 1917-1986, Singers & Crooners*, Mechelen, Belgium, 1989-1990.

D. Russell Connor, *The Record Of A Legend...Benny Goodman*, New York City, 1984.

D. Russell Connor & Warren W. Hicks, *BG On The Record, A Bio-Discography Of Benny Goodman*, New Rochelle, N.Y., 1975.

Gerhard Conrad, *Discographie der Jazz- und Semijazz aufnahmen im Bereich der heutigen Volksdemokratien* (11 vols) Menden, Germany, 1982-1991.

O. Flückiger, *Lionel Hampton, Selected Discography 1966-1978*, First Revised Edition, Reinach, Switzerland, 1980.

Kiyoshi Koyama, *Keynote Discography, A Chronological Listing*, Tokyo, Japan, n.d.

Ralph Laing & Chris Sheridan, *Jazz Records, The Specialist Labels* (2 vols), Copenhagen, Denmark, 1981.

Vincent Pelote, *The Complete Commodore Jazz Recordings, A Discography*, Stamford, Conn., 1990

Erik Raben (ed.), *Jazz Records 1942-80, A Discography*, Copenhagen, Denmark, 1989- (in progress).

Michel Ruppli & Jean-Pierre Tahmazian, *Black & Blue*, Paris, France, 1995.

Brian A.L. Rust, *Jazz Records 1897-1942*, 5th Revised and Enlarged Edition, Chigwell, Essex, England, n.d [1984].

Richard S. Sears, *V-Discs, A History And Discography*, Westport, Conn. & London, 1980

Richard S. Sears, *V-Discs First Supplement*, Westport, Conn. & London, 1986

Various editions of the *Bielefelder Katalog Jazz* (ed. Manfred Scheffner), and of *Bulletin du Hcf* and *Collectors Items* magazines.

1932
June 23 – New York City
Benny Carter and His Orchestra
Louis Bacon, Frank Newton, unknown (tp), Dicky Wells (tb), Benny Carter (cl, as), Wayman Carver (as, fl), Chu Berry (ts), Teddy Wilson (p), unknown (g), Richard Fulbright (b), Sid Catlett (dr), unknown female vocalist.

1765-1	Tell All Your Day Dreams To Me	
		Crown 3321

1932
October 5 – New York City
Benny Carter and His Orchestra
Unknown (tb) and (ts) added.

73772-2	Hot Toddy	Victor unissued
73773-3	Jazz Cocktail	—
73374-2	Black Jazz	—

1933
January 26 – Chicago
Louis Armstrong and His Orchestra
Louis Armstrong (tp, vo), Elmer Whitlock, Zilner Randolph (tp), Keg Johnson (tb), Scoville Brown, George Oldham (cl, as), Budd Johnson (cl, ts), Teddy Wilson (p), Mike McKendrick (bj, g), Bill Oldham (b, tu), Yank Porter (dr).

74891-1	I've Got The World On A String	
		Victor 24245
74892-1	I Gotta Right To Sing The Blues	24233
74893-1	Hustlin' And Bustlin' For Baby	24233
74894-1	Sittin' In The Dark	24245
74895-1	High Society (no vo)	24233
74896-1	He's A Son Of The South	24257

1933
Louis Armstrong and His Orchestra
As before.
January 27 – Chicago

75102-1	Some Sweet Day	Victor 24557
75103-1	Basin Street Blues	24351
75104-1	Honey, Do	24369

1933
Louis Armstrong and His Orchestra
As before.
January 28 – Chicago

75105-1	Snowball	Victor 24369
75106-1	Mahogany Hall Stomp (no vo)	24232
75107-1	Swing, You Cats (no vo)	
		Bluebird B-10225

1933
October 10 – New York City
The Chocolate Dandies
Max Kaminsky (tp), Benny Carter (tp-1, as-2), Floyd O'Brien (tb), Chu Berry (ts), Teddy Wilson (p), Lawrence Lucie (g), Ernest Hill (b), Sid Catlett (dr-3), Mezz Mezzrow (dr-4).

265156-2	Blue Interlude (2)(3)	Decca 18255
265157-1	I Never Knew (1)(3)	Columbia 2875-D
265158-1	Once Upon A Time (1)(3)	OKeh 41568
265159-2	Krazy Kapers (1)(4)	OKeh 41568

1933
October 16 – New York City
Benny Carter and His Orchestra
Eddie Mallory, Bill Dillard, Dick Clark (tp); J.C. Higginbotham, Fred Robinson, Keg Johnson (tb); Benny Carter (cl, as), Wayman Carver (as, fl), Glyn Paque (as), Johnny Russell (tb), Teddy Wilson (p), Lawrence Lucie (g), Ernest Hill (b), Sid Catlett (dr).

265160-1	Devil's Holiday	Columbia CB698
265161-1	Lonesome Nights	Columbia CB720
265162-2	Symphony In Riffs	Columbia CB698
265163-2	Blue Lou	Columbia CB720

1933
November 6 – New York City
Mezz Mezzrow and His Orchestra
Max Kaminsky, Freddy Goodman, Ben Gusick (tp); Floyd O'Brien (tb) Mezz Mezzrow (cl, as), Benny Carter (tp, as, vo-1), Johnny Russell (ts), Teddy Wilson (p), Jack Sunshine (g), Pops Foster (b), Jack Maisel (dr).

14272-A	Free Love	Brunswick 7551
14273-A	Dissonance	
14274-A	Swingin' With Mezz	Brunswick 6778
14275-A	Love, You're Not The One For Me (1)	—

1934
May 14 – New York City
Benny Goodman and His Orchestra
Charlie Teagarden, George Thow (t), Jack Teagarden (tb, vo-1), Benny Goodman (cl), Hank Ross (ts), Teddy Wilson (p), Benny Martel (g), Art Bernstein or Harry Goodman (b), Ray McKinley (dr).

152736-1	I Ain't Lazy - I'm Just Dreamin' (1)	
		Parlophone R2695
152737-1	As Long As I Live (1)	
152738-1	Moonglow	Columbia CB786
152739-2	Breakfast Ball	—

1934
May 22 – New York City
Teddy Wilson
Piano solos.

152751-1	Somebody Loves Me	CBS 66370
152751-2	Somebody Loves Me	—
152752-1	Sweet And Simple	—
152752-2	Sweet And Simple	—
152753-1	Liza	—
152753-2	Liza	—
152754-2	Rosetta	—

1934
August 15 – New York City
Wingy Mannone and His Orchestra
Wingy Mannone (tp), Dicky Wells (tb), Artie Shaw (cl), Bud Freeman (ts), Teddy Wilson (p), Frank Victor (g), John Kirby (b), Kaiser Marshall (dr).

15629-A	Easy Like	Meritt 6
15629-B	Easy Like	—
15630-A	In The Slot	—
15630-B	In The Slot	—

1934
September 26 – New York City
Red Norvo and His Swing Septet
Jack Jenney (tb), Artie Shaw (cl), Charlie Barnet (ts),
Teddy Wilson (p), Bobby Johnson (g), Red Norvo (xyl),
Hank Wayland (b), Billy Gaussak (dr).

16021-A	Old Fashioned Love	Columbia 3059-D
16021-B	Old Fashioned Love	Meritt 3
16021-C	Old Fashioned Love (Shaw out)	—
16022-A	I Surrender, Dear	Columbia 2977-D
16022-B	I Surrender, Dear	Meritt 3

1934
October 4 – New York City
Red Norvo and His Swing Septet
As before.

16033-A	Tomboy	Columbia 2977-D
16033-B	Tomboy	Meritt 3
16034-A	The Night is Blue	Columbia 3026-D

1934
October 16 – New York City
Benny Goodman Orchestra
Unknown (tp), poss. Jack Lacey (tb), Benny Goodman
(cl), unknown (ts), Teddy Wilson (p), unknown (g),
unknown (b), unknown (dr), Tony Socco (vo).

16132-1	Stars	Sunbeam SB148
16132-2	Stars	—

1934
December 13 – New York City
Benny Carter and His Orchestra
Russell Smith, Otis Johnson, Irving Randolph (tp);
Benny Morton, Keg Johnson (tb); Benny Carter (cl, as),
Ben Smith, Russell Procope (as), Ben Webster (ts),
Teddy Wilson (p), Clarence Holiday (g), Elmer James
(b), Walter Johnson (dr), Charles Holland (v-1).

16412-1	Shoot The Works	Vocalion 2898
16413-1	Dream Lullaby	—
16414-1	Everybody Shuffle	Vocalion 2870
16415-1	Synthetic Love -1	—

1935
January 2 – New York City
Bob Howard and His Orchestra
Benny Carter (tp, as), Buster Bailey (cl), Teddy Wilson
(p), Clarence Holiday (g), Elmer James (b), Cozy Cole
(dr), Bob Howard (vo).

39217-A	It's Unbelievable	Brunswick 02097
39217-B	It's Unbelievable	Decca 347
39218-A	Whisper Sweet	Brunswick RL-221
39218-B	Whisper Sweet	Decca 347
39219-A	Throwin' Stones At The Sun	Decca 343
39220-A	You Fit Into The Picture	—

1935
January 4 – New York City
Willie Bryant and His Orchestra
Robert Cheek, Richard Clark (tp), Edgar "Pudding
Head" Battle (tp, vtb), John Haughton, Robert Horton,
George Matthews (tb), Glyn Paque (cl, as), Stanley
Payne (as), Johnny Russell (ts), Teddy Wilson (p),
Arnold Adams (g), Louis Thompson (b), Cozy Cole
(dr), Willie Bryant (vo-1).

87265-1	Throwin' Stones At The Sun	
		Victor 24847
87266-1	It's Over Because We'reThrough (1)	
		24858
87267-1	A Viper's Moan (1)	24858
87268-1	Chimes At The Meetin' (1)	24847

1935
January 25 – New York City
Red Norvo and His Swing Octet:
Bunny Berigan (tp), Jack Jenney (tb), Johnny Mince
(cl), Chu Berry (ts), Teddy Wilson (p), Red Norvo (xyl),
George Van Eps (g), Artie Bernstein (b), Gene Krupa
(dr).

16703-1	Honeysuckle Rose	Sony SOPL187
16703-2	Honeysuckle Rose	Columbia 3059-D
16709-1	With All My Heart And Soul	3026-D
16710-1	Bug House	Columbia 3079-D
16711-1	Blues In E Flat	—

1935
February 21 – New York City
Taft Jordan and The Mob
Taft Jordan (tp), Ward Silloway (tb), Johnny Mince
(cl), Elmer Williams (tb), Teddy Wilson (p), Bobby
Johnson (g), John Kirby (b), Eddie Dougherty (dr).

16906-2	Night Wind	Meritt 8
16906-2	Night Wind	Banner 33385
16907-2	If The Moon Turns Green	—

Matrix 16906-1 may have appeared on European
78 r.p.m. issues.

1935
February 22 – New York City
Same.

16914-2	Devil In The Moon	Banner 33398
16915-2	Louisiana Fairy Tale	

1935
February 25 – New York City
Bob Howard and His Orchestra
As on January 2, 1935, except Ben Webster (ts-1, cl-2)
replaces Bailey.

39387-A	The Ghost Of Dinah (2)	Decca 400
39388-A	Pardon My Love (1)	—
39388-B	Pardon My Love (1)	Rarities 61

1935
March 4 – New York City
Bob Howard and His Orchestra
Rex Stewart (co) added; Barney Bigard (cl) replaces
Webster.

39390-A	Stay Out Of Love	Decca 439
39391-A	I'll Never Change	—
39392-A	Where Were You On The Night Of	
	June The Third	Decca 407
39393-A	Breakin' The Ice	—

1935
May 7 – New York City
Bob Howard and His Orchestra
Stewart omitted; Russell Procope (cl, as), Billy Taylor
(b) replace Bigard and James.

39518-A	Corinne Corinna	Decca 484

39519-A	Ev'ry Day	Decca 460
39520-A	A Porter's Love Song	—
39521-A	I Can't Dance	Decca 484

1935
May 8 – New York City
Willie Bryant and His Orchestra
As on January 4, 1935 except Eddie Durham (tb) replaces Matthews and Benny Carter (tp) replaces Cheek. Ben Webster (ts) added.

89817-1	Rigamorale	Victor 25038
89818-1	'Long About Midnight (1)	25045
89819-1,2	The Sheik	25038
89820-1	Jerry The Junker (1)	25045

1935
July 2 – New York City
Teddy Wilson and his Orchestra
Roy Eldridge (tp), Benny Goodman (cl), Ben Webster (ts), Teddy Wilson (p), John Trueheart (g), John Kirby (b), Cozy Cole (dr), Billie Holiday (vo).

17766-1	I Wished On The Moon	Brunswick 7501
17767-1	What A Little Moonlight Can Do	7498
17768-1	Miss Brown To You	7501
17769-1	A Sunbonnet Blue (BG out)	7498

1935
July 13 – New York City
Benny Goodman Trio
Benny Goodman (cl), Teddy Wilson (p), Gene Krupa (dr).

92704-1	After You've Gone	Meritt 3
92704-2	After You've Gone	Victor 25115
92705-1	Body And Soul	—
92705-2	Body And Soul	Meritt 3
92706-2	Who?	Victor 25181
92707-2	Someday, Sweetheart	—

1935
July 31 – New York City
Teddy Wilson and His Orchestra
Roy Eldridge (tp), Cecil Scott (cl), Hilton Jefferson (as), Ben Webster (ts), Teddy Wilson (p), Lawrence Lucie (g), John Kirby (b), Cozy Cole (dr), Billie Holiday (vo-1); or: Teddy Wilson (p solo-2).

17913-1	What A Night, What A Moon, What A Girl (1)	Brunswick 7511
17914-1	I'm Painting The Town Red (1)	7520
17915-1	It's Too Hot For Words (1)	7511
17916-1	Sweet Lorraine	7520
17917-1	Liza (2)	CBS 54297
17918-1	Rosetta	Columbia unissued

1935
August 2 – New York City
Putney Dandridge and His Orchestra
Putney Dandridge (vo), acc. by Henry Allen (tp), Buster Bailey (cl, as), Teddy Wilson (p), Lawrence Lucie (g), John Kirby (b), Walter Johnson (dr).

17934-1	I'm In The Mood For Love	Vocalion 3007
17935-1	Isn't This A Lovely Day?	3006
17936-1	Cheek To Cheek	—
17937-1	That's What You Think	3007

17938-1	Shine	3024

1935
September 20 – New York City
Mildred Bailey and Her Swing Band:
Mildred Bailey (vo), acc. by Chris Griffin (tp), Chu Berry (ts), Teddy Wilson (p), Red Norvo (xyl-1), Dick McDonough (g), Artie Bernstein (b), Eddie Dougherty (dr).

18090-1	I'd Love To Take Orders From You	Vocalion 3056
18091-1	I'd Rather Listen To Your Eyes	—
18092-1	Someday, Sweetheart	3057
18093-1	When Day Is Done (1)	—

1935
October 7 – New York City
Teddy Wilson
Piano solos.

18129-1	Every Now And Then	Brunswick 7543
18130-I	It Never Dawned On Me	—
18131-1	Liza	7563
18132-1	Rosetta	—

1935
October 21 – New York City
Putney Dandridge and His Orchestra
Putney Dandridge (vo), acc. by Shirley Clay (tp), Kenneth Hollon (ts), Teddy Wilson (p), Clarence Holiday (g), John Kirby (b), Walter Johnson (dr).

18183-1	I'm On A See-Saw	Vocalion 3082
18184-1	Eeny Meeny Miney Mo	3083
18185-1	Double Trouble	3082
18186-1	Santa Claus Came In The Spring	3083

1935
October 25 – New York City
Teddy Wilson and His Orchestra
Roy Eldridge (tp), Benny Morton (tb), Chu Berry (ts), Teddy Wilson (p), Dave Barbour (g), John Kirby (b), Billie Holiday (vo).

18196-1	Twenty-Four Hours A Day	Brunswick 7550
18197-1	Yankee Doodle Never Went To Town	—
18199-1	Eeny Meeny Miney Mo	7554
18209-1	If You Were Mine	—

1935
November 22 – New York City
Piano solos.

18295-1	I Found A Dream	Brunswick 7572
18296-1	On Treasure Island	—

1935
December 3 – New York City
Teddy Wilson and His Orchestra
Dick Clark (tp), Tom Macey (cl), Johnny Hodges (as), Teddy Wilson (p), Dave Barbour (g), Grachan Moncur (b), Cozy Cole (dr), Billie Holiday (vo-1).

18316-1	These 'N' That 'N' Those (1)	Brunswick 7577
18317-1	Sugar Plum	—
18318-1	You Let Me Down (1)	7581
18319-1	Spreadin' Rhythm Around (1)	—

1935
December 6 – New York City
Mildred Bailey and Her Alley Cats
Mildred Bailey (vo) acc. by Bunny Berigan (tp), Johnny Hodges (as), Teddy Wilson (p), Grachan Moncur (b).

60201-A	Willow Tree	Decca 18108
60202-A	Honeysuckle Rose	—
60203-A	Squeeze Me	18109
60204-A	Down-Hearted Blues	—

1935
December 6 – New York City
Putney Dandridge and His Orchestra
Richard Clarke (tp), Tom Mace (cl+ts-1), Teddy Wilson (p), Dave Barbour (g), Grachan Moncur (b), Cozy Cole (dr), Putney Dandridge (vo) .

18342-1	No Other One (1)	Vocalion 3122
18343-1	A Little Bit Independent	—
18344-1	You Took My Breath Away	3123

1936
January 17 – New York City
Teddy Wilson
Piano solos.

18517-1	I Feel Like A Feather In The Breeze	
		Brunswick 7599
18518-1	Breaking In A Pair Of Shoes	—

1936
January 30 – New York City
Teddy Wilson and His Orchestra
Chris Griffin (tp), Rudy Powell (cl), Ted McRae (ts), Teddy Wilson (p), John Trueheart (g), Grachan Moncur (b), Cozy Cole (dr), Billie Holiday (vo-1).

18612-1	Life Begins When You're In Love (1)	Brunswick 7612
18613-1	Rhythm In My Nursery Rhymes	—

1936
March 2 – New York City
Putney Dandridge and His Orchestra
Putney Dandridge (vo) acc. by Richard Clarke (tp), Johnny Russell (ts), Teddy Wilson (p), Arnold Adams (g), Ernest Hill (b), Cozy Cole (dr).

18741-1	Sweet Violets	Vocalion 3190
18742-1	Dinner For One, Please James	3189
18743-1	A Beautiful Lady In Blue	—
18744-1	Honeysuckle Rose	3190

1936
March 12 – Demonstration Of Swing Broadcast, New York City
Bunny Berigan's All Stars
Bunny Berigan (t), Joe Marsala (cl), Bud Freeman (ts), Teddy Wilson (p), Stan King (d), with unknown studio musicians.

Old Man Mose	Bamboo ISM1980
Discourse On Jazz 1	—
Tiger Rag	—
Discourse On Jazz 2	—
Sweet Sue	—
Stardust	—
Bugle Call Rag	—
Discourse On Jazz 3	—

Honeysuckle Rose	—
Basin Street Blues	—

1936
March 17 – New York City
Teddy Wilson and His Orchestra
Frank Newton (tp), Benny Morton (tb), Jerry Blake (cl,as), Ted McRae (ts), Teddy Wilson (p), John Trueheart (g), Leemie Stanfield (b), Cozy Cole (dr), Ella Fitzgerald (vo-1).

18829-1	Christopher Columbus	Brunswick 7640
18830-1	My Melancholy Baby (1)	7729
18831-1	I Know That You Know	unissued
18832-1	All My Life (1)	Brunswick 7640

1936
April 24 – Chicago
Benny Goodman Trio
As on July 13, 1935; Helen Ward (vo-1) added.

100395-1	China Boy	Victor 25333
100396-1	More Than You Know	25345
100397-1	All My Life (1)	25324

1936
Benny Goodman Trio
As before.
April 27 – Chicago

100500-1	Oh, Lady Be Good!	Victor 25333
100501-1	Nobody's Sweetheart	25345
100502-1	Too Good To Be True (1)	25324

1936
May 14 – Chicago
Teddy Wilson and His Orchestra
Roy Eldridge (tp, vo-1), Buster Bailey (cl), Chu Berry (ts), Teddy Wilson (p), Bob Lessey (g), Israel Crosby (b), Sid Catlett (dr).

C-1376-1	Mary Had A Little Lamb (1)	
		Brunswick 7663
C-1377-2	Too Good To Be True	—
C-1378-1	Warmin' Up	7684
C-1379-1	Blues In C Sharp Minor	—

1936
June 1– New York City
Putney Dandridge and His Orchestra
Putney Dandridge (vo) acc. by Bobby Stark (tp), Teddy McRae (ts) Teddy Wilson (p), John Trueheart (g), John Kirby (b), Cozy Cole (dr).

19352-1	It's A Sin To Tell A Lie	Vocalion 3252
19353-2	All My Life	—
19354-1	Ol' Man River	3269
19355-1	Why Was I Born?	—

1936
June 30 – New York City
Teddy Wilson and His Orchestra
Jonah Jones (tp), Johnny Hodges (as), Harry Carney (cl-1, bars-2), Teddy Wilson (p), Lawrence Lucie (g), John Kirby (b), Cozy Cole (dr), Billie Holiday (vo-3).

19495-2	It's Like Reaching For The Moon (1, 2, 3)	Brunswick 7702
19496-2	These Foolish Things (2, 3)	7699
19497-2	Why Do I Lie To Myself About You? (2)	—

19498-2   I Cried For You (2, 3)   7729
19499-2   Guess Who (1, 2, 3)   7702

1936
August 21 – Hollywood
Benny Goodman Quartet:
Benny Goodman (cl), Teddy Wilson (p), Lionel
Hampton (vb), Gene Krupa (dr).
97752-1   Moon Glow   Victor 25398

1936
August 24 – Los Angeles
Teddy Wilson and His Orchestra
Chris Griffin (tp), Benny Goodman (cl-1), Vido Musso
(ts), Teddy Wilson (p), Lionel Hampton (vb), Allen
Reuss (g), Harry Goodman (b), Gene Krupa (dr), Helen
Ward (as "Vera Lane") (vo-2), Rod Harper (vo-3).
LA1158-AYou Came To My Rescue (1, 2)
                            Brunswick 7739
LA1159-AHere's Love In Your Eyes (1, 2)   —
LA1160-AYou Turned The Tables On Me (3) 7736
LA1161-ASing, Baby, Sing (3)   —

1936
August 26 – Hollywood
Benny Goodman Trio/Quartet
As on August 21, 1936. Hampton (vo-1).
97772-1   Dinah   Victor 25398
97773-1   Exactly Like You (1) (trio)   25406
97774-1   Vibraphone Blues (1)   25521

1936
October 21 – New York City
Teddy Wilson and His Orchestra
Irving Randolph (tp), Vido Musso (cl), Ben Webster
(ts), Teddy Wilson (p), Allen Reuss (g), Milt Hinton
(b), Gene Krupa (dr), Billie Holiday (vo).
20105-1   Easy To Love   Brunswick 7762
20106-2   With Thee I Sing   7768
20107-1   The Way You Look Tonight
                            Affinity(E) AFF1044
20107-2   The Way You Look Tonight
                            Brunswick 7762

1936
October 28 – New York City
Teddy Wilson and His Orchestra
As before.
20142-1/3 Who Loves You?   Brunswick 7768

1936
November 9 – New York City
Mildred Bailey and Her Orchestra
Ziggy Elman (tp), Artie Shaw (cl-1), Johnny Hodges
(as-2), Francis Lowe (ts), Teddy Wilson (p), Dave
Barbour (g), John Kirby (b), Cozy Cole (dr), Mildred
Bailey (vo).
20217-1   For Sentimental Reasons (1)
                            Vocalion 3367
20218-1   It's Love I'm After (1, 2)   —
20219-1   'Long About Midnight (1)   3378
20220-1   More Than You Know   —

1936
November 18– New York City
Benny Goodman Quartet
Benny Goodman (cl), Teddy Wilson (p), Lionel
Hampton (vb), Gene Krupa (dr).
03062-1   Sweet Sue, Just You   Victor 25473
03063-1   My Melancholy Baby   —
03064-1   Tiger Rag   rejected

1936
November 19 – New York City
Teddy Wilson and His Orchestra
Jonah Jones (tp), Benny Goodman (as "John Jackson")
(cl), Ben Webster (ts), Teddy Wilson (p), Allen Reuss
(g), John Kirby (b), Cozy Cole (dr), Billie Holiday
(vo-1).
20290-1   Pennies From Heaven (1)
                            Brunswick 7789
20290-2   Pennies From Heaven (1)
                            Columbia CEK47724-2
20291-1   That's Life I Guess (1)   Brunswick 7789
20291-1   That's Life I Guess (1)
                            Columbia CEK47724-2
20292-2   Sailin'   Brunswick 7781
20293-1   I Can't Give You Anything But
          Love (1)   —

1936
November 25 – New York City
Teddy Wilson and His Orchestra
Jonah Jones (t), Ben Webster (ts), Stuff Smith (vn),
Teddy Wilson (p), Lawrence Lucie (g), John Kirby (sb),
Cozy Cole (dr).
I Got Rhythm   Jazz Archives JA15

1936
November 25 – Hotel Pennsylvania, New York
City, CBS broadcast
Benny Goodman Quartet
As on November 18, 1936.
Sweet Sue, Just You   Jazz Archives JA49

1936
December 2 – New York City
Benny Goodman Quartet
As before.
03064-2   Tiger Rag (omit LH)   Victor 25481
03514-1   Stompin' At The Savoy   25521
03514-2   Stompin' At The Savoy   —
03515-1   Whispering   25481

1936
December 10 – New York City
Putney Dandridge and His Orchestra
Putney Dandridge (vo) acc. by Doc Cheatham (tp),
Tom Mace (cl), Teddy Wilson (p), Allen Reuss (g),
Ernest Hill (b), Sid Catlett (dr).
20384-1   I'm In A Dancin' Mood   Vocalion3399
20385-2   With Plenty Of Money And You   —
20386-1   That Foolish Feeling   3409
20387-1   Gee! But You're Swell   —

1936
December 16 – New York City
Teddy Wilson and His Orchestra
Irving Randolph (tp), Vido Musso (cl) Ben Webster (ts), Teddy Wilson (p), Allen Reuss (g), John Kirby (b), Cozy Cole (dr), Midge Williams (vo-1).
20410-1/2   I'm With You (Right Or Wrong)(1)
Brunswick7797
20411-1   Where The Lazy River Goes By (1) —
20412-2   Tea For Two   7816
20413-1/4   I'll See You In My Dreams   —

1937
January 6 – New York City, CBS short-wave broadcast to BBC
Benny Goodman Trio/Quartet
As on November 18, 1936.
Medley – a) Body And Soul/b) Dinah (Hampton out)
Doctor Jazz W2X40350
Stompin' At The Savoy   —

1937
January 12 – New York City
Billie Holiday and Her Orchestra
Billie Holiday (vo) acc. by Jonah Jones (tp), Edgar Sampson (cl, as), Ben Webster (ts), Teddy Wilson (p), Allen Reuss (g), John Kirby (b), Cozy Cole (dr).
20506-1   One Never Knows, Does One?
Vocalion 3431
20507-1   I've Got My Love To Keep Me Warm
Columbia CL2426
20507-2   I've Got My Love To Keep Me Warm
Vocalion 3431
20508-1   If My Heart Could Only Talk
Vocalion 3440
20509-2   Please Keep Me In Your Dreams   —

1937
January 25 – New York City
Teddy Wilson and His Orchestra
Buck Clayton (tp), Benny Goodman (cl), Lester Young (ts), Teddy Wilson (p), Freddie Green (g), Walter Page (b), Jo Jones (dr), Billie Holiday (vo).
20568-1   He Ain't Got Rhythm   Brunswick 7824
20569-2   This Year's Kisses   —
20570-1   Why Was I Born?   7859
20571-1   I Must Have That Man   —

1937
February 3 – New York City
Benny Goodman Quartet
As on November 18, 1936.
04559-2   Ida, Sweet As Apple Cider Victor 25531
04560-1   Tea For Two   25529
04561-1   Runnin' Wild   —

1937
February 6 – New York City
Benny Goodman Trio/Quartet
As on November 18, 1936.
Dinah   Doctor Jazz W2X40350

1937
February 18 – New York City
Teddy Wilson and His Orchestra
Henry Allen (tp), Cecil Scott (cl, as, ts), Prince Robinson (ts), Teddy Wilson (p), James McLin (g), John Kirby (b), Cozy Cole (dr), Billie Holiday (vo).
20698-2   The Mood That I'm In   Brunswick 7844
20699-2   You Showed Me The Way   7840
20700-2   Sentimental And Melancholy   7844
20701-1   (This Is) My Last Affair   7840

1937
March 9 – New York City
Benny Goodman Trio/Quartet
As on November 18, 1936.
Shine   Doctor Jazz W2X40350

1937
March 11 or 16 – New York City, Mutual broadcast
Benny Goodman Quartet
As before.
Limehouse Blues   MGM E3789

1937
March 16 – New York City, CBS *Camel Caravan* broadcast
Benny Goodman Trio/Quartet
As on November 18, 1936.
Body And Soul   Doctor Jazz W2X40350

1937
March 18 – New York City, broadcast
Benny Goodman Quartet
As before.
I Know That You Know   unissued

1937
March 25 – New York City, Mutual broadcast
Benny Goodman Quartet
As on November 18, 1936.
Runnin' Wild   Columbia ML4591

1937
March 31 - New York City
Teddy Wilson and His Orchestra
Cootie Williams (tp), Johnny Hodges (as) Harry Carney (cl), Teddy Wilson (p), Allen Reuss (g), John Kirby (b), Cozy Cole (dr), Billie Holiday (vo-1).
20911-3   Carelessly (1)   Brunswick 7867
20912-1   How Could You? (1)   —
20913-1   Moanin' Low (1)   7877
20914-1   Fine And Dandy   —

1937
April 1– New York City
Billie Holiday and Her Orchestra
Billie Holiday (vo) acc. by Eddie Tompkins (tp), Buster Bailey (cl), Joe Thomas (ts), Teddy Wilson (p), Carmen Mastren (g), John Kirby (b), Alphonse Steele (dr).
20918-1   Where Is The Sun?   Vocalion 3543
20919-1   Let's Call The Whole Thing Off   3520
20920-1   They Can't Take That Away From Me
—

20920-2	They Can't Take That Away From Me	
		Raretone(It) RTR24011
20921-1	Don't Know If I'm Comin' Or Goin'	
		Vocalion 3543
20921-2	Don't Know If I'm Comin' Or Goin'	
		Raretone(It) RTR24011

1937
April 23 – New York City
Teddy Wilson and His Orchestra
As on March 31, 1937, except Harry James (tp), Buster
Bailey (cl) and Helen Ward (vo-1) replace Williams,
Carney, Holiday.

21034-1	There's A Lull In My Life (1)	
		Brunswick 7884
21035-2	It's Swell Of You (1)	—
21036-2	How Am I To Know (1)	7893
21037-1	I'm Coming Virginia	—

1937
April 28 – New York City, CBS broadcast
Benny Goodman Quartet
As on November 18, 1936.

| Ida | Sounds Great SG8004 |

1937
April 29 – New York City, WNEW *Make Believe*
Ballroom broadcast
Benny Goodman Quartet
As on November 18, 1936.

| I Got Rhythm | MGM E3789 |

1937
May 11 – New York City
Teddy Wilson and His Orchestra
Buck Clayton (tp), Buster Bailey (cl), Johnny Hodges
(as), Lester Young (ts) Teddy Wilson (p), Allen Reuss
(g), Artie Bernstein (b), Cozy Cole (dr), Billie Holiday
(vo-1).

21117-2	Sun Showers (1)	Brunswick 7917
21118-2	Yours And Mine (1)	—
21119-1	I'll Get By (1)	7903
21119-2	I'll Get By (1)	Columbia CL2487
21120-1	Mean To Me (1)	Brunswick 7903
21120-2	Mean To Me (1)	Columbia CL2487

1937
May 18 – New York City, CBS *Camel Caravan*
broadcast
Benny Goodman Quartet
As before.

| Digga Digga Doo | MGM E3788 |

1937
June 1 – New York City
Teddy Wilson and His Orchestra
Buck Clayton (ts), Buster Bailey (cl), Lester Young (ts),
Teddy Wilson (p), Freddie Green (g), Walter Page (b),
Jo Jones (dr), Billie Holiday (vo-1).

21217-1	Foolin' Myself (1)	Brunswick 7911
21218-2	Easy Living (1)	—
21219-2	I'll Never Be The Same (1)	7926
21220-1	I've Found A New Baby	—

1937
June 12 – Pittsburgh, Pa., CBS *Saturday Night*
Swing Session broadcast
Benny Goodman Trio/Quartet
As before.
There's A Lull In My Life (trio; Hampton out)

| | Jazz Archives JA40 |
| Nagasaki | unissued |

1937
June 15 – Pittsburgh, Pa., CBS *Saturday Night*
Swing Session broadcast
Benny Goodman Quartet
As before.

| The Sheik of Araby | Columbia ML4590 |

1937
June 22 – Columbus, Ohio, CBS *Camel Caravan*
broadcast
Benny Goodman Quartet
As before.

| A Handful Of Keys | unissued |

1937
June 29 – New York City, CBS *Camel Caravan*
broadcast
Benny Goodman Trio/Quartet
As before.

| Sweet Leilani (trio) | Columbia ML459 |
| Avalon | MGM E3789 |

1937
July/August – Hollywood, Cal., *Hollywood Hotel*
film soundtrack
Benny Goodman Quartet
As before.

| I've Got A Heartful Of Music | |
| | Extreme Rarities 1002 |

1937
July 16 – Palomar Ballroom, Los Angeles, broad-
cast
Benny Goodman Quartet
As before, Harry James (tp-1).

| Handful Of Keys | MGM E3790 |
| Twilight In Turkey (1) | — |

1937
July 20, Los Angeles, CBS *Camel Caravan* broad-
cast
Benny Goodman Trio/Quartet:
As before.

| Tea For Two (quartet) | MGM E3788 |
| Tiger Rag (trio) | Sunbeam SB149 |

1937
July 27 – Los Angeles, CBS *Camel Caravan* broad-
cast
Benny Goodman Trio
As before.

| Marie | MGM E3790 |

1937
July 30 – Hollywood
Benny Goodman Quartet
As before.
09627-1   Avalon   Bluebird AXM2-5568
09627-2   Avalon   Victor 25644
09628-1   Handful Of Keys   25705
09632-1   The Man I Love   25644

1937
July 30 – Los Angeles
Teddy Wilson and His Orchestra
Harry James (tp), Benny Goodman (cl), Vido Musso (ts), Teddy Wilson (p), Allen Reuss (g), Harry Goodman (b), Gene Krupa (dr), Boots Castle (vo-1).
LA1380-A   You're My Desire (1)   Meritt 3
LA1380-B   You're My Desire (1) Brunswick 7940
LA1381-A   Remember Me (1)   —
LA1381-B   Remember Me (1)   Meritt 3
LA1382-A   The Hour Of Parting (1)
                                    Brunswick 7943
LA1382-B   The Hour Of Parting (1)
                                    Nostalgia NR1003
LA1383-A   Coquette   Brunswick 7943
LA1383-B   Coquette   Meritt 3

1937
August 2 – Hollywood
Benny Goodman Quartet
As before.
09633-2   Smiles   Victor 25660
09634-3   Liza   —

1937
August 10 – Los Angeles, broadcast
Benny Goodman Trio/Quartet
As before.
Sailboat In The Moonlight (trio)   Sunbeam SB146
Shine (quartet)   Columbia ML4590

1937
August 13 – Los Angeles, broadcast
Benny Goodman Quartet
As before, Lionel Hampton (vo).
Vibraphone Blues   Columbia ML4590

1937
August 17 – Los Angeles, Columbia broadcast
Benny Goodman Trio
As before.
So Rare   MGM E3790
Liza   Columbia ZLP12690

1937
August 19 – Palomar Ballroom, Los Angeles, CBS broadcast
Benny Goodman Trio/Quartet
As before.
Where Or When (trio)   unissued
Sweet Sue, Just You (quartet)   unissued

1937
August 24 – Los Angeles, broadcast
Benny Goodman Trio/Quartet
As before.

My Cabin Of Dreams (trio)   Sunbeam SB147
Stompin' At The Savoy (quartet)   —

1937
August 29 – Los Angeles
Teddy Wilson and His Orchestra
Harry James (tp), Archie Rosati (cl), Vido Musso (ts), Teddy Wilson (p), Allen Reuss (g), John Simmons (b), Cozy Cole (dr), Frances Hunt (vo-1).
LA1404-A   Big Apple (1)   Brunswick 7954
LA1404-B   Big Apple (1)   Meritt 3
LA1405-B   You Can't Stop Me From Dreaming
                                            —
LA1405-B   You Can't Stop Me From Dreaming
LA1406-B   If I Had You (1)   7960
LA1407-B   You Brought A New Kind Of Love
                                      To Me (1)
Teddy Wilson Quartet
Harry James (tp), Teddy Wilson (p), Red Norvo (xyl), John Simmons (b).
LA1408-B   Ain't Misbehavin'   Meritt 3
LA1408-B   Ain't Misbehavin'   —

1937
August 31 – Los Angeles, CBS *Camel Caravan* broadcast
Benny Goodman Trio /Quartet
As before, Lionel Hampton (vo-1).
Whispers In The Dark (trio)   MGM E3788
Vibraphone Blues (quartet; 1)   Sunbeam SB147

1937
September 5, Los Angeles
Teddy Wilson Quartet
As on August 29, 1937.
LA1408-C   Ain't Misbehavin'   Brunswick 7964
LA1429-A   Just A Mood (Blue Mood) - part 1
                                            7973
LA1430-A   Just A Mood (Blue Mood) - part 2 —
LA1431-A   Honeysuckle Rose   7964

1937
September 7 – Los Angeles, CBS *Camel Caravan* broadcast
Benny Goodman Quartet
As before.
Smiles   MGM E3790

1937
September 12, Dallas, Tex., CBS broadcast
Benny Goodman Quartet
As before.
Ida Sweet As Apple Cider   Sunbeam SB149

1937
October 13 – Madhattan Room, New York City, CBS broadcast
Benny Goodman Trio/Quartet
As before.
Whispers In The Dark (trio)   Sunbeam SB116
Avalon (quartet + band in coda)   —

1937
October 16 – Madhattan Room, New York City,
CBS broadcast
Benny Goodman Trio/Quartet
As before.
Roses In December (trio)   Sunbeam SB117
Ding Dong Daddy From Dumas (quartet)   —

1937
October 19 – New York City, CBS *Camel Caravan*
broadcast
Benny Goodman Trio/Quartet
As before.
Remember Me (trio)   MGM E3789
Everybody Loves My Baby   Columbia ML4591

1937
October 20 – Madhattan Room, New York City,
CBS broadcast
Benny Goodman Trio/Quartet
As before.
Body And Soul (trio)   Sunbeam SB118
Sweet Sue (quartet)   —

1937
October 23 – Madhattan Room, New York City,
CBS broadcast
Benny Goodman Trio/Quartet
As before.
Where Or When (trio)   Sunbeam SB120
Nagasaki (quartet)   —

1937
October 27 – Madhattan Room, New York City,
CBS broadcast
Benny Goodman Trio/Quartet
As before.
A Handful Of Keys   Sunbeam SB121

1937
October 29 – New York City
Benny Goodman Trio/Quartet
As before, Martha Tilton (vo-1).
015575-1 Where Or When (trio)   Victor 25725
015576-1 Silhouetted In The Moonlight (trio, 1)
                                               25711
015577-2 Vieni, Vieni (quartet)   25705

1937
October 30 – Madhattan Room, New York City,
CBS broadcast
Benny Goodman Trio/Quartet
As before.
Oh, Lady Be Good (trio)   Sunbeam SB122
Everybody Loves My Baby (quartet)   —

1937
November 1 – New York City
Teddy Wilson and His Orchestra
*Buck Clayton (tp), Prince Robinson (cl), Vido Musso
(ts), Teddy Wilson (p), Allen Reuss (g), Walter Page
(b), Cozy Cole (dr), Billie Holiday (vo).*
21982-1   Nice Work If You Can Get It
                                      Brunswick 8015

21983-1   Things Are Looking Up   —
21984-1   My Man (Mon Homme)   8008
21985-1   Can't Help Lovin' That Man   —

1937
November 2 – New York City, CBS *Camel Caravan*
broadcast
Benny Goodman Trio
As before.
Time On My Hands   Columbia ML4591

1937
November 6 – Madhattan Room, New York City,
CBS broadcast
Benny Goodman Trio/Quartet
As before.
More Than You Know (trio)   Sunbeam SB127
Vieni, Vieni (quartet)   —

1937
November 12 – New York City
Teddy Wilson
Piano Solos.
22025-1   Don't Blame Me   Brunswick 8025
22025-2   Don't Blame Me   CBS 66370
22026-1   Between The Devil And The Deep
          Blue Sea   Brunswick 8025
22026-2   Between The Devil And The Deep
          Blue Sea   Columbia CL2428

1937
November 16 – New York City, CBS *Camel
Caravan* broadcast
Benny Goodman Trio/ Quartet
As before.
Nagasaki (quartet)   Columbia ML4590
After You've Gone (trio)   Fanfare LP13-113

1937
November 20 – Madhattan Room, New York City,
CBS broadcast
Benny Goodman Trio/Quartet
As before.
Who (trio)   Sunbeam SB125
Limehouse Blues (quartet)   —

1937
November 23 – New York City, CBS *Camel
Caravan* broadcast
Benny Goodman Trio
As before.
Nice Work If You Can Get It   Columbia ML4590

1937
November 30 – New York City, CBS *Camel
Caravan* broadcast
Benny Goodman Quartet
As before.
Moonglow   Columbia ML4590

1937
December 2 – New York City
Benny Goodman Quartet
As before.

017451-1/2   I'm A Ding Dong Daddy
Victor 25725

1937
December 7 – New York City, CBS *Camel Caravan*
broadcast
Benny Goodman Trio/Quartet
As before.
Have You Met Miss Jones? (trio)
Columbia ML4591
Killer Diller (quartet)   —

1937
December 14 – New York City, CBS *Camel
Caravan* broadcast
Benny Goodman Quartet
As before.
My Gal Sal   Columbia ML4591

1937
December 17 – New York City
Teddy Wilson and His Orchestra
*Possibly Hot Lips Page (tp), Pee Wee Russell (cl), Chu
Berry (ts), Teddy Wilson (p) Allen Reuss (g), unknown
(b), unknown (dr), Sally Gooding (vo-1).*
22192-2   My First Impression Of You (1)
Meritt 21
22193-1   With A Smile And A Song (1)
I.A.J.R.C 28
22193-2   With A Smile And A Song (1) Meritt 21
22194-2   When You're Smiling   —
22195-2   I Can't Believe That You're In Love
With Me (1)   —

1937
December 18 – Madhattan Room, New York City,
CBS broadcast
Benny Goodman Trio/Quartet
As before.
Where Or When (trio)   Sunbeam SB126
Dinah (quartet)   —

1937
December 21 – New York City
Benny Goodman Quartet
As before, Martha Tilton (vo).
017754-1   Bei Mir Bist Du Schön - part 1
Victor 25751

1937
December 22 – Madhattan Room, New York City,
CBS broadcast
Benny Goodman Trio/Quartet
As before.
I Can't Help Lovin' That Man (trio)
Sunbeam SB124
Avalon (quartet + band in coda)   —

1937
December 25 – Hotel Pennysylvania, New York
City
Benny Goodman Trio
As before.
Once In A While   Sunbeam SB149

1937
December 29 – New York City
Benny Goodman Quartet
*As before,. Ziggy Elman (t) added, Martha Tilton
(vo).*
017783-1   Bei Mir Bist Du Schön - part 2
Victor 25751

1938
January 6 – New York City
Teddy Wilson and His Orchestra
*Buck Clayton (tp), Benny Morton (tb) Lester Young
(ts), Teddy Wilson (p), Freddie Green (g), Walter Page
(b), Jo Jones (dr), Billie Holiday (vo).*
22192-3   My First Impression Of You
Columbia CL2427
22192-4   My First Impression Of You
Brunswick 8053
22194-3   When You're Smiling   8070
22194-4   When You're Smiling   Columbia 36208
22195-3   I Can't Believe That You're In Love
With Me   36335
22195-4   I Can't Believe That You're In Love
With Me   Brunswick 8070
22255-1   If Dreams Come True   8053
22255-2   If Dreams Come True
Columbia JG34837

1938
January 10 – New York City
Mildred Bailey and Her Orchestra
*Mildred Bailey (vo) acc. by Jimmy Blake (tp), Hank
D'Amico (cl), Chu Berry (ts) Teddy Wilson (p), Allen
Reuss (g), Pete Peterson (b), Dave Tough (dr).*
22265-2   I See Your Face Before Me Vocalion 3931
22266-1   Thanks For The Memory   Meritt 12
22266-2   Thanks For The Memory   Vocalion 3931
22267-2   From The Land Of Sky-Blue Water 3932
22268-1   Lover, Come Back To Me   —
22268-2   Lover, Come Back To Me   Meritt 12

1938
January 12 – New York City
Billie Holiday and Her Orchestra
*Billie Holiday (vo) acc. by the same personnel as Teddy
Wilson and His Orchestra on January 6, 1938.*
22281-1   Now They Call It Swing
Columbia CL2427
22281-2   Now They Call It Swing   Vocalion 3947
22282-1   On The Sentimental Side
Columbia CL1759
22282-2   On The Sentimental Side Vocalion 3947
22283-1   Back In Your Own Backyard   4929
22284-2   When A Man Loves A Woman   —

1938
January 16 – Carnegie Hall, New York City
Benny Goodman Trio/Quartet
As before.
Body And Soul (trio)   Columbia CL815
Avalon (quartet)   —
The Man I Love (quartet)   —
China Boy (trio)   Columbia CL816
Stompin' At The Savoy (quartet)   —

Dizzy Spells (quartet)   —
I Got Rhythm (quartet)   Columbia CL815

1938
January 29 – New York City, CBS *Saturday Night Swing Session* broadcast
Benny Goodman Quartet
As before.
I'm A Ding Dong Daddy   Columbia ML4590

1938
March 23 – New York City
Teddy Wilson and His Orchestra
Bobby Hackett (co), Pee Wee Russell (cl), Tab Smith (as), Gene Sedric (ts), Teddy Wilson (p), Allen Reuss (g), Al Hall (b), Johnny Blowers (dr), Nan Wynn (vo-1).

22610-2	Alone With You (1)	I.A.J.R.C. 28
22611-1	Moments Like This (1)	Brunswick 8112
22612-2	I Can't Face The Music (1)	—
22613-1	Don't Be That Way	8116
22613-2	Don't Be That Way	Meritt 11

1938
March 25 – New York City
Benny Goodman Trio/Quartet
Benny Goodman (cl), Teddy Wilson (p), Lionel Hampton (vb, vo-1), Dave Tough (dr).

021625-1	Sweet Lorraine (trio, omit Hampton)	Victor 25822
021626-1	The Blues In Your Flat	26044
021627-1	The Blues In My Flat (1)	—
021628-1	Sugar	Meritt 3
021628-2	Sugar	Victor 26240
021629-1	Dizzy Spells	25822

1938
March 31 – Hotel Pennsylvania, New York City, Mutual broadcast
Benny Goodman Quartet
As before.
The Man I Love   Sunbeam SB152

1938
April 5 – New York City, CBS *Camel Caravan* broadcast
Benny Goodman Trio
As before.
Tiger Rag   Sunbeam SB152

1938
April 21 – Hotel Pennsylvania, New York City, Mutual broadcast
Benny Goodman Quartet
As before.
Shine   Sunbeam SB152

1938
April 23 – Hotel Pennsylvania, New York City, CBS broadcast
Benny Goodman Trio/Quartet
As before.
I'm A Ding Dong Daddy From Dumas (quartet)   unissued

Nice Work If You Can Get It (trio)   unissued

1938
April 25 – New York City, CBS *Eddie Cantor Program* broadcast
Benny Goodman Quartet
As before.
Don't Be That Way   Aircheck 1

1938
April 26 – New York City, CBS *Camel Caravan* broadcast
Benny Goodman Trio
Benny Goodman (cl), Teddy Wilson (p), Lionel Hampton (d).
Nobody's Sweetheart   MGM E3789

1938
April 29 – New York City
Teddy Wilson and His Orchestra
As March 23, 1938, but Johnny Hodges (as) replaces Smith and Sedric is omitted.

22822-1	If I Were You (1)	Meritt 10
22822-2	If I Were You (1)	Brunswick 8150
22823-1	You Go To My Head (1)	8141
22824-1	I'll Dream Tonight (1)	—
22824-1	I'll Dream Tonight (1)	Meritt 10
22825-1	Jungle Love	New World NW250
22825-2	Jungle Love	Brunswick 8150

Teddy Wilson
Piano solos.

22826-3	That Old Feeling	Brunswick unissued
22827-1	My Blue Heaven	Meritt 23

1938
May 3 – New York City, CBS *Camel Caravan* broadcast
Benny Goodman Quartet
Benny Goodman (cl), Teddy Wilson (p), Lionel Hampton (vb), Gene Krupa (dr)
Nagasaki   Sunbeam SB152

1938
May 10 – New York City, CBS *Camel Caravan* broadcast
Benny Goodman Quartet
As before.
Lillie Stomp   unissued

1938
May 13 – New York City
Teddy Wilson
Piano solos.

22826-3	That Old Feeling	Meritt 23
22826-4	That Old Feeling	Teddy Wilson School For Pianists
22827-2	My Blue Heaven	—
22827-3	My Blue Heaven	Meritt 23

1938
May 17 – New York City, CBS *Camel Caravan* broadcast
Benny Goodman Trio/Quartet
As before.

Moon Glow (quartet)   Blu-Disc T5001/02
Who? (trio)   unissued

1938
May 24 – New York City, CBS *Camel Caravan*
broadcast
Benny Goodman Quartet
As before.
Joseph, Joseph   Giants Of Jazz GOJ1005

1938
June 7 – Cleveland, Ohio, CBS *Camel Caravan*
broadcast
Benny Goodman Quartet
As before.
Diga Diga Doo   Blu-Disc T5001/02

1938
June 11 – New York City, NBC *Magic Keys Of
Radio* broadcast
Benny Goodman Quartet
As before.
Avalon   unissued
The Man I Love (fragment)   unissued

1938
June 14 – Boston, Mass., CBS *Camel Caravan*
broadcast
Benny Goodman Quartet
As before; Martha Tilton (vo-1).
I Hadn't Anyone Till You (1)   Columbia ML4590
I Found A New Baby   Blu-Disc T5001/02

1938
June 21 – Boston, Mass., CBS *Camel Caravan*
broadcast
Benny Goodman Trio
*Benny Goodman (cl), Teddy Wilson (p), Lionel
Hampton (dr).*
Chinatown, My Chinatown   unissued

1938
June 28 – Forum Arena, Montreal, CBS *Camel
Caravan* broadcast
Benny Goodman Quartet
*Benny Goodman (cl), Teddy Wilson (p), Lionel
Hampton (vb), Gene Krupa (dr).*
Canadian Capers   unissued

1938
July 5 – Glen Park Casino, Williamsville, N.Y.,
CBS *Camel Caravan* broadcast
Benny Goodman Trio/Quartet
As before.
I Hadn't Anyone Till You (trio) Blu-Disc T5001/02
I'm A Ding Dong Daddy (From Dumas) (quartet)
                                         unissued

1938
July 12 – New York City, CBS *Camel Caravan*
broadcast
Benny Goodman Quartet
As before.
Margie   unissued

1938
July 19 – New York City, CBS *Camel Caravan*
broadcast.
Benny Goodman Trio
Lionel Hampton (vb), Teddy Wilson (p), Jo Jones (d).
Coquette   unissued

1938
July 26 – New York City, CBS *Camel Caravan*
broadcast.
Benny Goodman Trio
As 19 July 1938, plus Ben Bernie (vo).
Dinah   unissued

1938
July 29 – New York City
Teddy Wilson and His Orchestra
*Jonah Jones (tp) Benny Carter (as), Ben Webster (ts),
Teddy Wilson (p), John Kirby (b), Cozy Cole (dr), Nan
Wynn (vo).*
23305-1   Now It Can Be Told   Brunswick 8199
23306-2   Laugh And Call It Love   8207
23307-1   On The Bumpy Road To Love   —
23308-1   A-Tisket, A-Tasket   8199

1938
August 1 – New York City
Teddy Wilson
Piano solos.
23311-1   Loch Lomond   unissued
23312-1   Tiger Rag   —

1938
August 2 – New York City, CBS *Camel Caravan*
broadcast, New York City
Benny Goodman Quartet
*Benny Goodman (cl), Lionel Hampton (vb), Teddy
Wilson (p), Jo Jones (d).*
Lambeth Walk   unissued

Benny Goodman Trio
*Benny Goodman (cl), Teddy Wilson (p), Lionel
Hampton (d)*
The World Is Waiting For The Sunrise   unissued

1938
August 5 – prob. New York City, unknown
broadcast
Benny Goodman Quartet
*Benny Goodman (cl), Teddy Wilson (p), Lionel
Hampton (vb), poss. Jo Jones (dr).*
Dinah   Blu-Disc T5001/02

1938
August 9 – New York City, CBS *Camel Caravan*
broadcast.
Benny Goodman Quartet
*Benny Goodman (cl), Teddy Wilson (p), Lionel
Hampton (vb), Dave Tough (dr).*
Honeysuckle Rose   unissued

1938
August 11 – New York City
Teddy Wilson
Piano solos.

23311-2	Loch Lomond	Meritt 23
23311-3	Loch Lomond	
	Teddy Wilson School For Pianists	
23312-2	Tiger Rag	Meritt 23
23312-3	Tiger Rag	
	Teddy Wilson School For Pianists	
23327-1	I'll See You In My Dreams	—
23328-1	Alice Blue Gown	—

1938
August 16 – unknown location, CBS *Camel Caravan* broadcast
Benny Goodman Quartet
As before.
Runnin' Wild   Blu-Disc T5001/02

1938
August 23 – State Fairgrounds, Detroit, Mich., CBS *Camel Caravan* broadcast
Benny Goodman Quartet
As before.
Stompin' At The Savoy   unissued

1938
August 30 – Detroit, CBS *Camel Caravan* broadcast
Benny Goodman Quartet
As on March 25, 1938.
Benny Sent Me   Columbia ML4591

1938
September 1 – Chicago, broadcast
Benny Goodman Quartet
As before.
I Found A New Baby   Spook Jazz SPJ6602

1938
September 6 – Chicago, CBS *Camel Caravan* broadcast.
Benny Goodman Quartet
As before.
Shine   Blu-Disc T5001/02

1938
September 13 – Chicago, CBS *Camel Caravan* broadcast.
Benny Goodman Trio
Benny Goodman (cl), Teddy Wilson (p), Lionel Hampton (dr).
I Surrender Dear   MGM E3788

Benny Goodman Quartet
As before.
Some Of These Days   MGM E3790

1938
September 20 – Chicago, CBS *Camel Caravan* broadcast.
Benny Goodman Trio
As before.
Don't Let That Moon Get Away   Soundcraft LP1020

1938
September 27 – Chicago, CBS *Camel Caravan* broadcast.
Benny Goodman Trio/Quartet
As before.
You're Blase (trio)   Soundcraft LP1021
The Sheik Of Araby (quartet)   —

1938
October 4 – Orpheum Theater, Minneapolis, CBS *Camel Caravan* broadcast
Benny Goodman Quartet
As before.
Opus1/2   unissued

1938
October 11, Chicago, CBS *Camel Caravan* broadcast
Benny Goodman Trio
Benny Goodman (cl), Teddy Wilson (p), Lionel Hampton (dr).
I Know That You Know   unissued

1938
October 12 – Chicago
Benny Goodman Trio/Quartet
Trio: Goodman (cl), Wilson (p), Hampton (dr).
Quartet: Goodman (cl), Wilson (p), Hampton (vb), Tough (dr).

025876-1	Opus ½ (quartet)	Victor 26091
025877-1	I Must Have That Man (trio)	26090
025878-2	Sweet Georgia Brown (quartet)	26051
025879-1	'S Wonderful (quartet)	26090
025879-2	'S Wonderful (quartet)	
		Bluebird AXM2-5568

1938
October 25 – New York City, CBS *Camel Caravan* broadcast.
Benny Goodman Quartet
As before.
I Got Rhythm   unissued

1938
October 31 – New York City
Teddy Wilson and His Orchestra
Harry James (tp), Benny Morton (tb), Edgar Sampson & Benny Carter (as), Lester Young, Herschel Evans (ts), Teddy Wilson (p) Albert Casey (g), Walter Page (b), Jo Jones (dr), Billie Holiday (vo).

23642-1	Everybody's Laughing	Brunswick 8259
23643-1	Here It Is Tomorrow Again	—

1938
November 1 – New York City, CBS *Camel Caravan* broadcast
Benny Goodman Trio
Benny Goodman (cl), Teddy Wilson (p), Lionel Hampton (dr).
I Must Have That Man   unissued

1938
November 8 – New York City, CBS *Camel Caravan*
broadcast
Benny Goodman Quartet
Harry James (t); Benny Goodman (cl), Teddy Wilson
(p), Lionel Hampton (vb), Hannah Williams (vo).
Stay On The Right Side, Sister   unissued

1938
November 9 – New York City
Teddy Wilson and His Orchestra
As October 31, 1938.

23687-1	Say It With A Kiss	Brunswick 8270
23688-1	April In My Heart	8265
23688-2	April In My Heart	Meritt 19
23689-1	I'll Never Fail You	Brunswick 8265
23690-1	They Say	8270
23690-2	They Say	Columbia CL2427

1938
November 15, New York City, broadcast
Benny Goodman Quartet:
As on October 12, 1938.
Dizzy Spells   Blu-Disc T5001/02

1938
November 28 – New York City
Teddy Wilson and His Orchestra
Bobby Hackett (co), Trummy Young (tb), Toots
Mondello, Ted Buckner (as), Bud Freeman, Chu Berry
(ts), Teddy Wilson (p), Al Casey (g), Milton Hinton (b),
Cozy Cole (dr), Billie Holiday (vo).

23760-1	You're So Desirable	Brunswick 8283
23761-1	You're Gonna See A Lot Of Me	8281
23762-1	Hello, My Darling	—
23763-2	Let's Dream In The Moonlight	8283

1938
December 18 – New York City, CBS *Fitch*
Bandwagon broadcast.
Benny Goodman Quartet
Benny Goodman (cl), Teddy Wilson (p), Buddy Schutz
(dr), Lionel Hampton (vb).
I'm A Ding-Dong Daddy (From Dumas)
                          Blu-Disc T5001/02

1938
December 20 – New York City, CBS *Camel*
Caravan broadcast.
Benny Goodman Quartet
Benny Goodman (cl), Teddy Wilson (p), Don Budge
(dr), Lionel Hampton (vb).
Dinah   unissued

1938
December 29 – New York City
Benny Goodman Quintet
Benny Goodman (cl), Teddy Wilson (p), Lionel
Hampton (vb), John Kirby (b), Buddy Schutz (dr).

030774-1	Pick-A-Rib part 1	Victor 26166
030774-2	Pick-A-Rib part 1	Time-Life STL-J05
030775-1	Pick-A-Rib part 2	Victor 26166
030775-2	Pick-A-Rib part 2	LPM1226
030776-1	I Cried For You	LPM6702

030776-2	I Cried For You	26139

Benny Goodman Quartet (as Benny Goodman
Trio)
As Quintet, except Hampton switches to (dr) and
Schutz is omitted.

030777-1	I Know That You Know	
		Bluebird AXM2-5568
030777-2	I Know That You Know	Victor 26139

1939
January 10 – New York City, CBS *Camel Caravan*
broadcast
Benny Goodman Trio
Benny Goodman (cl), Teddy Wilson (p), prob. Buddy
Schutz (dr).
Softly, As In A Morning Sunrise
                      Giants Of Jazz GOJ1030

Benny Goodman Sextet
Benny Goodman (cl), Teddy Wilson (p), Leonard Ware
(elg), Al Hall (b), Buddy Schutz (dr), Lionel Hampton
(vb).
Umbrella Man   Giants Of Jazz GOJ1030

1939
January 17 – Paramount Theater, New York City,
CBS *Camel Caravan* broadcast.
Benny Goodman Quartet
Benny Goodman (cl), Teddy Wilson (p), Buddy Schutz
(dr), Lionel Hampton (vb).
Lillie Stomp   unissued

1939
January 20 – Hickory House, New York City
Hickory House Jam Session compered by Alistair
Cooke
Harry James, Charlie Teagarden (tp), Jack Teagarden
(tb, vo-1), Joe Marsala (cl), Chu Berry (ts), Teddy
Wilson (p), John Kirby (b), George Wettling (dr).

Someday Sweetheart	Jazz Panorama(Sd) LP9
Basin Street Blues (1)	—
Honeysuckle Rose	—
Boogie Woogie Blues	—

1939
January 27 – New York City
Teddy Wilson
Piano solos.

24024-1/2	Coquette	
	Teddy Wilson School For Pianists	
24025-1	China Boy	—
24026-1	Melody In F	—
24027-1	When You And I Were	
	Young, Maggie	—

1939
January 30 – New York City
Teddy Wilson and His Orchestra
Roy Eldridge (tp), Benny Carter (as, ts), Ernie Powell
(cl, ts), Teddy Wilson (p), Danny Barker (g), Milton
Hinton (b), Cozy Cole (dr), Billie Holiday (vo).

24044-1	What Shall I Say	Brunswick 8314
24045-1	It 's Easy To Blame The Weather	—
24046-1	More Than You Know	8319

24046-2 More Than You Know
                              Columbia CL2428
24047-1 Sugar   Brunswick 8319

1939
January 31 – Paramount Theater, New York City,
CBS *Camel Caravan* broadcast
Benny Goodman Quartet
As 17 January 1939.
Umbrella Man   unissued

1939
February 7 – Paramount Theater, New York City,
CBS *Camel Caravan* broadcast
Benny Goodman Quartet
As 17 January 1939.
I've Found A New Baby Giants Of Jazz GOJ1033

1939
February 14 – Philadelphia, Pa., CBS *Camel Caravan* broadcast
Benny Goodman Quartet
As last.
Deep Purple   I.A.J.R.C. 8

1939
February 21 – Shubert Theater, Newark, N.J., CBS
Camel Caravan broadcast
Benny Goodman Trio
Benny Goodman (cl), Teddy Wilson (p), Lionel Hampton (dr).
The World Is Waiting For The Sunrise   unissued

1939
February 28 – Fox Theater, Detroit, Mich., CBS
Camel Caravan broadcast
Benny Goodman Quartet
As 17 January 1939.
I Found A New Baby   unissued

1939
May 10 New York City
Teddy Wilson and His Orchestra
Karl George, Harold Baker (tp), Jack Wiley (tb), Pete Clark (cl, as, bars), Rudy Powell (cl, as), Ben Webster, George Irish (ts), Teddy Wilson (p), Albert Casey (g), Al Hall (b), J.C. Heard (dr), Thelma Carpenter (vo-1).
24497- If Anything Happened To You (1)
                              Brunswick unissued
24498- Why Begin Again? (1)   Tax(Sd) m-8018

1939
June 28 – New York City
Teddy Wilson and His Orchestra
As last.
24824-B Jumpin' For Joy (1)   Brunswick 8438
24825-A Booly-Ja-Ja   Columbia 35220
24826-A The Man I Love (1)   Brunswick 8438
24827-A Exactly Like You   Columbia 35220

1939
July 26 – New York City
Teddy Wilson and His Orchestra
As last.

24931-A Love Grows On The White Oak Tree (1)
                              Brunswick 8455
24932-A This Is The Moment (1)   —
24933-A Early Session Hop   Columbia 35207
24934-A Lady Of Mystery

1939
August 10 – New York City, BBC *America Dances* broadcast
Teddy Wilson and His Orchestra
Uncertain personnel probably similar to 10 May 1939 (Baker, Webster, Wilson, Heard certain), Thelma Carpenter (vo-1).
Little Things That Mean So Much
                              Fanfare LP14-114
I Know That You Know   —
Stairway To The Stars (1)   —
Exactly Like You   —
The Man I Love   —
Booly-Ja-Ja   —
Back To Back (1)   —
Body And Soul   —
Lonesome Road   Unissued
Dear Old Southland   —
Little Things That Mean So Much   —

1939
August 11 – New York City
Redd Evans and His Billy Boys
Lewis 'Redd' Evans (vo, hot sweet potato-1) acc. by Willie Kelly (tp), Floyd Brady (tb), Reggie Merrill (as), Clark Galehouse (ts), Teddy Wilson (p), Al Casey (g), Al Hall (b), Cozy Cole (dr).
25189-1 Milenberg Joys (1)   Vocalion 5173
25190-1 In The Baggage Coach Ahead   —
25191-2 Am I Blue (1)   unissued
25192-2 When It's Springtime In The Rockies —

1939
September 12 – New York City
Teddy Wilson and His Orchestra
Karl George, Harold Baker (tp), Jack Wiley (tb), Pete Clark (cl, as, bars), Rudy Powell (cl, as), Ben Webster, George Irish (ts), Teddy Wilson (p), Albert Casey (g), Al Hall (b), J.C. Heard (dr), Jean Eldridge (vo).
26058-A Jumpin' On The Blacks And Whites
                              Columbia 35232
26059-A Little Things That Mean So Much   —
26060-A Hallelujah   35298
26061-A Some Other Spring   —

1939
December 11 – New York City
Teddy Wilson and His Orchestra
As last, Doc Cheatham (tp) and Floyd Brady (tb) added, J.C. Heard (vo-1), Jean Eldridge (vo-2), band vo-1.
25735-1 Wham (Re-Bop-Boom-Bam) (1)
                              Columbia 35354
25736-1 Sweet Lorraine (1)   35711
25737-1 Moon Ray (2)   35354
25738-1 Liza   35711
25738-2 Liza   Tax m8018

1939/40
Unknown date – Hollywood, Cal.
Jerry Jerome Trio
Jerry Jerome (ts), Teddy Wilson (p), unknown (b-1),
Cozy Cole (d).
Back Home Again In Indiana (1)   Vantage 503
Between The Devil And The Deep Blue Sea (1) —
Embraceable You (1)   —
Stompin' At The Savoy (1)   —
Exactly Like You (1)   —
Just You, Just Me (1)   —
When It's Sleepy Time Down South   —
I'll See You In My Dreams   —
My Gal Sal   —
Serenade   —
I Love You Truly   —
Who's Sorry Now   —
Save The Bread   —
Break It Up   —
The above titles are taken from Keystone 16" ETs.
Many more titles were issued on ET, but details of
the Keystone issues are not available.

1940
January 15 – New York City
Mildred Bailey (vo) acc. by Orchestra
Mildred Bailey (vo), acc. by Roy Eldridge (tp), Jimmy
Carroll, Robert Burns (cl), Carl Prager (bcl), Eddie
Powell (fl), Teddy Wilson (p), John Collins (g), Pete
Peterson (b), Bill Beason (dr) .
26413-A   Wham (Re-Bop-Boom-Bam)
                                   Columbia 35370
26414-A   Little High Chairman   —
26415-A   Easy To Love   35921

1940
January 18 – New York City
Teddy Wilson and His Orchestra
As on December 11, 1939.
26435-A   Crying My Soul Out For You (2)
                                   Columbia 35372
26436-A   In The Mood   —
26437-A   Cocoanut Groove   35737
26437-B   Cocoanut Groove   Tax m-8018
26438-A   71   Columbia 35737

1940
January 25 – New York City
Mildred Bailey (vo) acc. by orchestra
As on January 15, 1940.
26460-B   Give Me Time   Columbia unissued
26461-A   They Can't Take That Away From Me
                                          unissued
26462-A   A Bee Gezindt   35409
26464-A   After All I've Been To You   —
26464-A   Don't Take Your Love From Me   35921
26464-B   Don't Take Your Love From Me   DO-
2226

1940
April 2 – New York City
Mildred Bailey (vo) acc. by orchestra
As on January 15, 1940, Mitch Miller (ob) added.
26460-C   Give Me Time   Columbia 35626

26696-A   Fools Rush In   35463
26697-A   From Another World   —
26698-A   I'm Nobody's Baby   35626

1940
May 15 – New York City
Mildred Bailey (vo) acc. by orchestra
As on January 15, 1940, Irving Horowitz (bcl), Kenny
Clarke (dr), replace Prager and Beason.
27302-1   How Can I Ever Be Alone?
                                   Columbia 35532
27303-1   Tennessee Fish Fry   —
27304-1   I'll Pray For You   35589
27305-1   Blue And Broken-Hearted   —

1940
June 7 – New York City
Billie Holiday
Billie Holiday (vo), acc. by Roy Eldridge (tp), Bill
Bowen, Joe Eldridge (as), Kermit Scott, Lester Young
(ts), Teddy Wilson (p), Freddie Green (g), Walter Page
(b), J.C. Heard (dr).
26900-A   I'm Pulling Through   OKeh 5991
26901-A   Tell Me More   5719
26902-A   Laughing At Life   —
26903-A   Time Only Hands   5991

1940
September 12 – New York City
Billie Holiday
Billie Holiday (vo), acc. by Roy Eldridge (tp), George
Auld, Don Redman (as), Don Byas, Jimmy Hamilton
(ts), Teddy Wilson (p), John Collins (g), Al Hall (b),
Kenny Clarke (dr).
28617-1   I'm All For You   Okeh 5831
28617-2   I'm All For You   Columbia CL2428
28618-1   I Hear Music   Okeh 5831
28618-2   I Hear Music   Columbia CL2428
286191   The Same Old Story   Meritt 25
28619-1   The Same Old Story   Okeh 5806
28619-2   The Same Old Story   Columbia CL2428
28619-3   The Same Old Story
                            Jazz Unlimited(Sd) JUCD2014
28620-1   Practice Makes Perfect   Okeh 5806
28620-2   Practice Makes Perfect   Epic LN24030
28620-3   Practice Makes Perfect
                                   ColumbiaCL2428

1940
October 4 – New York City
Eddy Howard
Eddy Howard (vo), acc. by Bill Coleman (tp), Benny
Morton (tb), Edmond Hall (cl), Bud Freeman (ts),
Teddy Wilson (p), Charlie Christian (elg), Billy Taylor
(b), Yank Porter (dr).
28794-1   Old Fashioned Love   Columbia 35771
28795-1   Star Dust   —
28796-1   Exactly Like You   35915
28797-1   Wrap Your Troubles In Dreams   —

1940
October 7 – New York City, NBC *Chamber Music*
Society of Lower Basin Street broadcast
Jimmy Hamilton (cl), Teddy Wilson (p), Yank Porter
(d).

China Boy   Spook Jazz(E) SPJ6606
Body And Soul   —

1940
December 6 – New York City
Chick Bullock and His All-Star Orchestra
Chick Bullock (vo), acc. by Bill Coleman (tp), Benny Morton (tb), Edmond Hall (cl) Bud Freeman (ts) Teddy Wilson (p), Eddie Gibbs (g), Billy Taylor (b), Yank Porter (dr).

29221-1	Smiles	Okeh 6013
29222-1	It Had To Be You	—
29222-2	It Had To Be You	Meritt 8
29223-1	My Melancholy Baby	Okeh 6261
29223-3	My Melancholy Baby	Meritt 10
29224-1	Back Home Again In Indiana	Okeh 6261

1940
December 9 – New York City
Teddy Wilson and His Orchestra
Bill Coleman (tp), Benny Morton (tb), Jimmy Hamilton (cl), George James (bars), Teddy Wilson (p), Eddie Gibbs (g), Al Hall (b), Yank Porter (dr), Helen Ward (vo-1).

29233-1	I Never Knew	Columbia 35905
29234-1	Embraceable You (1)	—
292~5-1	But Not For Me (1)	36084
29236-1	Oh! Lady, Be Good	—

1940
December 19 – New York City
Billie Holiday and Her Orchestra
Hot Lips Page (tp), Charlie Barnet (as), Coleman Hawkins, Lester Young (ts), Teddy Wilson (p), unknown (g), unknown (b), unknown (dr), Billie Holiday (vo).
The Man I Love (part only)   Saga(E) ER08014

1941
14 January – New York City.
Benny Goodman and His Orchestra
Alec Fila, Jimmy Maxwell, Irving Goodman (tp), Cootie Williams (tp, vo-1), Lou McGarity, Cutty Cutshall (tb), Benny Goodman (cl, vo-2), Skip Martin, Gus Bivona, Bob Snyder (as), George Auld, Jackie Henderson (ts), Teddy Wilson (p), Mike Bryan (g), Artie Bernstein (b), Dave Tough (dr), Helen Forrest (vo-3).

29502-	Let The Door Knob Hitcha (1)	
	Phontastic(Sd) NOST7612	
29502-	Let The Door Knob Hitcha (1)	
	Blu-Disc T1009	
29502-1	Let The Door Knob Hitcha (1)	
	Columbia 35962	
29503-	I Hear A Rhapsody (3)	
	Phontastic(Sd) NOST7612	
29503-	I Hear A Rhapsody (3)	Blu-Disc T1009
29503-1	I Hear A Rhapsody (3)	Columbia 35937
29504-	It's Always You (3)	Columbia KG32822
29504-1	It's Always You (3)	Columbia 36002
29505-	Corn Silk (3)	Phontastic(Sd) NOST7612
29505-	Corn Silk (3)	Blu-Disc T1009
29505-1	Corn Silk (2)	Columbia 35992
29507-	Birds Of A Feather (3)	Blu-Disc T1009

29507-	Birds Of A Feather (3)	
	Phontastic(Sd) NOST7612	
29507-1	Birds Of A Feather (3)	Columbia 35977

1941
January 21 – New York City.
Benny Goodman and His Orchestra
Hymie Schertzer (as) replaces Martin.

29530-	Time On My Hands	
	Phontastic(Sd) NOST7612	
29530-1	Time On My Hands	Columbia 36180
29530-	Time On My Hands	Columbia PG33405
29531-	You're Dangerous (3)	
	Phontastic(Sd) NOST7612	
29531-1	You're Dangerous (3)	Columbia 35977
29532-	The Mem'ry Of A Rose (3)	
	Phontastic(Sd) NOST7612	
29532-1	The Mem'ry Of A Rose (3)	
	Columbia 35992	

1941
January 28 — New York City.
Benny Goodman and His Orchestra
Les Robinson (as) replaces Snyder, Skip Martin (bars) added.

29577-	This Is New (breakdown) (3)	
	Phontastic(Sd) NOST7615	
29577-	This Is New (3)	
	Phontastic(Sd) NOST7615	
29577-1	This Is New (3)	Columbia 35944
	Jenny (2, 3)	Blu-Disc T1006
	Jenny (breakdown) (2, 3)	Blu-Disc T1006
	Jenny (2, 3)	Blu-Disc T1006
29578-	Perfidia (Tonight) (3)	Meritt 11
29578-	Perfidia (Tonight) (3)	
	Phontastic(Sd) NOST7615	
29578-1	Perfidia (Tonight) (3)	Columbia 35962
29579-	Bewitched (3)	
	Phontastic(Sd) NOST7615	
29579-1	Bewitched (3)	Columbia 35944

1941
February 12 – New York City
Chick Bullock and His All-Star Orchestra
Chick Bullock (vo), acc. by Bill Coleman (tp), Benny Morton (tb), Jimmy Hamilton (cl), George James (bsx), Teddy Wilson (p), Eddie Gibbs (g), Al Hall (b) J.C. Heard (dr).

29703-1	Dolores	Okeh 6123
29704-1	Amapola (Pretty Little Poppy)	6100
29705-1	Oh! How I Hate To Get Up In The Morning	6123
29706-1	There'll Be Some Changes Made	6100

1941
April 7 – Chicago
Teddy Wilson
Piano solo.

CCO 3653-1		Smoke Gets In Your Eyes
		Columbia 36631

Teddy Wilson Trio
Teddy Wilson (p), Al Hall (b), J.C. Heard (dr).

CCO 3654-1	Rosetta	Columbia 36632
CCO 3654-2	Rosetta	Parlophone R2981

CCO 3654-3   Rosetta   CBS 66370
CCO 3654-4   Rosetta   CBS 66370

1941
April 11 – Chicago
Teddy Wilson Trio
As last.
CCO 3686-1   I Know That You Know
                                             Columbia 36633
CCO 3686-2   I Know That You Know CBS 66370
CCO 3687-1   Them There Eyes   Columbia 36631
CCO 3687-2   Them There Eyes   CBS 66370
CCO 3687-3   Them There Eyes   —
CCO 3688-2   China Boy   Columbia 36634
CCO 3688-3   China Boy   CBS 66370
CCO 3688-4   China Boy   —
CCO 3688-5   China Boy   —
CCO 3688-6   China Boy   —
CCO 3688-7   China Boy   —

Teddy Wilson
Piano solos.
CCO 3693-1   I Surrender Dear
                                       Columbia unissued
CCO 3694-1   Body And Soul   36634
CCO 3695-1   I Can't Get Started   36633
CCO 3695-2   I Can't Get Started   CBS 66370

1941
May 5 – New York City
Benny Goodman and His Orchestra
*Billy Butterfield, Jimmy Maxwell, Irving Goodman,
Cootie Williams (t), Lou McGarity, Cutty Cutshall
(tb), Benny Goodman (cl), Les Robinson, Jimmy
Horvath (as), George Auld, Pete Mondello (ts), Skip
Martin (bars), Teddy Wilson (p), Mike Bryan (g), Artie
Bernstein (b), Jo Jones (d), Helen Forrest (vo-1).*
30419-1   Good Evenin', Good Lookin' (1)
                                       Columbia 36136
30419-2   Good Evenin', Good Lookin' (1)
                                  Phontastic(Sd) NOST7616
30420-   Something New (Negra Soy)   —
30420-1   Something New (Negra Soy)
                                       Columbia 36209
30421-1   Air Mail Special   Columbia 36254
30422-1   I Found A Million Dollar Baby (1)
                                  Phontastic(Sd) NOST7616
30422-2   I Found A Million Dollar Baby (1)
                                       Columbia 36136
Test 104   Don't Be That Way
                                  Phontastic(Sd) NOST7616

1941
May 5 – WJZ 'What's New' broadcast, New York
City.
Benny Goodman and His Orchestra/Trio/Sextet
Orchestra as before, Helen Forrest (vo-1).
*Trio: Benny Goodman (cl), Teddy Wilson (p), Gene
Krupa (dr).*
*Sextet: Cootie Williams (t), Benny Goodman (cl), Teddy
Wilson (p), Charlie Christian (elg), Artie Bernstein (b),
Jo Jones (dr).*
Walkin' By The River (trio)   Phontastic(Sd) BG01
Hot-Cha-Chornya (trio)   Unissued

Fancy Meeting You (1)   Unissued
Superman   Fanfare Lp19-119
G'Bye Now (1)   Unissued
Flying Home (sextet/orch in coda)
                                  Queen-Disc(It) Q016
Let's Dance (theme)   Unissued

1941
June 4 – New York City
Benny Goodman and His Orchestra
*As May 5, 1941, except Chris Griffin (t), Gene Kinsey
(as), Charlie Christian (elg); Walter Ioss (b), J.C. Heard
(d), replace Maxwell, I. Goodman, Horvath, Bryan,
Bernstein, Jones.*
30598-   When The Sun Comes Out (1)
                                  Phontastic(Sd) NOST7616
30598-1   When The Sun Comes Out (1)
                                       Columbia 36209
30599-   Smoke Gets In Your Eyes (1)
                                  Phontastic(Sd) NOST7616
30599-1   Smoke Gets In Your Eyes (1)
                                       Columbia 36284
Ref. rec. Tuesday At Ten   Columbia unissued
Sources differ as to whether Teddy Wilson or
Johnny Guarnieri is the pianist on this session.

1941
August 7 – New York City
Billie Holiday (vo) acc. by Teddy Wilson and His
Orchestra
*Emmett Berry (tp), Jimmy Hamilton (cl), Hymie
Schertzer (cl, as), Babe Russin (cl, ts) Teddy Wilson (p),
Albert Casey (g), John Williams (b), J.C. Heard (dr).*
31002-1   Jim   Okeh 6369
31002-2   Jim   Columbia KG30782
31003-1   I Cover The Waterfront Columbia 37493
31004-1   Love Me Or Leave Me   Okeh 6369
31005-1   Gloomy Sunday   6451
31005-2   Gloomy Sunday   Queen-Disc Q4501
31005-3   Gloomy Sunday   Columbia KG30782

1941
September 16 – New York City
Teddy Wilson and His Orchestra
*Emmett Berry (tp), Benny Morton (tb), Jimmy
Hamilton (cl), Teddy Wilson (p), John Williams (b),
J.C. Heard (dr), Lena Horne (vo-1).*
31319-1   A Touch Of Boogie Columbia unissued
31320-1   Out Of Nowhere (1)   Columbia 36737
31321-1   Prisoner Of Love (1)   V-Disc 317
31322-1   The Sheik Of Araby Columbia KG31564
31322-2   The Sheik Of Araby   Meritt 10

1941
September/October – Cafe Society Downtown,
New York City
Teddy Wilson and His Orchestra
As before, Pete Johnson (p) added.
Unlucky Woman (1)   Jazz Classics JCVC108
This title is from the soundtrack of the film *Boogie
Woogie Dream* (dir. Hans Berger). The issue quoted
is a commercial video.

1942
January 21 – New York City
Teddy Wilson
Piano solos.

32282-1	These Foolish Things	Columbia 36632
32282-2	These Foolish Things	CBS 66370
	Teddy Wilson Original	—
	Studio Doodling	—

1942
February 10 – New York City
Billie Holiday (vo) acc. by Teddy Wilson and His Orchestra
As on August 7, 1941, except Gene Fields (g) replaces Casey.

32405-1	Wherever You Are	Harmony 1075
32406-1	Mandy Is Two	Columbia CL2428
32407-1	It's A Sin To Tell A Lie	Harmony 1075
32408-1	Until The Real Thing Comes Along	
		Columbia 37493
32408-	Until The Real Thing Comes Along	
		Columbia KG30782

The last item is a spliced version combining take -1 with the final two bars of take 2.

1942
July 31 – New York City
Teddy Wilson and His Orchestra
As on September 16, 1941, except Edmond Hall (cl) replaces Hamilton, Helen Ward (vo-1).

33083-1	You're My Favorite Memory (1)	
		Columbia 36632
33084-1	Something To Shout About - pt .1	
		unissued
33085-1	Something To Shout About - pt. 2	
		unissued
33086-2	B Flat Swing	Meritt 8

1942
September 7 – Cafe Society, New York City, CBS broadcast
Teddy Wilson Sextet
Joe Thomas (tp), Benny Morton (tb), Edmond Hall (cl), Teddy Wilson (p), Johnny Williams (b), Sid Catlett (d).

| Unknown title | unissued |
| I Got Rhythm | unissued |

1943
August 13 – New York City
Teddy Wilson Quartet
Joe Thomas (tp), Edmond Hall (cl), Teddy Wilson (p), Sid Catlett (d).

VP84	How High The Moon	V-Disc 16
	Unknown title	V-Disc unissued
VP85	Russian Lullaby	V-Disc 16
	Russian Lullaby (incomplete alternative	
	take)	Vintage Jazz Classics VJC1013-2

1943
c. November – New York City
Teddy Wilson and His Sextet
Emmett Berry (tp), Benny Morton (tb), Edmond Hall (cl), Teddy Wilson (p), Johnny Williams (b), Sid Catlett (d).

Honeysuckle Rose	
	AFRS Basic Music Library P186
Lady Be Good	Queen-Disc(It) Q020
B-Flat Swing	—

The last two titles were first issued on AFRS Jubilee 55, with various edits.

1943
November 4 – New York City
Mildred Bailey
Mildred Bailey (vo), acc. by Teddy Wilson (p).

VP309	Rockin' Chair	V-Disc 105
VP310	Sunday, Monday Or Always	—
VP311	Scrap Your Fat	135
VP312	More Than You Know	202

1944
January 26
Esquire All Stars – Metropolitan Opera House, New York City
Roy Eldridge (tp), Jack Teagarden (tb-1), Barney Bigard (cl-2), Coleman Hawkins (ts-3), Teddy Wilson (p), Red Norvo (vb-4), Al Casey (g), Oscar Pettiford (b), Sid Catlett (dr), Mildred Bailey (vo-6).

I've Got A Feeling I'm Falling (2)	FDC(It) 1007
More Than You Know (3) (6)	1010
Squeeze Me (1) (2) (6)	V-Disc 665
Honeysuckle Rose (2) (6)	FDC(It) 1010
Rockin' Chair (6)	FDC(It) 1010

1944
January 25 – New York City
Edmond Hall's All Star Quintet
Edmond Hall (cl,) Teddy Wilson (p), Red Norvo (vb), Carl Kress (g), John Williams (b).

BN908-1	Rompin' In 44	Mosaic MR6-109
BN908-2	Rompin' In 44	Blue Note 30
BN909	Blue Interval	31
BN910-1	Smooth Sailing	Mosaic MR6-109
BN910-2	Smooth Sailing	Blue Note 30
BN911	Seein' Red	31

1944
January 31 — New York City
Coleman Hawkins Quintet Featuring Teddy Wilson
Roy Eldridge (tp), Coleman Hawkins (ts), Teddy Wilson (p), Billy Taylor (b), Cozy Cole (dr).

KHL9-1	I Only Have Eyes For You	
		Keynote(J) 18PJ1052
KHL9-2	I Only Have Eyes For You	
KHL9-3	I Only Have Eyes For You	K609
KHL10-1	'S Wonderful	18PJ1052
KHL10-2	'S Wonderful	K609
KHL11-1	I'm In The Mood For Love	K610
KHL12-1	"Bean" At The Met	18PJ1052
KHL12-2	"Bean" At The Met	—
KHL12-3	"Bean" At The Met	Keynote K610

1944
February 17 – New York City
Coleman Hawkins Quintet
Coleman Hawkins (ts), Teddy Wilson (p), Israel Crosby (b), Cozy Cole (dr) .

HL13	Flame Thrower	Keynote K611
HL14	Imagination	K612
HL15	Night And Day	K611
HL16	Cattin' At Keynote	K612

1944
March – New York City.
Teddy Wilson
Piano solo.
I Know That You Know   Folkways FJ2852

1944
May 2 – New York City.
Edmond Hall Sextet
Hot Lips Page (tp), Benny Morton (tb), Edmond Hall (cl), Teddy Wilson (p), Al Hall (b), Sid Catlett (dr).
Honeysuckle Rose   Jazz Archives JA17
Get The Mop   —

1944
May 7 – New York City, AFRS *Radio Hall Of Fame* broadcast
Benny Goodman Trio/Quartet
Benny Goodman (cl), Teddy Wilson (p), Sid Weiss (b in quartet), Cozy Cole (dr).
Body And Soul (trio)   Sunbeam SB145
Who? (trio)   —
After You've Gone (quartet)   —
The first two titles were originally issued on an AFRS ET.

1944
May 28 – New York City, *Philco Hall of Fame* broadcast
Benny Goodman Quartet
Benny Goodman (cl), Teddy Wilson (p), Sid Weiss (b), Cozy Cole (dr).
Intro/I Surrender Dear   Sunbeam SB145
Hallelujah   unissued

1944
May 29 – New York City
Coleman Hawkins' All American Four
Coleman Hawkins (ts), Teddy Wilson (p), John Kirby (b), Sid Catlett (dr).

HL33-1	Make Believe	Keynote(J) 18PJ1056
HL33-2	Make Believe	K1317
HL34-1	Don't Blame Me	18PJ1056
HL34-2	Don't Blame Me	K1320
HL35-1	Just One Of Those Things	K1317
HL36-1	Hallelujah	K1320

1944
New York City
Teddy Wilson
Piano solos.
Bye Bye Blues   Spook Jazz(E) SPJ6608
On The Sunny Side Of The Street   —
You Took Advantage Of Me   —
Just One Of Those Things   —
Jealous   —
Louise   —
I Surrender Dear   —
Isn't It Romantic   —

I've Got The World On A String   —
Rosetta   —

1944
June – New York City, concert
Benny Goodman Trio
Benny Goodman (cl), Teddy Wilson (p), Specs Powell (dr).
Poor Butterfly   V-Disc 274
The World Is Waiting For The Sunrise   —

1944
June 12 – New York City
Benny Goodman and His Orchestra
Billy Butterfield, Charlie Shavers, Mickie McMickle (tp); Vernon Brown Jack Satterfield (tb), Benny Goodman (cl), Hymie Schertzer, Jules Rubin (as), Art Rollini, Don Byas (ts), Ernie Caceres (bars), Teddy Wilson (p), Allan Reuss (g), Sid Weiss (b), Cozy Cole (dr).
12368   All The Cats Join In   Capitol EAP1-519
Benny Goodman Quartet
Goodman/Wilson/Weiss/Cole only.
12451   After You've Gone   —

1944
June 15 – New York City
Teddy Wilson Sextet
Emmett Berry (tp), Benny Morton (tb), Edmond Hall (cl), Teddy Wilson (p), Slam Stewart (b), Sid Catlett (dr).

I Got Rhythm	Musak 185
Lady Be Good	Musak 185
Honeysuckle Rose	Musak 185
Honeysuckle Rose	Sound Off 202
Rose Room	Musak 186
Indiana	Musak 186
Don't Be That Way	Musak 186
A Touch Of Boogie Woogie	Jazz Archives JA28
Flying Home	—
B Flat Swing	—
Embraceable You	—
Mop Mop	—
The Way You Look Tonight	—
Stompin' At The Savoy	—
You're My Favorite Memory	—
The Sheik Of Araby	—

The titles originally issued by Muzak were all issued commercially on Jazz Archives JA28.

1944
July – New York City
Benny Goodman Trio
Benny Goodman (cl), Teddy Wilson (p), Specs Powell (dr).
Poor Butterfly   AFRS Something For The Girls #13
The World Is Waiting For The Sunrise   —

1944
July 11 – New York City
Edmond Hall Quartet with Teddy Wilson
Edmond Hall (cl), Teddy Wilson (p), Billy Taylor (b), Arthur Trappier (dr).

A4790-TK1	Sleepy Time Gal #2	
		Commodore 6.25893
A4790-1	Sleepy Time Gal #4	
		Mosaic MR23-128
A4790-2	Sleepy Time Gal	Commodore C581
A4790-3	Sleepy Time Gal #3	
		Mosaic MR23-128
A4791-1	Where Or When	Commodore C579
A4791-2	Where Or When #2	
		Commodore 6.25893
A4791-	Where Or When #3	
		Mosaic MR23-128
A4792-1	It Had To Be You #1	
		Commodore 6.25893
A4793-1	Caravan #2	—
A4793-2	Caravan	Commodore C557
A4793-3	Caravan #3	Mosaic MR23-128
A4793-4	Caravan #4	—

1944
July 12 – New York City, CBS *Mildred Bailey And Company* broadcast
Teddy Wilson Sextet
Charlie Shavers (t), Red Norvo (vb), Teddy Wilson (p), Remo Palmieri (g), Al Hall (b), Specs Powell (d).
Undecided   AFRS Mildred Bailey Show #1

1944
July 20 – New York City
Edmond Hall Quartet with Teddy Wilson
Edmond Hall (cl), Teddy Wilson (p), Billy Taylor (b), Arthur Trappier (dr).

A4797-TK1	It's Only A Shanty In Old Shanty	
	Town #3	Mosaic MR23-128
A4797-TK2	It's Only A Shanty In Old Shanty	
	Town #4	—
A4797-1	It's Only A Shanty In Old Shanty	
	Town #2	Commodore 6.25893
A4797-2	It's Only A Shanty In Old Shanty	
	Town	Commodore C557
A4798-1	Night And Day #2	
		Commodore 6.25893
A4798-2	Night And Day	Commodore C579
A4799-TK1	I Want To Be Happy #2	
		Commodore 6.25893
A4799-1	I Want To Be Happy	
		Commodore C580
A4799-	I Want To Be Happy #3	
		Mosaic MR23-128
A4800-TK1	Show Piece #2	Commodore 6.25893
A4800-1	Show Piece	Commodore C580
A4800-2	Show Piece #3	Mosaic MR23-128

1944
July 26 – New York City, CBS *Mildred Bailey And Company* broadcast
Teddy Wilson Sextet
Roy Eldridge (tp), Teddy Wilson (p), Red Norvo (vb), Remo Palmieri (g), Al Hall (b), Specs Powell (dr).
After You've Gone   Jazz Archives JA36

Teddy Wilson with the Paul Baron Orchestra
Teddy Wilson (p) with unknown personnel.
Sweet Lorraine   Jazz Archives JA36

1944
July 27 – New York City
Red Norvo All Star Sextet
Aaron Sachs (c), Teddy Wilson (p), Red Norvo (vb), Remo Palmieri (g), Slam Stewart (b), Ed Dell (dr).

HL49-1	Subtle Sexology	Keynote K1310
HL50-1	Blues A La Red	Keynote(J) 18PJ1059
HL50-2	Blues A La Red	Keynote K1319
HL51-1	The Man I Love	K1314
HL52-1	Seven Come Eleven	
		Keynote(J) 18PJ1059
HL52-2	Seven Come Eleven	Keynote K1314

1944
July 31 – New York City
Benny Goodman and His V-Disc All Star Band
Charlie Shavers, Yank Lawson, Roy Eldridge, Mickey McMickle (tp), Vernon Brown, Ward Silloway (tb), Benny Goodman (cl, vo-1), Hymie Schertzer, Reggie Merrill (as), Art Rollini, Wolfe Tayne (ts), Ernie Caceres (bars), Teddy Wilson (p), Tommy Kay (g), Gene Traxler (b), Specs Powell (dr), Mildred Bailey (vo-2), Perry Como (vo-3).
Benny Goodman and His V-Disc Quartette
Goodman, Wilson, Traxler, Powell.

	After You've Gone	unissued
	There'll Be A Jubilee (2)	unissued
	Goodbye, Sue (1)	unissued
	Hallelujah! (quartet)	unissued
VP848	After You've Gone	V-Disc 322
VP849	Goodbye Sue (3)	V-Disc 312
VP850	There'll Be A Jubilee (2)	V-Disc 494
VP859	These Foolish Things Remind Me Of	
	You (2)	V-Disc 302
VP859	Hallelujah (quartet)	V-Disc 302
	At The Darktown Strutters Ball	
		AFRS BML P307

The final title as by Benny Goodman and His Orchestra and issued commercially on Giants Of Jazz GOJ1017.

1944
Summer to Fall – New York City
Paul Baron and His Orchestra
32 pieces inc. Teddy Wilson (p).
Begin The Beguine
          Vintage Jazz Classics VJC1013-2

1944
August 2 – New York City, CBS *Mildred Bailey And Company* broadcast.
Paul Baron and His Orchestra
32 pieces inc. Billy Butterfield, Roy Eldridge, Chris Griffin, Yank Lawson, Jimmy Maxwell, Charlie Shavers (tp), Will Bradley, Ward Silloway (tb), Ernie Caceres, Nick Caiazza, Hank D'Amico, Paul Ricci (saxes), unknowns (woodwinds), unknowns (strings), Teddy Wilson (p), Remo Palmieri (g), Al Hall (b), Specs Powell (d), Red Norvo (vb), Elaine Vito (harp), Mildred Bailey (vo-1).
Four In A Bar   IAJRC 17

Teddy Wilson Sextet
As on July 26, 1944.
If Dreams Come True   Jazz Archives JA36

1944
August 11 – CBS *Music Till Midnight* broadcast,
New York City.
Teddy Wilson with Paul Baron's Orchestra
As before.
Hallelujah   V-Disc 456
It is not certain that this issue is from this broadcast.

1944
August 14 – New York City
Red Norvo's Quintet
Aaron Sachs (cl), Teddy Wilson (p) Red Norvo (vb),
Remo Palmieri (g), Al Hall (b), Specs Powell (dr).
Which Switch Which   V-Disc 324
Bass On The Bar Floor Room   —

1944
August 18 – New York City, CBS *Music Till*
Midnight broadcast
Paul Baron Orchestra
As before, plus Coleman Hawkins (ts-2), Slam Stewart
(b-3).
From The Land Of Sky Blue Water (MB-vo)
                                             Hindsight HSR133
I'll Never Be The Same (1)   —
Four In A Bar   —
The Man I Love (2)   —
Play Fiddle Play (as Bass Feature)(3)
                                             Swing House(E) SWH13
The Man I Love (2)   Jazz Society AA504

Teddy Wilson Sextet.
As on July 26, 1944.
Untitled Original   Jazz Archives JA36
The first four titles are from the rehearsal for the
broadcast.

1944
August 25 – New York City, Reheearsal for CBS
Music Till Midnight broadcast
Paul Baron Orchestra
As before.
Please Don't Talk About Me When I'm Gone (1)
                                             Hindsight HSR133
Body And Soul   —

Teddy Wilson Sextet.
As on July 26, 1944.
China Boy   —

1944
September 1 – New York City, CBS *Music Till*
Midnight broadcast.
Paul Baron and His Orchestra
As before, plus Stuff Smith (vn-2).
Lover Come Back To Me (1)   Hindsight HSR133
St. Louis Blues   —
Bugle Call Rag (2)   Swing House(E) SWH13
The first two titles are from the rehearsal for the
broadcast.

1944
September 4 – New York City, CBS *Music In The*
Air broadcast

Paul Baron and His Orchestra
As before.
Hallelujah   Fanfare LP14-114
Come Out Wherever You Are   —
I Used To Love You   —

1944
September 8 – New York City, CBS *Music Till*
Midnight broadcast
Paul Baron and His Orchestra
As before, plus Charlie Shavers (t).
Summertime   Swing House(E) SWH14

1944
September 18 – New York City
Buck Ram All Stars
Frank Newton, Shad Collins (tp), Tyree Glenn (tb),
Earl Bostic (as), Don Byas (ts), Ernie Caceres (bars),
Teddy Wilson (p), Red Norvo (vb), Remo Palmieri (g),
Slam Stewart (b), Cozy Cole (dr).
S5714   Twilight In Teheran   Savoy 572
S5715   Morning Mist   SJL2208
S5716   Swing Street   572
S5717   Ram Session   XP8077

1944
September 25 – New York City.
Benny Goodman Quintet
Benny Goodman (cl), Red Norvo (vb), Teddy Wilson
(p), Sid Weiss (b), Morey Feld (dr).
VP942   Sweet Georgia Brown/The Sheik Of
         Araby   V-Disc 366

1944
September 29 – New York City, Rehearsal for
CBS *Music Till Midnight* broadcast
Paul Baron and His Orchestra
As before.
I'll Get By (MB-vo)   Hindsight HSR133

1944
September 29 – New York City, CBS *Music Till*
Midnight broadcast
Teddy Wilson Sextet:
As on July 26, 1944 except Charlie Shavers (tp)
replaces Eldridge.
Rose Room   Jazz Archives JA36

1944
October 10 – New York City
Red Norvo's All Star Septet
Joe Thomas (tp), Vic Dickenson (tb), Hank D'Amico
(cl), Teddy Wilson (p), Red Norvo (vb-1, xyl-2), Slam
Stewart (b), Specs Powell (dr).
HL61-2   Russian Lullaby (2) Keynote(J) 18PJ1060
HL61-2   Russian Lullaby (2)   Keynote K1310
HL62-1   I Got Rhythm (1)   Keynote(J) 18PJ1060
HL62-2   I Got Rhythm (1)   18PJ1060
HL62-3   I Got Rhythm (1)   Keynote K1319
HL63-1   Sing Something Simple (2)
                               Keynote(J) 18PJ1060
HL63-2   Sing Something Simple (2)   18PJ1060
HL63-3   Sing Something Simple (2)   18PJ1060

1944
October 11 – New York City
Benny Goodman Quintet
Benny Goodman (cl), Teddy Wilson (p), Red Norvo (vb), Sid Weiss (b), Morey Feld (dr).

Untitled		V-Disc344
Rose Room		394
Just One Of Those Things		446

1944
October 13 – New York City, CBS *Music Till Midnight* broadcast
Mildred Bailey/Trummy Young, acc. Paul Baron Orchestra
Collective personnel: Billy Butterfield, Roy Eldridge, Chris Griffin, Yank Lawson, Jimmy Maxwell, Charlie Shavers (tp), Will Bradley, Ward Silloway, Trummy Young (tb), Ernie Caceres, Hank D'Amico, Paul Ricci (reeds), Nick Caiazza (ts), unknowns (woodwind), unknowns (strings), Red Norvo (vb), Teddy Wilson (p), Remo Palmieri (g), Al Hall (b), Specs Powell (d), Elaine Vito (harp), Mildred Bailey (vo-1).

I Didn't Know About You (1)	Hindsight HSR133
Tain't Me (1)	AFRS Mildred Bailey #2
I Didn't Know About You (1)	—
More Than You Know (1)	—
I'm Gonna See My Baby (1)	—
I'm Seeing Her Tonight (1)	—
I'm Livin' For Today	—

Teddy Wilson Sextet
Charlie Shavers (tp), Red Norvo (vb), Teddy Wilson (p), Remo Palmieri (g), Billy Taylor (b), Specs Powell (dr).

Sweet Georgia Brown	AFRS Mildred Bailey #2

The first title is from the rehearsal.

1944
October 17 – New York City
Coleman Hawkins Quintet:
Buck Clayton (tp), Coleman Hawkins (ts), Teddy Wilson (p), Slam Stewart (b), Denzil Best (dr).

HL64-1	I'm Yours	Keynote(J) 18PJ1061
HL64-2	I'm Yours	—
HL64-3	I'm Yours	EmArcy MG26011
HL65-1	Under A Blanket Of Blue	Keynote K655
HL66-1	Beyond The Blue Horizon	Keynote(J) 18PJ1061
HL66-2	Beyond The Blue Horizon	EmArcy MG26011
HL66-3	Beyond The Blue Horizon	Keynote K622
HL67-1	A Shanty In Old Shanty Town	Keynote(J) 18PJ1061
HL67-2	A Shanty In Old Shanty Town	—
HL67-4	A Shanty In Old Shanty Town	Keynote K622

1944
October 17 – New York City.
Benny Goodman Quintet
As before.

VP1245	Rachel's Dream	V-Disc 446
VP1271	Let's Fall In Love	V-Disc 475

1944
October 18 – New York City.
Charlie Shavers' All American Five
Charlie Shavers (tp), Coleman Hawkins (ts), Teddy Wilson (p), Billy Taylor (b), Denzil Best (dr).

HL68-1	My Man	Keynote(J) 18PJ1061
HL68-2	My Man	Keynote K619
HL69-1	El Salon De Gutbucket	K619
HL69-2	El Salon De Gutbucket	18PJ1061
HL70-1	Embraceable You	EmArcy MG26011
HL71-1	Undecided	Keynote(J) 18PJ1061
HL71-2	Undecided	—
HL71-3	Undecided	—

1944
October 20 – New York City, CBS *Music Till Midnight* broadcast
Paul Baron Orchestra
As before, Hank D'Amico (cl-1), Coleman Hawkins (ts-2), Mildred Bailey (vo-3).

Hold On, Keep Your Hands On The Plow (3)	V-Disc 328
I'll Walk Alone (3)	AFRS Mildred Bailey Show #3
Evelina (3)	—
Hold On, Keep Your Hands On The Plow (3)	—
Summertime (3)	V-Disc 414
Mad About The Boy (1)	V-Disc 833
Bugle Call Rag	AFRS Mildred Bailey Show #3
Yesterdays (2)	Jazz Panorama JPLP2

Teddy Wilson Sextet
As before.

Stompin' At The Savoy	AFRS Mildred Bailey Show #3

The whole session is on AFRS Mildred Bailey Show #3, except that the title on V-Disc 328 is thought to be from the rehearsal.

1944
October 27 – New York City, CBS *Music Till Midnight* broadcast
Paul Baron Orchestra
Charlie Shavers, Chris Griffin, two unknowns (tp), three unknowns (tb), five unknowns (reeds), unknowns (strings), Red Norvo (vb), Teddy Wilson (p), Remo Palmieri (g), Al Hall (b), Specs Powell (d), Benny Goodman (cl-1)/John Sebastian (hca-2), Mildred Bailey (vo-3).

Somebody Loves Me (3)	AFRS Mildred Bailey Show #4
I'm Making Believe (3)	—
I'll Never Be The Same (3)	—
Tain't Me (3)	—
Four In A Bar	—
Holiday For Strings (2)	—
Henderson Stomp	—

Benny Goodman Quintet
As before.

Rachel's Dream — Opus 2	—

Four In A Bar has been issued commercially on Swing House SWH13.

1944
ʹc. November – New York City.
Teddy Wilson Sextet
*Charlie Shavers (tp), Red Norvo (vb), Teddy Wilson
(p), Remo Palmieri (g), Al Hall (b), Specs Powell (dr).*

Stompin' At The Savoy	Standard Q208
China Boy	—
I'm Confessin'	—
Rose Room	—
After You've Gone	—
How High The Moon	—
I Surrender Dear	—
Whispering	—
I Know That You Know	
Body And Soul	—
Talk Of The Town	Standard Q210
The Sheik Of Araby	—
Dinah	—
Undecided	—
Speculation	—
Sweet Georgia Brown	—
Flying Home	—
Central Avenue Blues	—

This session has been issued commercially on
Vintage Jazz Classics VJC1013-2.

1944
November 3 – New York City, CBS *Music Till
Midnight* broadcast
Mildred Bailey/Stuff Smith, acc. Paul Baron
Orchestra.
As before, Stuff Smith (vn-1), Mildred Bailey (vo-2)

I'll Get By (2)	AFRS Mildred Bailey Show #5
He's Funny That Way (2)	—
St. Louis Blues (2)	—
Right As The Rain	V-Disc 387
Dark Eyes	Swing House(E) SWH13
Reckonin' With Specs	—
Humoresque (1)	AFRS Mildred Bailey Show #5

Teddy Wilson Sextet
As before.

Flyin' Home	—

All titles issued on AFRS Mildred Bailey Show #5.
I'll Get By may not be from this session.

1944
November 10 – New York City, CBS *Music Till
Midnight* broadcast
Paul Baron Orchestra
*As before, Will Bradley (tb-1), Sal Franzella, Jr. (cl-2),
Carl Kress (g-3), Mildred Bailey (vo-4).*

I Never Knew (4)	Hindsight HSR133
Evalina (4)	—
I Never Knew (4)	AFRS Mildred Bailey Show #6
Wish You Were Waitin' For Me (4)	—
Together	—
Evelina	—
What Is This Thing Called Love (2)	—
Oh, Lady Be Good (1)(3)	—
Am I Blue	V-Disc 373

Teddy Wilson Sextet
As before.

How High The Moon	Jazz Archives JA36

The last two titles were also issued on AFRS
Mildred Bailey Show #6. The first two titles are
from the rehearsal.

1944
November 6 – New York City.
Benny Goodman Quintet
As before.

Avalon	AFRS BML P244

1944
November 16 – New York City.
Benny Goodman Quintet
As before, Peggy Mann (vo-1).

33816-	Ev'ry Time We Say Goodbye (1)	
		Phontastic(Sd) NOST7648
33816-1	Ev'ry Time We Say Goodbye (1)	
		Columbia 36767
33817-	After You've Gone	Blu-Disc T1002
33817-	After You've Gone	Meritt 11
33817-1	After You've Gone	AFRS BML P307
33817-2	After You've Gone	Columbia 4-11G
33818-	Only Another Boy And Girl (1)	
		Phontastic(Sd) NOST7648

1944
November 17 – New York City, CBS *Music Till
Midnight* broadcast
Paul Baron Orchestra
*As before, inc, Trummy Young (tb), Bill Coleman (tp-
1), Tony Pastor (ts/vo-2), Mildred Bailey (vo-3).*

I Didn't Know About You (3)	
	AFRS Mildred Bailey Show #7
I'm Confessin' (3)	—
From The Land Of The Sky Blue Water (3)	V-Disc 414
Accentuate The Positive (3	
	AFRS Mildred Bailey Show #7
Toreador Song	—
Russian Lullaby (1)	—
On The Sunny Side Of The Street (2)	—

Teddy Wilson Sextet
As before.

Speculatin'	—

1944
December 8 – New York City, CBS *Music Till
Midnight* broadcast
Paul Baron Orchestra
As before, Ed Hall (cl-1), Mildred Bailey (vo-2).

Sometimes I Feel Like A Motherless Child (2)	
	V-Disc 434
Someday Sweetheart (2)	
	AFRS Mildred Bailey Show #10
Wish You Were Waitin' For Me (2)	—
Accentuate The Positive (2)	—
Sometimes I Feel Like A Motherless Child (2)	—
Besame Mucho (1)	—
Nostalgia	—

Teddy Wilson Sextet
As before.

Sweet Georgia Brown	Fanfare Lp14-114

The last title also was issued on AFRS Mildred

Bailey Show #10. The V-Disc issue is thought to be from a rehearsal.

1944
December 15 – New York City, CBS *Music Till Midnight* broadcast
Mildred Bailey/Delta Rhythm Boys, acc. Paul Baron's Orchestra.
As before, Mildred Bailey (vo-1), Delta Rhythm Boys (vo-2).

Hold On, Keep Your Hands On The Plow (1)	
	AFRS Mildred Bailey Show #11
I Didn't Know About You (1)	—
He's Funny That Way (1)	—
Evelina (1)	—
A Second Breath	—
Stop Calling Me Jo Jo (1)	—

Teddy Wilson Sextet
As before, plus Trummy Young (tb-1), Jimmy Dorsey (cl-1).

I Got Rhythm (1)	Jazz Archives JA36
Dinah	V-Disc 656

The last two titles were also issued on AFRS Mildred Bailey Show #11.

1944
December 21 – New York City
Benny Goodman Quintet
As on November 16, 1944, except Jane Harvey (vo-1) replaces Mann.

34030-1A	Rachel's Dream	Phontastic(Sd) NOST7648
34030-2	Rachel's Dream	Blu-Disc T1002
34031-	Only Another Boy And Girl (1)	—
34031-2	Only Another Boy And Girl (1)	Columbia 36767
34031-5	Only Another Boy And Girl (1)	Fontana(E) TFL5067

1944
prob. December – New York City
Benny Goodman Quintet
As before.

Only Another Boy And Girl (1)	AFRS BML P287

1944
prob. December – New York City
Benny Goodman Quintet
As before.

After You've Gone	
	AFRS Mail Call Series H-1 #117

1944
December 22 – New York City, CBS *Music Till Midnight* broadcast
Mildred Bailey/Count Basie, acc. Paul Baron's Orchestra
As before, Count Basie (p-1), Mildred Bailey (vo-2).

Don't Fence Me In (2)	
	AFRS Mildred Bailey Show #12
More Than You Know (2)	—
Home (2)	—
There'll Be A Jubilee (2)	—

Jingle Bells	—
I Got Rhythm (1)	—

Teddy Wilson Sextet
As before.

Red Bank Boogie	Jazz Archives JA36

The last title was originally issued on AFRS Mildred Bailey Show #12

1944
December 28 – New York City
Teddy Wilson Sextet
As before.

How High The Moon	Columbia unissued
Stompin' At The Savoy	—
After You've Gone	—
I Surrender Dear	—
I'm Confessin'	—
Body And Soul	—
Talk Of The Town	—
I Know That You Know	—
Whispering	—
Rose Room	—
China Boy	—

1944
December 29 – New York City, CBS *Music Till Midnight* broadcast
Mildred Bailey, acc. Paul Baron's Orchestra
As before, Mildred Bailey (vo-1).

Somebody Loves Me (1)	
	AFRS Mildred Bailey Show #13
All Of A Sudden My Heart Sings (1)	—
I'm Confessin' (1)	—
From Rockin' Horse To Rockin' Chair (1)	—
Invitation To A Trance	—

Teddy Wilson Quartet
Cootie Williams (tp), Red Norvo (vb), Teddy Wilson (p), Oscar Pettiford (b).

Tea For Two	Jazz Archives JA36

The last title was originally issued on AFRS Mildred Bailey Show #13.

1945
January 5 – New York City, CBS *Music Till Midnight* broadcast
Mildred Bailey/Tommy Dorsey, acc. Paul Baron's Orchestra
As before, Tommy Dorsey (tb-1), Mildred Bailey (vo-2).

It Had To Be You (2)	Hindsight HSR133
It Had To Be You (2)	Fanfare LP14-114
Sleighride In July (2)	AFRS Mildred Bailey Show #14
Swing Low, Sweet Chariot (2)	—
Which Of The Great 48 (Do You Hail From) (2)	V-Disc 444
Enchantment	AFRS Mildred Bailey Show #14
Summertime	—
Smoke Gets In Your Eyes (1)	—

Teddy Wilson Sextet
Charlie Shavers (t), Red Norvo (vb), Teddy Wilson (p), Tommy Kay (g), Al Hall (b), Specs Powell (dr).

Sheik Of Araby	Fanfare LP14-114

All titles were issued on AFRS Mildred Bailey Show #14, except the first, which is from the rehearsal.

1945
January 8 – New York City
Teddy Wilson Quintet
Charlie Shavers (tp), Teddy Wilson (p) Red Norvo (vb), Billy Taylor (b), Morey Feld (dr), Maxine Sullivan (vo-1).

5234	This Heart Of Mine (1)	
		Musicraft unissued
5235-3	Every Time We Say Goodbye (1)	317
5236-2	Just You Just Me (1)	316
5237-3	Just For You Blues	—

1945
January 12 – New York City, CBS *Music Till Midnight* broadcast
Mildred Bailey, acc. Paul Baron's Orchestra
As before, *Mildred Bailey (vo-1).*

Tain't Me (1)	AFRS Mildred Bailey Show #15
More And More (1)	Sunbeam SB209
Summertime (1)	—
Robin Hood (1)	—
Finiculi, Funicula	—

Teddy Wilson Sextet/Septet
As before, plus Woody Herman (vo/cl-1).

Smiles	AFRS Mildred Bailey Show #15
The Blues (WH-vo)(1)	Sunbeam SB209

All titles were issued on AFRS Mildred Bailey Show #15.

1945
January 15 – New York City
Teddy Wilson Quartet
Charlie Shavers (tp), Teddy Wilson (p), Red Norvo (vb), Al Hall (b), Specs Powell (d), Maxine Sullivan (vo-1).

5234-6	This Heart Of Mine (1)	Musicraft317
5238-3	Bugle Call Rag	318
5239-4	Running Wild	319
5240-2	I Surrender Dear	—
5241-1	Memories Of You	318

1945
January 17 – Philharmonic Auditorium, New York City
Benny Goodman Quintet
Benny Goodman (cl), Teddy Wilson (p), Red Norvo (vb), Sid Weiss (b), Morey Feld (d), Mildred Bailey (vo-1).

Down Hearted Blues (1)	AFRS OWS490
Air Mail Special	—
The World Is Waiting For The Sunrise	—

This session first issued commercially on FDC 1008.

1945
January 19 – New York City, CBS *Music Till Midnight* broadcast
Mildred Bailey, acc. Paul Baron's Orchestra
As before, plus Trummy Young (tb), Mildred Bailey (vo-1).

I'm Beginning To See The Light (1)	
	Sunbeam SB209
I Didn't Know About You (1)	—
He's Funny That Way (1)	—
I'm Gonna See My Baby (1)	
	AFRS Mildred Bailey Show #16
Night Music	—
Trummin' On A Riff	Sunbeam SB209

Teddy Wilson Sextet
As before.

VP-1163	Tiger Rag	V-Disc 424

All titles are on AFRS Mildred Bailey Show #16. The V-Disc issue of the last title and many reissues show the title as *Bugle Call Rag.*

1945
January 26 – New York City, CBS *Music Till Midnight* broadcast
Mildred Bailey/Milt Yaner/Cozy Cole, acc. Paul Baron's Orchestra
As before, Milt Yaner (as-1), Cozy Cole (dr-2), Mildred Bailey (vo-3).

Don't Fence Me In (3)	
	AFRS Mildred Bailey Show #17
Wish You Were Waitin' For Me (3)	—
Sometimes I Feel Like A Motherless Child(3)	—
Evelina(3)	—
Stardust (1)	—
Stompin' At The Savoy (2)	—

Teddy Wilson Sextet
Charlie Shavers (t), Teddy Wilson (p), Tommy Kay (g), Al Hall (b), Specs Powell (dr).

Dinah	Jazum 3

The last title was originally issued on AFRS Mildred Bailey Show #17.

1945
February 2 – New York City, CBS *Music Till Midnight* broadcast.
Mildred Bailey/Stuff Smith, acc. Paul Baron's Orchestra.
As before, Stuff Smith (vn-1), Mildred Bailey (vo-2).

Just Friends	AFRS Mildred Bailey Show #18
I'm Beginning To See The Light (2)	—
The Man I Love (2)	—
I Wish You Were Waitin' For Me	V-Disc 715

Teddy Wilson Sextet
Charlie Shavers (t), Red Norvo (vb), Teddy Wilson (p), Tommy Kay (g), Al Hall (b), Specs Powell (dr).

Just You, Just Me	V-Disc 444

All titles were issued on AFRS Mildred Bailey Show #18.

1945
February 4 – New York City.
Benny Goodman Quintet
Benny Goodman (cl), Red Norvo (vb), Teddy Wilson (p), Mike Bryan (g), Slam Stewart (b), Morey Feld (d), Jane Harvey (vo-1).

33817-	After You've Gone

	Phontastic(Sd) NOST7648	
33817-3	After You've Gone	Columbia 36781
34263-	Slipped Disc	Blu-Disc T1022
34263-2	Slipped Disc	AFRS BML P384
34263-	Slipped Disc	Blu-Disc T1011
34263-	Slipped Disc (breakdown)	
		Blu-Disc T1011
34263-1	Slipped Disc	Columbia 36817
34264-1	Oomph Fah Fah	Columbia 36817
34265-1	She's Funny That Way (1)	
		Columbia 36923
34265-2	She's Funny That Way (1)	
		Columbia(Br) 30-1276
34266-	Body And Soul	
		Phontastic(Sd) NOST7648

Norvo, Bryan and Stewart omitted.

34266-	Body And Soul	
		Phontastic(Sd) NOST7648
34266-1	Body And Soul	Columbia 36781

1945
February 9 – New York City, CBS *Music Till Midnight* broadcast
Mildred Bailey, acc. Paul Baron's Orchestra
As before, Mildred Bailey (vo-1).

The Man I Love	AFRS Mildred Bailey Show #19	
Cabaret		V-Disc 453
Sleighride In July (1)		
	AFRS Mildred Bailey Show #19	
Hold On, Keep Your Hands On The Plow (1)	—	
Old Rockin' Chair (1)		V-Disc 656
Honeysuckle Rose (1)		V-Disc 715
Sweet Lorraine		V-Disc 456

Teddy Wilson Sextet.
As before.

Rose Room		Caracol CAR426

All the above titles were issued on AFRS Mildred Bailey Show #19.

1945
May 7 – New York City.
Benny Goodman Sextet
Benny Goodman (cl), Red Norvo (vb), Teddy Wilson (p), Mike Bryan (g), Slam Stewart (b), Morey Feld (d).

34030-3	Rachel's Dream	
		Phontastic(Sd) NOST7650
34030-4	Rachel's Dream	Columbia 36925
34673-1	Just One Of Those Things	
		Columbia 36924
34673-2	Just One Of Those Things	
		Blu-Disc T1002

1945
May 24 – 400 Restaurant, New York City, Blue Network broadcast
Benny Goodman Sextet
As before.
Benny Goodman Trio
Benny Goodman (cl), Teddy Wilson (p), Morey Feld (d).

After You've Gone (sextet)		unissued
Body And Soul (trio)		unissued

1945

May 29 – 400 Restaurant, New York City, Mutual Network broadcast
Benny Goodman Sextet
As before.

Slipped Disc		Phontastic(Sd) BG01
Just One Of Those Things		Phontastic(Sd) BG01

1945
May/June – 400 Restaurant, New York City, Mutual Network broadcast
Benny Goodman Sextet
As before.

Rachel's Dream		Phontastic(Sd) NOST7605
Oomph Fah Fah		Phontastic(Sd) NOST7605

Note that a number of other recordings by the Benny Goodman Sextet survive from radio broadcasts from this engagement at the 400 Restaurant, New York City, but are as yet unissued.

1945
June 5 – Paramount Theater, New York City, WNEW 'Glenn Miller Day' broadcast
Benny Goodman Sextet
As before.
The World Is Waiting For The Sunrise
Metronome MNR1213

1945
June 6 – New York City
Red Norvo and His Selected Sextet
Dizzy Gillespie (tp), Charlie Parker (as), Flip Phillips (ts), Teddy Wilson (p), Red Norvo (vb), Slam Stewart (b), Specs Powell (dr).

T8-1	Hallelujah	Dial LP903
T8-2	Sing Hallelujah	1045
T8-3	Hallelujah	Comet T6
T9-3	Get Happy	Dial 1043
T9-4	Get Happy	Comet T7

J.C. Heard (dr) replaces Powell.

T10-1	Slam Slam Blues	Dial 1045
T10-2	Slam Slam Blues	Comet T6
T11-l	Congo Blues (ts,vb out) (incomplete)	
		Dial LP903
T11-2	Congo Blues -do	—
T11-3	Congo Blues (incomplete)	—
T11-4	Congo Blues	Dial 1035
T11-5	Congo Blues	Comet T7

1945
June 6 – New York City
Jerry Jerome Trio
Jerry Jerome (ts), Teddy Wilson (p), Specs Powell (dr).

510	Sunday	Stinson 359-3
511	Calling All Cats	359-2
511-B	What Is There To Say	359-1
512	You're Lucky To Me	359-3
513	Emaline	359-1
514	Wrap Your Troubles In Dreams	359-2

1945
June 7 – New York City
Buck Clayton Quintet
Buck Clayton (tp), Flip Phillips (ts), Teddy Wilson (p), Slam Stewart (b), Danny Alvin (dr).

MR105	Diga Diga Doo	Melrose 1201
MR106	Love Me Or Leave Me	—
MR107	We're In The Money	1202
MR108	B.C. Blues (Melrose Blues)	—

c. 1945
New York City?
Teddy Wilson (Sextet?)
No details available.

| Ay, Ay, Ay | Allegro LP1739 |
| Lady Be Good | — |

1945
June 9 – Town Hall, New York City
Red Norvo and His Orchestra
Shorty Rogers (tp), Eddie Bert (tb), Aaron Sachs (cl),
Flip Phillips (ts), Teddy Wilson (p), Red Norvo (vb),
Remo Palmieri (g), Slam Stewart (b), Specs Powell
_(dr)._

A4966	1-2-3-4 Jump	Baronet A47106
A4967	In A Mellotone I+II+III	
		Selson 7219/7220
A4968	The Man I Love	Baronet A47103
A4969	Seven Come Eleven I+II	Disc 6089
A4970	One Note Jive I+II	Baronet A47104
A4971	Ghost Of A Chance (no horns)	A47103

Don Byas And Slam Stewart
Don Byas (ts), Teddy Wilson (p), Remo Palmieri (g),
Slam Stewart (b).

| A4983 | Candy | Commodore FL20009 |

Teddy Wilson Duo
Teddy Wilson (p), Specs Powell (dr).

| A4984 | Where Or When | Selmer Y7085 |
| A4985 | I Know That You Know | — |

Teddy Wilson/Flip Phillips Quintet
Flip Phillips (ts), Remo Palmieri (g), Slam Stewart (b)
added.

A4979	Sweet And Lovely	Selmer Y7149
A4980	I Can't Believe That You're In Love	
	With Me	—

1945
August 14 – Barbizon Plaza Hotel, New York City
Teddy Wilson Sextet
Buck Clayton (tp), Ben Webster (ts), Teddy Wilson
(p), Al Casey (g), Al Hall (b), J.C. Heard (dr).

5296-1	If Dreams Come True	MGM 65055
5296-2	If Dreams Come True	Musicraft 336
5297-1	I Can't Get Started	Musicraft 332
5297-2	I Can't Get Started	MGM EP648
5298-2	Stomping At The Savoy	Musicraft 332
5298-3	Stomping At The Savoy	MGM EP648
5299-3	Blues Too	Musicraft 336

1945
October 6 – New York City.
Teddy Wilson
Teddy Wilson (p), unknown acc.

| Seven Come Eleven | Caracol(F) CAR426 |

1945
November 5 – New York City

Teddy Wilson
Piano solo.

| 5330 | You Go To My Head | Musicraft 341 |

1945/1946
Billy Daniels, acc. by Jerry Jerome Orchestra
Personnel includes Jerry Jerome (ts), Teddy Wilson (p),
Sid Weiss (b), Cozy Cole (dr), Billy Daniels (vo).

	Butterfly	Apollo 1077
	Diane	—
AP3029/M	That Old Black Magic	1101
AP3114	Love's A Lovely Thing	—
	My Yiddische Mamma I	1172
	My Yiddische Mamma II	—
	Charmaine	1188
	Trees	—

1946
January 15 – New York City
Metronome All Stars
Harry Edison, Cootie Williams, Rex Stewart, Pete
Candoli, Neal Hefti, Sonny Berman (tp), Tommy
Dorsey, Will Bradley, Bill Harris, J.C. Higginbotham
(tb), Buddy DeFranco (cl), Johnny Hodges (as), Herbie
Fields, Flip Phillips, George Auld (ts), Harry Carney
(bars), Teddy Wilson (p), Tiny Grimes, Billy Bauer (g),
Chubby Jackson (b), Dave Tough (dr), Sy Oliver (cond).

| D6VC5026 | Look Out | Victor 40-4000 |

Red Norvo (vb) added; Williams, Stewart and Bradley
omitted; Duke Ellington (cond).

| D6VC5027 | Metronome All Out | Victor 40-4000 |

1946
May 1 – New York City
Teddy Wilson
Piano solos.

5461	Cheek To Cheek	Musicraft 369
5462	Sunny Morning	371
5463	Why Shouldn't I	—
5464	Strange Interlude	370

1946
May 2 – New York City
Teddy Wilson
Piano solos.

5476	All Of Me	Musicraft 372
5477	Hallelujah	370
5478	You're My Favorite Memory	369
5479	Long Ago And Far Away	372

1946
August 19 – New York City
Teddy Wilson Octet
Buck Clayton (tp), Scoville Brown (as), Don Byas (ts),
George James (bars) Teddy Wilson (p), Remo Palmieri
(g), Billy Taylor (b), J.C. Heard (dr), Sarah Vaughan
_(vo-1)._

5652	Penthouse Serenade (1)	Musicraft 505
5653	Don't Worry 'Bout Me (1)	421
5654	I Want To Be Happy	—
5655	Just One Of Those Things	MVS2001

1946
Fall – New York City.

Teddy Wilson.
Piano solos.

5734	Fine And Dandy	Musicraft MVS2008
5735	I've Got The World On A String	—
5736	Ain't Misbehavin'	—
5737	You Too Advantage Of Me	—
5743	Living In Dreams	—
5744	I'm Yours	—
	Isn't It Romantic	Musicraft MVS2007
	These Foolish Things	—
	When We're Alone	Musicraft MVS2001

Nothing definite is known about the recording dates of the titles which do not have matrix numbers, except that they were recorded in 1945-47.

1946
November 19 – New York City
Teddy Wilson Quartet:
Charlie Ventura (ts), Teddy Wilson (p), Remo Palmieri (g), Billy Taylor (b), Sarah Vaughan (vo-1).

5809	Time After Time (1)	Musicraft 462
5810	Moon Faced, Starry Eyed (1)	—
5811	September Song (1)	446
5812	Moonlight On The Ganges	—

1946
December 4 – New York City
Esquire All-American Award Winners   .
Charlie Shavers, Buck Clayton (tp), J.J. Johnson (tb), Coleman Hawkins (ts), Harry Carney (bars), Teddy Wilson (p), John Collins (g), Chubby Jackson (b), Shadow Wilson (dr).

D6VB3369-1	Indian Winter	Victor 40-0137
D6VB3370-1	Indian Summer (omit Clayton)	
		40-0136
D6VB3371-1	Blow Me Down	40-0134
D6VB3372-1	Buckin' The Blues	40-0135
D6VB3373-1	Dixieland Stomp (omit Clayton)	
		Camden CAL446

Matrix D6VB3373 issued as by Chubby Jackson and His Jackson-Ville Seven and is titled *Moldy Fig Stomp* on some reissues.

1947
January 13
A Billie Holiday title from this date has been issued as a Teddy Wilson accompaniment, but it is not.

1947
February 25 – New York City
Tommy Dorsey and His Orchestra
Charlie Shavers (t), Tommy Dorsey (tb), Johnny Mince (cl), Boomie Richman (ts), Teddy Wilson (p), Billy Bauer (g), Sid Bloch (b), Alvin Stoller (d), Hannah Williams (vo).

D7VB171	That's Life I Guess	Victor 20-2302
D7VB172	But I Do Mind If Ya Don't	—

1947
Autumn – New York City
Helen Humes acc. by Buck Clayton and His

Orchestra
Buck Clayton (tp), Scoville Brown (cl), Rudy Williams (ts), Teddy Wilson (p), Jimmy Butts (b), probably Denzil Best (dr), Helen Humes (vo).

1641-2	Mad About You	Mercury 8074
1641-3	Mad About You	Verve 525.609
1642-1	Jumpin' On Sugar Hill	Mercury 8077
1643-2	Flippity Flop Flop	Verve 525.609
1643-3	Flippity Flop Flop	Mercury 8074
1644-2	Today I Sing The Blues	Verve 525.609
1644-3	Today I Sing The Blues	Mercury 8077

1947
November 7 – New York City
Benny Goodman Trio
Benny Goodman (cl), Teddy Wilson (p), Jimmy Crawford (dr).

1996	Blue And Broken-Hearted	Capitol 15888
1997	After Hours	Capitol 15888
1998	All I Do Is Dream Of You	T795
1999	I'll Never Be The Same	H343
2500	Bye, Bye, Pretty Baby	15887
2501	Shoe Shine Boy	H/T441

1947
November 16 – New York City, NBC *Fred Allen Show* broadcast
Benny Goodman Trio
As before.

All I Do Is Dream Of You		unissued

1947
November 17 – New York City
Benny Goodman Trio
As before.

2517	At Sundown	Capitol 15888
2518	When You're Smiling	15887
2519	All I Do Is Dream Of You	15886
2520	Stompin' At The Savoy	H343

1947
November 19 – New York City
"Jazz Band"
Canada Lee (narration, vo) with Buck Clayton (tp), Edmond Hall (cl), Teddy Wilson (p), Sid Weiss (b), Jimmy Crawford (dr).

4108	Jazz Band	Young People's Record 410

1947
c. December 1 – New York City.
Teddy Wilson Trio
Teddy Wilson (p), Billy Taylor (b), Keg Purnell (dr).

Chinatown, My Chinatown		Vernon VM505

1947
December 3 – New York City.
Teddy Wilson Quartet
Buck Clayton (tp), Teddy Wilson (p), Billy Taylor (b), Denzil Best (dr)

5998	The Sheik Of Araby	Musicraft 547
	Limehouse Blues	Vernon VM505
	After You've Gone	—
	Georgia On My Mind	—

1947
December 15 & 18 – New York City.
Teddy Wilson Trio
Teddy Wilson (p), Billy Taylor (b), Keg Purnell (dr),
Kay Penton (vo-1).

6006	Whispering	Musicraft 580
6026	Something I Dreamed Last Night (1)	
		547
6027	As Time Goes By (1)	580
	Bess, You Is My Woman	Vernon VM505
	Just Like A Butterfly	—

1948
May 24 – Click Restaurant, Philadelphia, NBC
broadcast
Benny Goodman Septet
Benny Goodman, Stan Hasselgard (cl), Wardell Gray
(ts), Teddy Wilson (p), Billy Bauer (g), Arnold Fishkind
(b), Mel Zelnick (d), Patti Page (vo-1).

Stompin' At The Savoy	unissued
Limehouse Blues	—
Body And Soul (trio: BG/TW/MZ only)	—
On The Sunny Side Of The Street (1)	—
Cookin' One Up	Dragon(Sd) DRLP16
Poor Butterfly (quintet: BG/TW/BB/AF/MZ	
only)	unissued
After You've Gone	—
Good-Bye	—

1948
May 27 – Click Restaurant, Philadelphia, NBC
broadcast
Benny Goodman Septet
As before.

Swedish Pastry	Dragon(Sd) DRLP16
All The Things You Are	
You Turned The Tables On Me (1)	unissued
Where Or When (trio: BG/TW/MZ only)	—
The World Is Waiting For The Sunrise	
(quartet: +AF)	—
The Man I Love (1)	—
Mary's Idea	Dragon(Sd) DRLP16
Don't Blame Me (1)	unissued
Good-Bye	—

1948
May 28 – Click Restaurant, Philadelphia, NBC
broadcast
Benny Goodman Septet
As before.

Swedish Pastry	Dragon(Sd) DRLP16
There's A Small Hotel (trio: BG/TW/MZ only)	
	unissued
On The Sunny Side Of The Street (PP-vo)	—
Body And Soul (trio: BG/TW/MZ only)	—
The World Is Waiting For The Sunrise	
(quartet: trio + AF)	—
It Had To Be You (PP-vo)	—
After You've Gone	Swedisc(J) 25-9016
Good-Bye	unissued

1948
May 29 – Click Restaurant, Philadelphia, NBC
broadcast

Benny Goodman Septet
As before.

Bye, Bye, Pretty Baby	Dragon(Sd) DRLP16
I'm In The Mood For Love (PP-vo)	unissued
Mary's Idea	Dragon(Sd) DRLP16
Just One Of Those Things (quintet: as before)	
	unissued
Mel's Idea	—

1948
June 1 – Click Restaurant, Philadelphia, NBC
broadcast
Benny Goodman Septet
As before.

Mary's Idea	Swedisc(J) 25-9016
If I Had You (1; trio: BG/TW/MZ only)	
	unissued
Indiana	—
Poor Butterfly (quartet: as before)	—
Don't Blame Me (1)	—
Bye Bye Blues	Dragon(Sd) DRLP16

1948
June 3 – Click Restaurant, Philadelphia
Benny Goodman Septet
As before.

Limehouse Blues	AFRS 1722
The Man I Love (1)	—
Back Home In Indiana	—
Confess (1)	—
Bye Bye Blues	—
Little White Lies (1)	—
Mel's Idea	—
Body And Soul (BG/TW/MZ only)	—

All titles from this session issued commercially on
Donna K0S1100.

late 1940s – New York City, broadcast
Teddy Wilson
Unknown studio orchestra with prob. Buck Clayton
(tp), Teddy Wilson (p).

The Sheik Of Araby	
	Vintage Jazz Classics VJC1013-2
I Want To Be Happy	—

early 1950s – New York City
Teddy Wilson
Piano solos.

Indiana	Eshron 1234
Say It Isn't So	—
Just One Of Those Things	—
But Not For Me	—
Our Love Is Here To Stay	—
Liza	—

1950
June 29 – New York City
Teddy Wilson Trio
Teddy Wilson (p), Arvell Shaw (b), J.C. Heard (dr).

44033	Just One Of Those Things	
		Columbia CL6153
44034	Just Like A Butterfly	—
44035	Runnin ' Wild	—
44036	I 've Got The World On A String	—

44037	Fine And Dandy	—
44038	Ghost Of A Chance	—
44039	Honeysuckle Rose	—

1950
August 25 – New York City
Teddy Wilson Trio
Teddy Wilson (p), Al McKibbon (b), Carl Fields (dr).

44273	Between The Devil And The Deep Blue Sea	Columbia CL6 153
44274	Bess You Is My Woman Now	—
44275	I Can't Give You Anything But Love	—
44276	After You've Gone	—

1950
September/October
A number of *Dumont Star Time* and other TV broadcasts by the Sextet which recorded on October 10 are known to survive, but none has been issued as far as is known.

1950
October 10 – New York City
Benny Goodman and His Sextet
Benny Goodman (cl), Teddy Wilson (p), Terry Gibbs (vb), Johnny Smith (g), Bob Carter (b), Terry Snyder (dr), Rickey (Jimmy Ricks) (vo-1), Nancy Reed (vo-2).

44431	Oh Babe (1, 2)	Columbia 39045
44432	You're Gonna Lose Your Gal	Harmony HL7278
44433	Walkin' With The Blues (1)	Columbia 39045

1950
October 25 – New York City
Leroy Holmes and His Orchestra
Doc Severinsen, Art Depew, Charlie Shavers (tp), Will Bradley, George Arus, Phil Giardina (tb), Hymie Schertzer, Al Klink (as), Babe Fresk, Boomie Richman (ts), Sol Schlinger (bars), Teddy Wilson (p), Carmen Mastren (g), Bob Carter (b), Buzzy Drootin (dr), The Starlings (vo-1).

50-S-342	Lyin' In The Hay	MGM 10892, 356
50-S-343	Oh, Babe (1)	356
	In Your Arms (1)	10892
	Billboard March	unissued

1950
October 26 – New York City
Anita O'Day acc. by Jack Pleis Orchestra
As Leroy Holmes and His Orchestra on October 25, 1950, except Billy Mure (g) replaces Mastren, Anita O'Day (vo).

50580	Tennessee Waltz	London 867
50581	Yeah Boo	—
	Something I Dreamed Last Night	879
	If I Could Be With You	—

1950
November 24 – New York City
Benny Goodman and His Sextet
As on October 10, 1950, except Charles Smith (dr) replaces Snyder.

| C44674 | Lullaby Of The Leaves | Columbia 39121 |
| C44675 | Then You've Never Been Blue | Harmony HL7278 |

| C44676 | Walkin' | — |
| C44677 | Temptation Rag | Columbia 39121 |

1951
April 1 – New York City, WNEW broadcast
Benny Goodman Trio Plays For Fletcher Henderson
Benny Goodman (cl), Teddy Wilson (p), Gene Krupa (dr) with: Eddie Safranski (b-1), Johnny Smith (g-2), Lou McGarity (tb-3), Buck Clayton (tp-4).

China Boy	Columbia MB1000
Body And Soul	—
Runnin' Wild	—
On The Sunny Side Of The Street (1)	—
After You've Gone (1, 2)	—
Basin Street Blues (1, 2, 3)	—
Rose Room	—
Honeysuckle Rose (1, 2, 4)	—
I Found A New Baby	—
One O'Clock Jump (1, 2, 3, 4)	—

1952
March 25 – New York City
Charlie Parker Quartet
Charlie Parker (as), Teddy Wilson (p), Eddie Safranski (b), Don Lamond (d).

| Cool Blues | Royal Jazz RJD505 |

1952
July 29 – New York City
The New Benny Goodman Sextet
Benny Goodman (cl), Teddy Wilson (p), Terry Gibbs (vb), Mundell Lowe (g), Sid Weiss (b), Terry Snyder (dr).

48131	I've Got A Feeling I'm Falling	Columbia CL552
48132	Bye Bye Blues	—
48133	I'll Never Be The Same	—
48134	Between The Devil And The Deep Blue Sea	—

1952
July 30 – New York City
The New Benny Goodman Sextet
As before, except Don Lamond (dr) replaces Snyder.

48135	Under A Blanket Of Blue	Columbia CL552
48136	East Of The Sun	unissued
48137	Four Or Five Times	—
48138	How Am I To Know?	Columbia CL552
48139	Undecided	—
48140	unknown title	unissued

1952
October 6 – Stockholm
Teddy Wilson Trio
Teddy Wilson (p), Yngve Akerberg (b), Jack Norén (dr).

390	You're Mine, You	Metronome BLP26
391-A	I Got Rhythm	—
392	Someone To Watch Over Me	—
393	Indiana	—
394-A	Time On My Hands	—
395-A	Sweet Georgia Brown	—

396-A	I Can' t Get Started	—
397	Takin' A Chance On Love	—

1952
December 16 – New York City
Teddy Wilson Trio
Teddy Wilson (p), John Simmons (b), Buddy Rich (dr).

985-1	The One I Love	Clef MGC140
986-1	Darn That Dream (2:13)	—
986-4	Darn That Dream (2:50)	unissued
987-4	Tea For Two	Clef MGC140
988-3	Lady Be Good	—

1953
April 13 – New York City
Teddy Wilson Trio
Teddy Wilson (p), Aaron Bell (b), Denzil Best (dr).

1200-4	Emaline	Clef MGC140
1201-2	Tenderly	—
1202-5	Everything Happens To Me	—
120S-1	Liza	—

1953
May 7 – New York City
Gene Krupa Sextet
Charlie Shavers (tp), Willie Smith (as), Teddy Wilson (p), Steve Jordan (g), Israel Crosby (b), Gene Krupa (dr).

1204-3	Capital Idea	Clef MGC703
1205-4	Coronation Hop	MGC687
1206-5	Paradise	MGC703
1207-11	Overtime	MGC687

1953
July 9 – New York City
Metronome All Stars
Roy Eldridge (tp), Kai Winding (tb), John LaPorta (cl), Warne Marsh , Lester Young (ts), Teddy Wilson (p), Terry Gibbs (vb), Billy Bauer (g), Eddie Safranski (b), Max Roach (dr), Billy Eckstine (vo).

53S507	How High The Moon part I	
		MGM X1078
53S508	How High The Moon part II	—
53S509	St. Louis Blues part I	—
53S510	St. Louis Blues part II	—

1953
September 4 – New York City
Teddy Wilson Trio
Teddy Wilson (p), Arvell Shaw (b), J.C. Heard (dr).

1296-5	Nice Work If You Can Get It	
		Clef MGC156
1297-1	Air Mail Special	—
1298-3	Night And Day	—
1299-1	Cheek To Cheek	—

1953
September 8 – New York City
Teddy Wilson Trio
As before.

1304-5	East Of The Sun	ClefMGC156
1305-14	Autumn In New York	—
1306-2	Isn't It Romantic?	—

1307-1	You Go To My Head (omit b+dr)	—

1953
September 10 – New York City
Gene Krupa Sextet
Charlie Shavers (tp), Bill Harris (tb), Ben Webster (ts), Teddy Wilson (p), Herb Ellis (g), Ray Brown (b), Gene Krupa (dr).

1308-1	Imagination	Clef MGC687
1309-1	Don't Take Your Love Away From Me	—
1310-5	Midgets	—
1311-3	I'm Coming Virginia	—
1312-3	Payin' Them Dues Blues	—
1313-3	Jungle Drums	—
1314-2	Showcase	—
1315-5	Swedish Schnapps	—

1954
February 2 – New York City
Gene Krupa Sextet
Charlie Shavers (tp), Bill Harris (tb) Eddie Davis (ts), Teddy Wilson (p), Ray Brown (p), Gene Krupa (dr).

1506-2	Bloozy Woozy	Clef MGC631
1507-4	Windy	—
1508-2	Meddle My Minor	—
1509-4	Who's Rhythm	—
1510	unknown title	unissued
1511-3	Ballad Medley: Dancing In The Dark	
		Clef MGC631
	The Nearness Of You	—
	You Are Too Beautiful	—
	Tenderly	—
	Autumn In New York	—
1512-1	Second Helping Blues	—

1954
March 30 – New York City
Ben Webster Quartet
Ben Webster (ts), Teddy Wilson (p), Ray Brown (b), Jo Jones (dr).

1527-1	Love's Away	Clef MGN1018
1528-4	You're Mine You	—
1529-1	My Funny Valentine	—
1530-5	Sophisticated Lady	—

1954
June 3 – New York City
Teddy Wilson Trio
Teddy Wilson (p), Milt Hinton (b), Sticks Evans (dr).

1741-3	Unforgettable	Clef unissued
1742-1	Almost Like Being In Love	—
1743-2	Lover	—
1744-2	If Dreams Come True	—
1745-2	Don't Be That Way	—
1746-1	Stompin' At The Savoy	—
1747-1	Love Is Here To Stay	—
1748-1	Sweet And Lovely	—

1954
September 20 – New York City
Benny Carter Trio

Benny Carter (as), Teddy Wilson (p), Jo Jones (dr).

1988-5	Little Girl Blue	Verve(J) 25J25156
1989-4	June In January	—
1990-2	Jeepers Creepers	—
1991-2	Rosetta	—
1992-1	Birth Of The Blues	—
1993-3	When Your Lover Has Gone	—
1994-1	The Moon Is Low	—
1995-3	This Love Of Mine	—

1954

December 15 – New York City
Ben Webster with Ralph Burns' Orchestra
Ben Webster (ts), Jimmy Hamilton (cl), Danny Bank (bars), Teddy Wilson (p), Wendell Marshall (b), Louis Bellson (dr), strings, Ralph Burns (arr, cond).

2134-5	Do Nothin ' Till You Hear From Me	
		Norgran EPN98
2135-3	Prelude To A Kiss	—
2136-5	Willow Weep For Me	MGN1039
2137-2	Come Rain Or Come Shine	EPN98

? 1955

unknown date – New York City, CBS *Teddy Wilson Show* broadcast
Teddy Wilson Trio with Coleman Hawkins and Buck Clayton
Dizzy Gillespie (tp-1), Coleman Hawkins (ts-2), Teddy Wilson (p), Milt Hinton (b), Jo Jones (dr).

Lover Come Back To Me (2)		Shoestring SS107
How High The Moon (1)(2)		—

1955

January 1 – New York City
Teddy Wilson Trio
Teddy Wilson (p), Milt Hinton (b), Jo Jones (dr).

2231-1	Blues For The Oldest Profession	
		Norgran MGN1019
2235-1	It Had To Be You	
2233-1	You Took Advantage Of Me	—
2234-1	Three Little Words	—
2235-1	If I Had You	—
2236-1	Who's Sorry Now	—
2237-1	Birth Of The Blues	—
2238-1	When Your Lover Has Gone	—
2239-1	Moonlight On The Ganges	—
2240-3	April In Paris	—
2241-1	Hallelujah	—
2242-1	Get Out Of Town	—

1955

February 3 – New York City.
Ben Webster and Teddy Wilson
Ben Webster (ts), Teddy Wilson (p), unknown strings and rhythm.

2250-1	Some Other Spring	Verve (J) J28J25091
2251-1	When Your Lover Has Gone	—
2252-3	Stars Fell On Alabama	—
2253-3	Under A Blanket Of Blue	—

1955

March 25 & 26 – Basin Street Club, New York City

Benny Goodman Octet
Ruby Braff (tp), Urbie Green (tb), Benny Goodman (cl), Paul Quinichette (ts), Teddy Wilson (p), Perry Lopez (g), Milt Hinton (b), Bobby Donaldson (dr).

Don't Be That Way	Philips 6379 001
Rose Room (1)	—
Between The Devil And The Deep Blue Sea	—
Body And Soul (1)	—
After You've Gone	—
Slipped Disc	—
On The Alamo	—
Just One Of Those Things (1)	—
Blue And Sentimenal	—
Airmail Special	—
I Found A New Baby (1)	Philips 6379 002
As Long As I Live	—
Flying Home	—
'Deed I Do	—
Avalon	—
Memories Of You	—
Stompin' At The Savoy	—
If I Had You	—
Sing, Sing, Sing	—
Lady Be Good (1)	Philips 6379 003
Stairway To The Stars	—
Honeysuckle Rose	—
Nice Work If You Can Get It	—
Rosetta	—
Mean To Me	—
S-h-i-n-e	—
Night And Day	—
One O'Clock Jump	—
Goodbye	—
Let's Dance	Musicmasters CIJ20156F
Honeysuckle Rose	—
Runnin' Wild	—
Mean To Me	—
Memories Of You	—
Stompin' At The Savoy	—
Blue And Sentimental	—
One O'Clock Jump	—
I Found A New Baby	—
Stairway To The Stars	—
Body And Soul	—
Air Mail Special	—
Nice Work If You Can Get It	—
Sing, Sing, Sing	—
Goodbye	—
(1): omit tp/tb/ts.	

1955

April – New York City, CBS *Teddy Wilson Show* broadcast
Teddy Wilson Trio with Coleman Hawkins and Buck Clayton
Buck Clayton (tp-1), Coleman Hawkins (ts-2), Teddy Wilson (p), Milt Hinton (b), Jo Jones (dr).

Sunny Morning	AFRS Teddy Wilson #7
Just One Of Those Things	—
Confessin' (1)(2)	—
Body And Soul (2)	—
One O'Clock Jump (1)(2)	—
Sunny Morning	—

The third, fourth and fifth titles were issued commercially on Shoestring SS107.

Content of other AFRS Teddy Wilson transcriptions is not known.

1955
July 31 – Los Angeles
Lionel Hampton - Gene Krupa - Teddy Wilson
Lionel Hampton (vb), Teddy Wilson (p), Red Callender (b), Gene Krupa (dr).

2360-4	Avalon	Clef MGC681
2361-6	I Got Rhythm	—
2362-4	Moonglow (5:54)	
2362-7	Moonglow (3.23)	Clef 89166
2363-2	Blues For Benny (7.38)	MGC681
2363-3	Blues For Benny (3.15)	89166
2364-4	Just You Just Me	MGC681
2365-1	The Man I Love	Verve MGV82 15
2366-2	Airmail Special	Clef MGC681
2367-4	Body And Soul	Columbia(E) SEB10086

1955
August – Hollywood
Benny Goodman and His Orchestra
Buck Clayton, Chris Griffin, John Best, Conrad Gozzo, Irving Goodman, Ray Linn (tp), Murray McEachern, Urbie Green, Jimmy Priddy (tb), Benny Goodman (cl), Hymie Schertzer, Blake Reynolds (as), Babe Russin, Stan Getz (ts), Teddy Wilson (p), Allen Reuss (g), George Duvivier (b), Gene Krupa (dr), Martha Tilton (vo-7).

89016	Let's Dance	Decca DL8252
89017	Down South Camp Meeting	—
89018	King Porter Stomp	—
89019	It's Been So Long	—
89020	Roll 'Em	—
89021	Bugle Call Rag	—
89022	Don't Be That Way	—
89023	You Turned The Tables On Me (7)	—
89024	Goody Goody	—
89025	Slipped Disc (1)	—
89026	Stompin' At The Savoy	—
89027	One O'Clock Jump	—
89028	Memories Of You (2)	Decca DL8253
89029	China Boy (2)	—
89030	Moonglow (3)	—
89031	Avalon (3)	—
89032	And The Angels Sing (4, 7)	—
89033	Jersey Bounce	—
89034	Sometimes I'm Happy	—
89035	Shine (5)	—
89036	Sing Sing Sing (5)	—
	Sing, Sing, Sing (With A Swing)(5)	
		Universal-International 78189
	Oh, Lady Be Good (2)	
		Universal-International unissued
	Body And Soul (2)	—
	Honeysuckle Rose (1)	—
	On The Sunny Side Of The Street (1)	—
	Memories Of You	
	Sensation Rag (1)(6)	
	Film ST 'Benny Goodman Story'	

*(1) Octet:Clayton/Green/Goodman/Getz/Wilson/
Reuss/Duvivier/Krupa.*
(2) Trio: Goodman/Wilson/Krupa.

(3) Quartet: As trio with Lionel Hampton (vb).
(4) Add Manny Klein (tp).
(5) Add Harry James (tp).
(6) Stan Getz out.

1955
December 14 – New York City, NBC TV *Tonight* telecast
Benny Goodman Sextet
Buck Clayton (tp), Urbie Green (tb), Benny Goodman (cl), Teddy Wilson (p), poss. George Duvivier (b), Don Lamond (dr).

Honeysuckle Rose	Giants Of Jazz GOJ1010
Memories Of You	Unissued

Doc Severinsen (tp), Lou McGarity (tb), Sol Yaged (cl), Sid Caesar (ts), added.

One O'Clock Jump	Unissued
Stompin' At The Savoy	Unissued

1956
January 12 – New York City
The Jazz Giants
Roy Eldridge (tp), Vic Dickenson (tb), Lester Young (ts), Teddy Wilson (p), Freddie Green (g), Gene Ramey (b), Jo Jones (dr).

2646-2	I Guess I'll Have To Change My Plans	
		Norgran MGN1056
2647-2	I Didn't Know What Time It Was	—
2648-4	Gigantic Blues	—
2649-2	This Year's Kisses	—
2650-2	You Can Depend On Me	—

1956
January 13 – New York City
Lester Young - Teddy Wilson
Lester Young (ts), Teddy Wilson (p), Gene Ramey (b), Jo Jones (dr).

2657-1	Pres Returns	Verve MGV8308
2658-1	Prisoner Of Love	Verve MGV8205
2659-1	Taking A Chance On Love	—
2660-1	All Of Me	—
2661-1	Louise	—
2662-2	Our Love Is Here To Stay	—
2663-1	Love Me Or Leave Me	—

1956
March 5 – Chicago
Teddy Wilson Trio
Teddy Wilson (p), Gene Ramey (b), Jo Jones (dr).

20104-1	Savoy	Verve MGV2073
20105-3	Say It Isn't So	—
20106-1	All Of Me	—
20107-2	Stars Fell On Alabama	—
20108-4	I Got Rhythm	—
	I Got Rhythm (alt. take)	
		GNP-Crescendo GNP9014
20109-1	Sunny Side Of The Street	—
20110-1	Sweet Georgia Brown	—
20111-1	As Time Goes By	—
20112-1	Smiles	—
20113-1	When Your Lover Has Gone	—
20114-1	Limehouse Blues	—
20115-1	Blues For Daryl	Verve MGV2073
20116-1	You're Driving Me Crazy	—

1956
September 13 – New York City
Teddy Wilson Trio
Teddy Wilson (p), Al Lucas (b), Jo Jones (dr).

3100-2	I Want To Be Happy	Verve MGV8272
3101-1	Ain't Misbehavin'	—
3102-2	Honeysuckle Rose	—
3103-2	Fine And Dandy	—
3104-3	Sweet Lorraine	—
3105-2	I Found A New Baby	—
3106-1	It's The Talk Of The Town	—
3107-1	Laura	—
3108-1	Undecided	—
3109-3	Time On My Hands	—
3110-2	Who Cares?	—
3111-1	Our Love Is Here To Stay	—
3112-3	When You're Smiling	Verve MGV8299
3113-1	Imagination	—
3114-1	The World Is Waiting For The Sunrise	—
3115-6	I've Got The World On A String	—
3116-3	Whispering	—
3117-1	Poor Butterfly	—
3118-1	Rosetta	—
3119-1	Basin Street Blues	—
3120-1	How Deep Is The Ocean?	—
3121-1	Just One Of Those Things	—
3122-2	Have You Met Miss Jones	—
3123-1	It Don't Mean A Thing	—

1957
July 6 – Newport Jazz Festival, Newport, R.I.
Teddy Wilson Trio
Teddy Wilson (p), Milt Hinton (b), Specs Powell (d).

Stompin' At The Savoy	Verve MGV8235
Airmail Special	—
Basin Street Blues	—
I Got Rhythm	—

1957
August 12 – New York City
Teddy Wilson Trio
Teddy Wilson (p), Arvell Shaw (b), Roy Burness (d).

21241-8	Avalon	Verve MGV8330
21242-2	The Little Things That Mean So Much	—
21243-2	'S Wonderful	—
21244-3	Someone To Watch Over Me	—
21245-2	Jeepers Creepers	—
21246-2	Rubinstein Medley	—
21247-2	Bye Bye Blues	—
21248-5	Sunny Morning	—
21249-1	Talking To The Moon	—
21250-1	Dream House	—
21251-1	Sometimes I'm Happy	—
21252-5	That Old Feeling	—

1957
October 7 – New York City
Teddy Wilson with Joe Lippman's Orchestra
Teddy Wilson (p), unknown large orchestra inc. strings.

21492	Little Things	Verve unissued
21493	Running World	—
21494	Sayonara	Verve 10110
21495	Sands Of Time	—

1958
July 5 – Newport Jazz Festival, Newport, R.I.
Teddy Wilson Trio
Teddy Wilson (p), Johnny Williams (b), Bert Dahlander (dr).

Stompin' At The Savoy	Columbia C2-38262
Flying Home	unissued
Birth Of The Blues	—
Airmail Special	—

1959
January 19 – New York City.
Teddy Wilson Trio
Teddy Wilson (p), Al Lucas (b), Bert Dahlander (dr).

62085	Somebody Loves Me	Columbia CL1318
62086	But Not For Me	—
62087	I've Got A Crush On You	—
62088	Liza	—
62089	Embraceable You	—
62090	Our Love Is Here To Stay	—
62091	The Man I Love	—

1959
early May – New York City.
Teddy Wilson Trio
Teddy Wilson (p), Arvell Shaw (b), Bert Dahlander (dr).

63185	All I Need	Columbia CL1352
63186	Some People	—
63187	Everything's Coming Up Roses	—
63188	Mama's Talking Soft	—
63189	It's A Small World	—

1959
May 10 – New York City.
Teddy Wilson Trio
As before.

63294	You'll Never Get Away	Columbia CL1352
63295	Together	—
63296	Little Lamp	—
63297	Mr. Goldstone I Love You	—
63298	Cow Song/Let Me Entertain You	—
63299	If Mama Was Married	—

circa **1959**
U.S.A.
Teddy Wilson and His Trio
As before.

Rose Room	Egmont AJS19
Just One Of Those Things	—
Shiny Stockings	—
Body And Soul	—
Sweet Lorraine	—
Moonglow	—
But Not For Me	—
Nice Work If You Can Get It	—
It Had To Be You	—
Someone To Watch Over Me	—

These items are a composite selection of recordings made during a tour, for Teddy Wilson's private use.

1959
December 3 – New York City
Teddy Wilson Trio
Teddy Wilson (p), Major Holley (b), Bert Dale (dr).
64452   Honeysuckle Rose   Columbia unissued
64453   Misty   —
64454   Rosetta   Columbia CL1442
64455   One O ' Clock Jump   —
64456   Sunny Morning   —
64457   'Round Midnight   —

1959
December 11 – New York City
Teddy Wilson Trio
As before.
64452   Honeysuckle Rose   Columbia CL1442
64453   Misty   —
64458   The Duke   —
64459   Artistry In Rhythm   —

1959
December 12 – New York City
Teddy Wilson Trio
As before.
64460   King Porter Stomp   Columbia CL1442
64461   Sophisticated Lady   —
64462   Lullaby Of Birdland   —
64463   If I Could Be With You   —

1961
October 27 – New York City, NBC *The Bell
Telephone Hour* telecast
Benny Goodman Trio
*Benny Goodman (cl), Teddy Wilson (p), Gene Krupa
(dr).*
Avalon   Rarities(Da) No. 30
Body And Soul   —
China Boy   —
Poor Butterfly   —
I Can't Give You Anything But Love   —
The Sheik Of Araby   —

1962
between July 1 and 8 – Moscow
Benny Goodman and His Orchestra
*Joe Newman, Joe Wilder, Jimmy Maxwell, John Frosk
(tp), Wayne Andre, Willy Dennis, Jimmy Knepper (tb),
Benny Goodman (cl), Phil Woods, Jerry Dodgion (as),
Zoot Sims, Tom Newsome (ts), Gene Allen (bars), Vic
Feldman (vb), John Bunch, Teddy Wilson (p), Turk Van
Lake (g), Bill Crow (b), Mel Lewis (dr).*
Meet The Band   RCA-Victor LSO/LOC6008-1

1962
between July 1 and 8 – Moscow
Benny Goodman Quintet /Septet /Octet
*Benny Goodman (cl), Teddy Wilson (p), Turk Van Lake
(g), Bill Crow (b), Mel Lewis (dr).*
Medley:
Avalon   RCA-Victor LSO/LOC6008-1
Body And Soul   —
Rose Room   —

The World Is Waiting For The Sunrise   —
*Joe Newman (tp), Zoot Sims (ts), Vic Feldman (vb)
added.*
On The Alamo   RCA-Victor LSO/LOC6008-2
Midgets   —

1963
February 13 – New York City
Benny Goodman Quartet
*Benny Goodman (cl), Teddy Wilson (p), Lionel
Hampton (vb), Gene Krupa (dr).*
K4PM6068 Who Cares? RCA-Victor LPM(S)2698
            Together   unissued
            September Song   —
            Just One Of Those Things   —
            Love Sends A Little Gift Of Roses —

1963
February 14 – New York City
Benny Goodman Quartet
As before.
K4PM6071 Dearest   RCA-Victor LPM(S)2698
            Love Sends A Little Gift Of Roses
                                  unissued
            Oh Gee, Oh Joy   —
            Bernie's Tune   —
            East Of The Sun   —

1963
August 26 – New York City
Benny Goodman Quartet
As before.
P4PM6064 Seven Come Eleven
                       RCA-Victor LPM(S)2698
P4PM6066 I've Found A New Baby   —
P4PM6067 Somebody Loves Me   —
P4PM6070 I'll Get By   —
            But Not For Me   unissued
            It's Allright With Me —
            It Had To Be You   —

1963
August 27 – New York City
Benny Goodman Quartet
As before.
P4PM6065 Say, It Isn't So!
                       RCA-Victor LPM (S)2698
P4PM6069 Runnin' Wild   —
P4PM6072 I Got It Bad And That Ain't Good —
P4PM6073 Four Once More   —
            Soft Light And Sweet Music unissued
            Nice Work If You Can Get It   —
            From This Moment On   —
            Liza   —
            If Dreams Come True   —

1963
September – New York City
Teddy Wilson acc. by Glen Osser's Orchestra
*Teddy Wilson (p) with large orchestra including
strings.*
Satin Doll   Cameo-Parkway C(S)1059A
A Second Chance   —
Nica's Dream   —

As Time Goes By —
Basin Street Blues —
Love Is A Many Splendored Thing —
Big Town —
Sidney's Soliloquy —
Strollin' —
How High The Moon —
Paris Theme —
Everything I Have Is Yours —

1966
July 3 – Newport, R.I.
Newport Jazz Festival All Stars
Teddy Wilson (p), Gene Taylor (b), Buddy Rich (dr).
Nice Work If You Can Get It
     Jazz Band(E) EBCD2120-2
Shiny Stockings —
Someone To Watch Over Me —
Somebody Loves Me —
Clark Terry (tp, vo-1) added.
Bye Bye Blackbird —
I Want A Little Girl (1) —
Mumbles (1) —

1967
June 18 – London
Teddy Wilson Quintet/Trio
Dave Shepherd (cl-1), Teddy Wilson (p), Ronnie Gleaves (vb), Peter Chapman (b), Johnny Richardson (dr).
Stompin' At The Savoy Black Lion BLP30114
I Can't Get Started —
Sometimes I'm Happy (1) —
Body And Soul —
I'll Never Be The Same (1) —
Easy Livin' —
Green Dolphin Street —
Honeysuckle Rose (1) —
Avalon   BLP20130
Honeysuckle Rose (alt.take?)(1) BLP30133
Flying Home —
Poor Butterfly —
Air Mail Special —
Omit Shepherd & Gleaves.
Moonglow   BLP30133
Ain't Misbehavin' —
Piano-solos.
As Time Goes By   BLP30133
I'm Thru With Love —

1968
March – London
Teddy Wilson
Piano solos.
Stella By Starlight Polydor 2310 060
Laura —
The Second Time Around —
Li'l Darlin —
Peter Chapman (b), Johnny Richardson (dr) added.
Love   Polydor 2310 060
Take The 'A' Train —
Dave Shepherd (cl), Ronnie Gleaves (vb) added.
Air Mail Special Polydor 2310 060
Seven Come Eleven —

Avalon —

1967
October 23 – Stuttgart, Germany
Don Byas – Teddy Wilson
Don Byas (ts), Teddy Wilson (p), Peter Trunk (b), Cees See (dr).
Stompin' At The Savoy Moon(It) MLP018-1/2
Fine And Dandy —
Medley: Tenderly/Don't Blame Me/Tenderly —

1968
December 12 – Copenhagen
Teddy Wilson Trio
Teddy Wilson (p), Niels-Henning Ørsted Pedersen (b), Bjarne Rostvold (dr).
My Silent Love Metronome(Sd) MLP15328
You Brought A New Kind Of Love —
Paradise —
My Heart Stood Still —
Serenata —
Indiana —
April In Paris —
'Deed I Do —
Autumn In New York —
Ain't Misbehavin' —
Serenade In Blue —
It's All Right With Me —

1968
December 14 – Copenhagen
Inez Cavanaugh with Teddy Wilson
As on December 12, 1968, Inez Cavanaugh (vo).
I've Got A Feelin' Sonet SLPS1005
I'll Never Be The Same —
You're Blase —
I Hadn't Anyone Till You —
You Gotta See Mama Every Night —
The Little Things That Mean So Much —
Easy Living —
If I Had You —
Is This To Be My Souvenir —
I Want Something To Live For —
Prelude To A Kiss —
Time On My Hands —
How Deep Is The Ocean —
When You're Smiling —

1969
March – London
JATP All Stars
Dizzy Gillespie, Clark Terry (t), Zoot Sims (ts), James Moody (ts, fl), Teddy Wilson (p), Bob Cranshaw (b), Louis Bellson (d).
Woman You Must Be Crazy Pablo Live 2620.119
Goin' To Chicago Blues —
Stormy Monday Blues —
Teddy Wilson Trio *(Wilson, Cranshaw, Bellson).*
Shiny Stockings —
Undecided —
I've Got The World On A String —
L.O.V.E —
JATP All Stars
Benny Carter (as), Coleman Hawkins (ts), Teddy

Wilson (p), Bob Cranshaw (b), Louis Bellson (d).
Blue Lou   —
I Can't Get Started   —
Body And Soul   —
Bean Stalkin'   —

1969
June – Jazz Festival, Ljubljana, Slovenia
Teddy Wilson Trio
Teddy Wilson (p), unknown (b) and (dr).
Sweet Georgia Brown   Helidon(Yu) 08-002

1969
November 11 — Odd Fellow Palæet, Copenhagen
Ben Webster Quartet
*Ben Webster (ts), Teddy Wilson (p), Niels-Henning
Ørsted Pedersen (b), Makaya Ntshoko (d).*
Stardust   Storyville SLP4118
Perdido   Storyville SLP4133
In A Mellow Tone   —

1970
April 14 – Stockholm
Teddy Wilson with The Ove Lind Swing Group
*Ove Lind (cl), Teddy Wilson (p), Lars Erstrand (vb),
Rolf Berg (g), Arne Wilhelmsson (b), Per Hultén (dr).*
Swing In F   Sonet SNTF618
Jam Session Cupol   —
Almost Bald   —
Nice To Have Them Around   —

1970
April 15 – Stockholm
Teddy Wilson with The Ove Lind Swing Group
As before, but omit Berg.
Fantasy In B   Sonet SNTF618
Melody In B   —
Inspired By You   —
Nobody Is Like You (no vb)   —
You Can't Be In Love With A Dream (no cl,vb) —

1970
April 16 – Stockholm
Teddy Wilson
Piano solo.
Too Late   Sonet SNTF618
My Love Is Yours   —

1970
April 17 – Stockholm
Marlene Widmark - Teddy Wilson
*Marlene Widmark (vo) acc. by Rolf Ericson (tp), Ove
Lind (cl, arr), Lennart Jansson (as), Bernt Rosengren,
Bjarne Nerem (ts), Lars Gullin, Erik Nilsson (bars),
Teddy Wilson (p), Staffan Broms (g), Arne
Wilhelmsson (b), Anders Burman (dr).*
I Let A Song Go Out Of My Heart
                           Odeon(Sd) E-062-34172
I Hear Music   —
Let's Fall In Love   —
Omit Gullin.
You're My Thrill   —
In A Sentimental Mood   —
Deep Night   —

Prelude To A Kiss (no cl)   —

1970
April 20 & May 11 – Stockholm
Marlene Widmark - Teddy Wilson
*Marlene Widmark (vo) acc. by Rowland Greenberg
(tp), Ove Lind (cl, arr), Lennart Jansson (as), Bjarne
Nerem (ts), Teddy Wilson (p), Staffan Broms (g), Arne
Wilhelmsson (b), Per Hultén (dr).*
I Had The Craziest Dream Last Night
                           Odeon(Sd) E-062-34172
Omit Jansson.
You Turned The Tables On Me   —
Keeping Out Of Mischief Now   —
I Concentrate On You   —
Add Lars Gullin (bars).
Gone With The Wind   —

c.1970
New York City
Teddy Wilson
Piano solos.
Cottage For Sale   Halcyon HAL106
Blues For Six   —
Shiny Stockings   —
Love   —

c.1970
New York City
Teddy Wilson - Marian McPartland
Piano duets.
Bluesette   Halcyon HAL106
Lover Man   —
Just One Of Those Things   —
Quiet Nights   —
Four-In-Hand Blues   —

1970
September 26 – Copenhagen, Denmark, broadcast
Ben Webster Quartet
*Ben Webster (ts), Teddy Wilson (p), Hugo Rasmussen
(b), Ole Streenberg (d).*
Old Folks   Storyville SLP4105

1970
October 5 – Tokyo
Teddy Wilson - Eiji Kitamura
*Eiji Kitamura (cl), Teddy Wilson (p), Ichiro Masuda
(vb), Masanaga Harada (b), Jimmy Takeuchi (dr).*
On The Sunny Side Of The Street Trio(J) RSP9015
Time On My Hands   —
I Can't Get Started   —
I've Found A New Baby   —
Stars Fell On Alabama   —
Whispering   —
Dream A Little Dream Of Me   —
Body And Soul   —
After You've Gone   —
Someday Sweetheart   —

1970
October 8 – Tokyo
Jimmy Takeuchi and Teddy Wilson
Teddy Wilson (p), Shoji Yokouchi (g), Masanaga

Harada (b), Jimmy Takeuchi (dr).

Star Dust	Toshiba(J) TP 7490
Isle Of Capri	—
The Girl From Ipanema	—
Besame Mucho	—
Blue Hawaii	—
Autumn Leaves	—
Kojyo No Tsuki	—

1970
October – Tokyo
Jimmy Takeuchi and Teddy Wilson
Shoji Suzuki (cl-1), Teddy Wilson (p), Shoji Yokouchi (g), Masanaga Harada (b), Jimmy Takeuchi (d).

Mack The Knife	Express(J) ETJ65015
Memories Of You (1)	—
Stardust —	
Sono Te Wa Naiyo	—
Sing Sing Sing	—
Stompin' At The Savoy	—
Take The "A" Train	—
Tea For Two	—
St. Louis Blues	—
I Got Rhythm	—
China Boy	—
Kojo No Tsuki	—

1971
July 5 – Tokyo
Teddy Wilson
Piano solos.

I Get A Kick Out Of You	Philips(J) RJ5001
Sweet Lorraine	—
Wrap Your Troubles In Dreams	—
My Ideal	—
On The Sunny Side Of The Street	—
Body And Soul	—
I Cried For You	—
Smoke Gets In Your Eyes	—
I'm Gonna Sit Right Down And Write Myself A Letter	—
Summertime	—
Runnin' Wild	—
She's Funny That Way	—
I've Got The World On A String	—
I Surrender Dear	—

1971
July 9 – Lino Hall, Tokyo, concert
Teddy Wilson - Eiji Kitamura
Akio Mitsui (tp), Kenichi Sonoda (tb), Eiji Kitamura (cl), Satoru Oda (ts), Teddy Wilson (p), Ichiroh Masuda (vb), Yukio Ikezawa (b), Hiroahi Sunaga (dr).

It's Been A Long Long Time	Trio(J) RSP9023
Stompin' At The Savoy	—
Sweet Lorraine	—
Tea For Two	—
When You're Smiling	—
St. James Infirmary	—
Ain't Misbehavin'	—
Someday Sweetheart	—

1971
September 5 – Colorado Jazz Party
Harry Edison and Joe Newman Quintet

Harry Edison, Joe Newman (tp), Teddy Wilson (p), Larry Ridley (b), Gus Johnson (dr).

Moten Swing	MPS(G) 49 21699
Yesterday	—
Caravan	—

1972
March 12 – New York City
Teddy Wilson
Piano solos.

One O'Clock Jump	Master Jazz MJR8117
Satin Doll	—
Honeysuckle Rose	Swaggie(Au) S1387
Teddy's Blues	—

1972
April – New School For Social Research, New York City, concert
Teddy Wilson
Piano solos.

Solitude	Chiaroscuro CR170
Take The "A" Train	—
Nice Work If You Can Get It	—
Li'l Darlin'	—

1972
May & September – New York City
Teddy Wilson
Piano solos.

What A Little Moonlight Can Do	ChiaroscuroCR111
This Year's Kisses	—
When You're Smiling	—
Easy To Love	—
Sugar	—
Easy Living	—
Body And Soul	—
Miss Brown To You	—
If You Were Mine	—
Them There Eyes	—
I'll Never Be The Same	—
I Wished On The Moon	—
Why Was I Born	—
What A Night, What A Moon, What A Girl	—

1972
October 23 – Philharmonic Hall, New York City
Benny Goodman Quartet
Benny Goodman (cl), Teddy Wilson (p), Lionel Hampton (vb), Gene Krupa (dr).

Avalon	unnumbered Timex LP
Ding Dong Daddy	—
Moonglow	unissued

1972
November 15 – Munich
The Dutch Swing College Band & Teddy Wilson
Bert de Kort (co), Dick Kaart (tb), Peter Schilperoort (ss, ts, bars), Bob Kaper (cl), Teddy Wilson (p), Arie Ligthart (g), Henk Bosch Van Drakestein (b), Huub Janssen (dr).

On The Sunny Side Of The Street	DSC Production(Du) PA 008
Basin Street Blues	—

Undecided (1) —
Limehouse Blues —
Riverboat Shuffle —
Time On My Hands (2) —
Poor Butterfly (3) —
I'm In The Market For You —
Rhythm King   DSC Production(Du) PA 2010
China Boy —
(1): Only Kaper (cl) with p/b/dr.
(2): Only Schilperoort (cl) & Wilson (p).
(3): As for 2, with b & dr.

1973
March 12 – Kaagdorp, Netherlands
The Dutch Swing College Band & Teddy Wilson
Bert de Kort (co), Teddy Wilson (p).
Ghost Of A Chance DSC Production(Du) PA 2010
Don't Blame Me —
Peter Schilperoort (cl) replaces De Kort.
Rosetta   DSC Production(Du) PA 2010
Someone To Watch Over Me —

1973
March 15 – Kaagdorp, Netherlands
Peter Schilperoort & Teddy Wilson
Peter Schilperoort (cl), Teddy Wilson (p).
When Sunny Gets Blue
        DSC Production(Du) PA 2010
Round Midnight —

1973
March 16 – Kaagdorp, Netherlands
The Dutch Swing College Band & Teddy Wilson
Teddy Wilson (p), Henk Bosch van Drakestein (b),
Huub Janssen (dr).
I'm Gonna Sit Right Down
        DSC Production(Du) PA 2010
I Wanna Be Happy —
My Blue Heaven —
Peter Schilperoort (cl) added.
Ain't Misbehavin' —
Bob Kaper (cl) replaces Schilperoort.
Street Of Dreams —
Spain —
Bert de Kort (co) added.
If I Had You —

1973
July 4 – Montreux, Switzerland
Teddy Wilson Trio/Quartet
Teddy Wilson (p), Kenny Baldock (b), Johnny
Richardson (dr).
One O'Clock Jump   Black Lion(E) BLP30149
Mood Indigo —
Take The 'A' Train —
Satin Doll —
Smoke Gets In Your Eyes (p-solo) —
Dave Shepherd (cl) added.
Runnin' Wild —
St. James Infirmary —
After You've Gone —
Poor Butterfly   BLP30148
1973
October 12 – Biel, Switzerland
The Dutch Swing College Band & Teddy Wilson

Dick Kaart (tb), Teddy Wilson (p).
Star Dust   DSC Production(Du) PA 2010
Full personnel as on November 15, 1972.
Honeysuckle Rose —
After You've Gone —
Sweet Georgia Brown —

1973
November 12 – Tokyo
Teddy Wilson - Eiji Kitamura
Eiji Kitamura (as, ts), Teddy Wilson (p), Masanaga
Harada (b), Hiroahi Sunaga (dr).
Ain't Misbehavin'   Trio(J) PA7097
I've Got The World On A String —
Someone To Watch Over Me —
I Want To Be Happy —
Deep Purple —
I Only Have Eyes For You —
Mean To Me —
Indiana —
Sleepy Time Gal —
I'm Getting Sentimental Over You —

1974
January 28 – New York City
Teddy Wilson
Piano solos.
Blue Turning Grey Over You
        Black Lion(E) BLP30156
Ain't Cha Glad —
I've Got A Feeling I'm Falling —
Zonky —
Black And Blue —
Ain't Misbehavin' —
Squeeze Me (take 1)   BLP30161
Honeysuckle Rose (take 1)   BLP30156
My Fate Is In Your Hands   BLP60131
Stealin' Apples —
Keepin' Out Of Mischief Now   BLCD760131

1974
January 31 – New York City
Teddy Wilson
Piano solos.
Striding After Fats   Black Lion(E) BLP30156
Blues For Thomas Waller —
Handful Of Keys —
Honeysuckle Rose (take 2)   BLP60131
Honeysuckle Rose (take 3)   BLCD760131
Squeeze Me (take 2)   BLP30156
Handful Of Keys (alt)   BLP60131

1974
May 2 – Rome
Teddy Wilson
Piano solos.
Blues For Roma   Horo(It) HHL 101-12
I Am Louis Armstrong —
Porgy And Bess Medley: It Ain't Necessarily So/
        Bess, You Is My Woman Now —
Summertime —
L'Atmosfera C'è —
Blues For Teddy —
Body And Soul —

Duke Ellington Medley: Sophisticated Lady/
    Prelude To A Kiss/Satin Doll   —

c.1974 – New York City
Lionel Hampton - Buddy Rich
Zoot Sims (ts), Teddy Wilson (p), Lionel Hampton (vb),
George Duvivier (b), Buddy Rich (dr).
Avalon   Groove Merchant GM3302
Air Mail Special   —
Ham Hock Blues   —
Ring Dem Bells   —

1974
November – Buenos Aires
Teddy Wilson
Piano solos.
Medley: It Ain't Necessarily So/Bess, You Is My
    Woman/Liza   Halcyon HAL113
Medley: Rhapsody In Blue/The Man I Love/
    Someone To Watch Over Me/Lady Be
    Good   —
Rosetta   —
Ain't Misbehavin'   —
Body And Soul   —
Flyin' Home   —

1975
November 13 – Kaasdorp, Netherlands
Teddy Wilson.
Teddy Wilson (p), Koos van der Sluis (b), Ted Easton
(dr).
Can't We Be Friends   Riff(Du) 659 010
Blue Skies   —
I Can't Get Started   —
Our Love Is Here To Stay   —
Sleepy Time Gal   —
Nice Work If You Can Get It   —
Embraceable You   —
Something To Remember You By   —
I've Got The World On A String   —
Moonglow   —
Porgy And Bess Medley   unissued
Liza   —
Tea For Two   —
Cheek To Cheek   —
Untitled Blues   —

1975
Unknown date – Tokyo, Japan
Martha Miyake
Martha Miyake (vo). acc by Teddy Wilson (p),
unknown (b), unknown (dr).
My Heart Belongs To Daddy Catalyst(J) CAT7907
Fools Rush In   —
Ain't Misbehavin'   —
Wrap Your Troubles In Dreams   —
The Days Of Wine And Roses   —
What A Little Moonlight Can Do   —
For Once In My Life   —
Give Me The Simple Life   —
My Baby Just Cares For Me   —
Don't Be That Way   —
The Good Life   —

1976
April 9 – Santa Tecla Jazzclub, Milan, Italy
Teddy Wilson Trio
Teddy Wilson (p), Lino Patruno (b), Carlo Sola (dr).
After You've Gone   Carosello(It) CLE21032
Sophisticated Lady   —
Don't Get Around Much Anymore   —
Flying Home   —
It Ain't Necessarily So   —
Bess, You Is My Woman Now   —
Summertime   —
Stompin' At The Savoy   —
Prelude To A Kiss   —
Take The 'A' Train   —
I Can't Get Started   —
One O'Clock Jump   —

1976
June – New York City
Teddy Wilson and His All Stars
Harry Edison (tp), Vic Dickenson (tb), Bob Wilber (cl,
as), Teddy Wilson (p), Major Holley (b), Oliver
Jackson (dr).
Hallelujah   Chiaroscuro CR150
Thinking Of You   —
Alice Blue Gown   —
Lonesome And Sorry   —
Fine And Dandy   —
Goodnight My Love   —
Just Friends   —
Miss You   —
June Night   —
I'll Get By   —
So Beats My Heart For You   —
Blues In D Flat   —

1976
July 14 – Nice, France
Teddy Wilson Trio
Teddy Wilson (p), Milt Hinton (b), Oliver Jackson
(dr).

76-140-3	Don't Be That Way		
		Black & Blue(F)	33094
76-141	Undecided		59.094-2
76-142-2	St. Louis Blues		33094
76-143	My Heart Stood Still		—
76-144	I Didn't Know What Time It Was		
			59.094-2
76-145	I've Got My Love To Keep Me Warm		
			33094
76-146	Where Or When		—
76-147	Sweet Lorraine		59.094-2
76-148	Sugar		950.505
76-149	I've Got The World On A String		33094
76-150	You Go To My Head		—
76-151-2	Three Little Words		—
76-152	Flyin ' Home		—
76-153	Basin Street Blues		—

1976/7
New York City
Teddy Wilson
Piano solos.

Manhattan   Chiaroscuro CR168
Thou Swell   —
My Heart Stood Still   —
You Took Advantage Of Me   —
Isn't It Romantic   —
You Are Too Beautiful   —
There's A Small Hotel   —
My Funny Valentine   —
Where Or When   —
Lady Is A Tramp   —
Have You Met Miss Jones?   —
Bewitched   —
Everything I've Got Belongs To You   —

1977
October 7 – New York City
Lionel Hampton presents Teddy Wilson
Gerry Fuller (cl-1), Lionel Hampton (vb-2), Teddy
Wilson (p), George Duvivier (b), Teddy Wilson, Jr. (d),
Sam Turner (cgs).
One O'Clock Jump   Who's Who WWLP21009
I Can't Get Started With You   —
The Man I Love (2)   —
Limehouse Blues   —
Dizzy Spells (1,2)   —
Liza (1,2)   —
Prelude To A Kiss   —
Sweet Sue (2)   —
Misty   RVC(J) RJL2644

1977
November 1 – London
Teddy Wilson
Piano solos.
Our Love Is Here To Stay Black Lion(E) unissued
Liza   —
Nice Work If You Can Get It   —
The Man I Love   —
Who Cares   —
Medley: Rhapsody In Blue/Bess You Is My
Woman
Now/It Ain't Necessarily So /Summertime   —
Lady Be Good   —
I Got Rhythm   —
Someone To Watch Over Me   —
I've Got A Crush On You   —
Blues For Gershwin   —
Embraceable You   —
A Foggy Day In London Town   —

1977
November 2 – London
Teddy Wilson
Piano solos.
Somebody Loves Me   Black Lion(E) unissued
But Not For Me   —
'S Wonderful   —
Love Walked In   —
Alexander's Ragtime Band   —
Cheek To Cheek   —
I've Got My Love To Keep Me Warm   —
What'll I Do   —
How Deep Is The Ocean   —
Blue Skies   —

I'm Dreaming Of A White Christmas   —
They Say That Falling In Love Is Wonderful   —
Russian Lullaby   —
Remember   —
This Year's Kisses   —
Easter Parade   —
Always   —
Berlin Blues   —

1977
November 3 – London
Teddy Wilson
Piano solos.
Easy To Love   Black Lion(G) BLM51505
I've Got You Under My Skin   —
Why Shouldn't I   —
Everytime We Say Goodbye   unissued
It's Alright With Me   BLM51505
I've Got You Under My Skin (2nd version)   unis
sued
Get Out Of Town   BLM51505
I Get A Kick Out Of You   —
I Love You   —
Just One Of Those Things   —
All Of You   unissued
What Is This Thing Called Love   BLM51505
Night And Day   unissued
Love For Sale   BLM51505
Porterhouse Blues   unissued
All Of You (2nd version)   —
Too Damn Blue   BLM51505

1978
July 1 – Carnegie Hall, New York City.
Lionel Hampton All-Star Band
Cat Anderson, Doc Cheatham (t), Jimmy Maxwell, Joe
Newman (t, flh), Eddie Bert, John Gordon, Benny
Powell (tb), Bob Wilber (cl), Charles McPherson (as),
Earl Warren (as, cl, fl), Arnett Cobb, Paul Moen (ts),
Pepper Adams (bar), Lionel Hampton (vb, vo-1), Teddy
Wilson (p), Billy Mackel (g), Chubby Jackson (b),
Panama Francis (d).
Tea For Two   Sultra SU2-1006
Avalon   —
Runnin' Wild   —

1978
July 2 – Newport Jazz Festival
Lionel Hampton All-Star Band
As before.
Sunny Side Of The Street (1) Timeless(Du) SJP142
Flying Home   —

1980
June 15 – Copenhagen
Teddy Wilson Trio
Teddy Wilson (p), Jesper Lundgard (b), Ed Thigpen
(d).
'S Wonderful   Storyville SLP4046
Someday Sweetheart   —
Sheik Of Araby   —
More Than You Know   —
Nobody's Sweetheart   —
Rose Room   —

China Boy	—
Sweet Sue	—
Moonglow	—
Exactly Like You	—
Sweet Lorraine	—
Whispering	—
How High The Moon	Storyville SLP4111
Keeping Out Of Mischief Now	—
Don't Be That Way	—
Somebody Loves Me	—
St. Louis Blues	—
I'll Remember April	—

1980
September 2 – Budohan, Tokyo, Japan
Benny Goodman Octet
Tony Terran (t), Dick Nash (tb), Benny Goodman (cl), Eddie Duran (g), Al Obidinski (b), John Markham (d), Rare Silk (vo-1).

Avalon (quintet: BG/TW/ED/AO/JM only)	
	East World(J) EWJ80187
Body And Soul (quintet: as before)	—
Oh, Lady Be Good! (quintet: as before)	—
The World Is Waiting For The Sunrise (quintet)	—
I Cover The Waterfront (DN/TW/ED/AO/JM only)	unissued
That's A Plenty	East World(J) EWJ80187
Broadway (1)	—
Girl Talk (1)	unissued
Goody Goody (1)	East World(J) EWJ80187
Medley: Don't Be That Way/Stompin' At The Savoy	
Memories Of You (quartet: BG/TW/AO/JM only)	—
Sing, Sing, Sing (1)	unissued
Sweet Georgia Brown	—
Good-Bye	—

1980
September 3 – Budohan, Tokyo, Japan
Gentlemen Of Swing/Helen Humes
Harry Edison (t), Benny Carter (as), Teddy Wilson (p), Milt Hinton (b), Shelley Manne (d), Helen Humes (vo-1).

Honeysuckle Rose	East World(J) EWJ80188
Undecided (TW/MH/SM only)	—
Misty (BC/TW/MH/SM only)	—
Sometimes I'm Happy	
Take The "A" Train (TW/MH/SM only; 1)	
	East World(J) EWJ80253
Prisoner Of Love (TW/MH/SM only; 1)	—

1980
September 6 – Bunraku Memorial Park, Osaka, Japan
Benny Goodman Quartet/Quintet/Octet
As September 2 1980.

Avalon (quintet	unissued
Body And Soul (quintet)	unissued
Oh, Lady Be Good! (quintet)	unissued
The World Is Waiting For The Sunrise (quintet)	unissued
I Cover The Waterfront (DN/TW/ED/AO/JM only)	

That's A Plenty	unissued
Broadway (1)	unissued
Tuxedo Junction (1)	unissued
Goody-Goody (1)	unissued
Memories Of You (quartet)	unissued
Medley: Don't Be That Way/Stompin' At The Savoy	—
Air Mail Special (1)	East World(J) EWJ80187
Sing, Sing, Sing (1)	unissued
Good-Bye	—
Sweet Georgia Brown	East World(J) EWJ80187

1980
September 7 – Yokohama Stadium, Japan
Gentlemen Of Swing
As before.

In A Mellowtone [sic]	East World(J) EWJ80188
It Don't Mean A Thing (TW/MH/SM only)	—
I'm Confessin' (HE/TW/MH/SM only)	—
St Louis Blues (TW/MH/SM only; 1)	—
Lover Man (TW/MH/SM only; 1)	—
Idaho	—
Honeysuckle Rose	unissued

1980
September 8 – Yokohama, Japan
Benny Goodman Quartet/Quintet/Octet
As September 2 1980.

Avalon (quintet)	unissued
Memories Of You (quintet)	—
Oh, Lady Be Good! (quintet)	—
If I Had You (quintet)	—
The World Is Waiting For The Sunrise (quintet)	—
I Cover The Waterfront (DN/TW/ED/AO/JM only)	unissued
That's A Plenty	—
Broadway (1)	—
Girl Talk (1)	—
Goody-Goody (1)	—
What Is This Thing Called Love? (TW/ED/AO/JM only	—
I've Found A New Baby (quintet)	—
Medley: Don't Be That Way/Stompin' At The Savoy	
Sing, Sing, Sing	East World(J) EWJ80187
Good-Bye	—

1981
August – San Francisco, Cal.
Eiji Kitamura Quintet/Sextet
Eiji Kitamura (cl), Teddy Wilson (p), Cal Tjader (vb-1), Eddie Duran (g), Bob Maize (b), Jake Hanna (d), Ernestine Anderson (v-2).

Avalon (1)	Concord Jazz CJ217
Misty	—
Old Lads (1)	—
Star Dust	—
The World Is Waiting For The Sunrise	—
Satin Doll (1)	—
Someone To Watch Over Me (2)	—
I Wanna Go Home	—

1982

April 15 – New York City.
Teddy Wilson
Piano solo.
But Beautiful   Palo Alto PA8028-2

1983
January 7/8 – Tokyo, Japan
Teddy Wilson
Piano solos.
Sophisticated Lady   Verve(J) 28MJ3444
Satin Doll   —
Stompin' At The Savoy   —
Lullaby Of Birdland   —
Moonglow   —
Mean To Me   —
I Can't Get Started   —
I'm Thru With Love   —
Cheek To Cheek   —
My Silent Love   —
Body And Soul   —
Shiny Stockings   —

1983
February 20 –
Teddy Wilson Trio
*Teddy Wilson (p), Slam Stewart (b), Sam Woodyard
(d).*
Take The "A" Train   Timeless(Du) SJP185/86
After You've Gone   —
Lil' Darlin'   —

1985
1/2 March –
Swing Reunion
*Benny Carter (as), Red Norvo (vb), Teddy Wilson (p),
Freddie Green, Remo Palmieri (g), George Duvivier (b),
Louis Bellson (d).*
Rosetta   Book Of The Month Club 71-7627
There'll Never Be Another You   —
Here's That Rainy Day   —
Swing Reunion   —
Evening Star   —
Porgy And Bess Medley   —
Undecided   —
How High The Moon   —
Exactly Like You   —
Star Dust   —
I Surrender Dear   —
All That Jazz   —
E.K.E.'s Blues   —
Green Dolphin Street   —
Body And Soul   —
After You've Gone   —
How About You   —
Dancers In Love   —
Polka Dots And Moonbeams   —
What Is This Thing Called Love   —
Town Hall Tonight   —
I Can't Get Started   —
Lush Life   —
A Train   —
Avalon   —

Index